New Jersey Quilts

1777 to 1950

New Jersey Quilts
1777 to 1950

CONTRIBUTIONS TO AN AMERICAN TRADITION

THE HERITAGE QUILT PROJECT OF NEW JERSEY

Text by Rachel Cochran, Rita Erickson, Natalie Hart & Barbara Schaffer
Edited by Rachel Cochran

With an Introduction by Carter Houck
Introductory Essay by John T. Cunningham
Quilt Photography by Chip Greenberg

American Quilter's Society

P. O. Box 3290 • Paducah, KY 42002-3290

Library of Congress Cataloging-in-Publication Data

New Jersey quilts 1777 to 1950: contributions to an American tradition/by The Heritage Quilt Project of New Jersey:
Rachel Cochran ... [et al.]; essay by John Cunningham; quilt photography by Chip Greenberg.
    p. cm.
Includes bibliographical references and index.
ISBN 0-89145-996-0: $29.95
1. Quilts – New Jersey – History. I. Cochran, Rachel. II. Cunningham, John T. III. The Heritage Quilt Project of New Jersey.
NK9112.N363 1992
746.9'7'09749 – dc20

92-30177
CIP

Grateful acknowledgment is made for permission to include the following:

Map of New Jersey from *Stories of New Jersey* by Frank R. Stockton. ©1961 by Rutgers, The State University.

Excerpts from *New Jersey from Colony to State 1609-1789* by Richard P. McCormick. ©1981. Reprinted by permission of the publisher, The New Jersey Historical Society.

Illustration in Figure 5 from *Smithville: The Results of Enterprise* by William C. Bolger. ©1980 by the Burlington County Cultural and Heritage Commission.

Excerpts from *Made in New Jersey* by John T. Cunningham. ©1954 by Rutgers, The State University.

Excerpts from the diary of Margaret Ten Eyck from *The Folklore and Folklife of New Jersey* by David S. Cohen. ©1983 by Rutgers, The State University.

Excerpts from the letters of Sarah Waln from The Eliza Smith Manuscript Collection, gift of Alice Blackwell Lewis, the Historical Society of Princeton.

Excerpts from the diary of Josephine Packer printed by permission of Josephine Fink.

Excerpts from the letter of Kay Haulenbeek printed by permission of the author.

Items in Plate 141 from the collections of Gladys Clegg, Rachel Cochran, Winifred Friese, Natalie Hart, Barbara Schaffer.

Excerpts from the letter of Bea Fleischman printed by permission of the author.

Items in Plate 172 from Rachel Cochran and The Heritage Quilt Project of New Jersey, Inc.

Quote by Jane Lutz from "Project Pinpoints Antique Quilt Origins," by Fran Miller from *The Hunterdon County Observer*, April 22, 1989.

All quiltmaker photographs courtesy of the quilt owners.

Front Cover: PIECED SAMPLER, 1842-1843, 102½" x 106". Made in Swedesboro, Gloucester County, New Jersey. This is a friendship quilt with each block having a signature and date (some dates written in the Quaker style), some stamped and others signed in ink. It is a wonderful collection of mostly pieced blocks in a variety of patterns and colors that continue on the back of the quilt with still more blocks and signatures. Owned by Marjorie R. Brooks. See page 76 for more information.

Additional copies of this book may be ordered from:
American Quilter's Society
P.O. Box 3290
Paducah, KY 42002-3290
@29.95. Add $1.00 for postage and handling.

Dedication

For all New Jersey quiltmakers
and those who treasure their quilt heritage

Exhibition Schedule

This book is the catalog for The Heritage Quilt Project of New Jersey's traveling exhibition, which is supported by grants from Johnson & Johnson and the Geraldine R. Dodge Foundation. Funding has been made possible in part by The New Jersey State Council on the Arts/Department of State.

THE MORRIS MUSEUM
Six Normandy Heights Road
Morristown, New Jersey
(201) 538-0454
December 19, 1992 - February 14, 1993

JERSEY CITY MUSEUM
472 Jersey Avenue
Jersey City, New Jersey
(201) 547-4514
March 24, 1993 - May 15, 1993

THE NOYES MUSEUM
Lily Lake Road
Oceanville, New Jersey
(609) 652-8848
May 30, 1993 - August 22, 1993

MONMOUTH MUSEUM
761 Newman Springs Road
Lincroft, New Jersey
(908) 747-2266
September 12, 1993 - November 28, 1993

ARCHIVES
Special Collections and Archives
Rutgers University Libraries
New Brunswick, New Jersey 08903
(908) 932-7006

Acknowledgments

HERITAGE QUILT PROJECT BOARD OF DIRECTORS: President: Barbara Schaffer, Livingston; Vice President: Rita Erickson, Montclair; Recording Secretary, Winifred Friese, Washington; Corresponding Secretary: Mariann Loughlin, Waldwick; Treasurer: Veronica Mitchell, Frenchtown. Board members: Helen Burkhart, Rachel Cochran, Barbara Finch, Natalie Hart, Aleta Johnson, Janet Krache, Olive Loper, Kay Lukasko, Leona Pancoast, Marti Porreca, Peggy Sloan.

We thank the following people for their help: Joy Bohanan, Martha Calderwood, Blair Cochran, Janice Cooke, Judy Dales, Barbara Dannenfelser, Pat Farace, Charlotte Froman, Barbara Julian, Lynn Kough, Rosemary Rehus, Virginia Saiia, Toni Schlegel, Kathy Schmidt, Beryl Sortino, Joe Stroble, Lois Weinberger, Marge Wetmore.

We also thank the Quilt Discovery Day coordinators listed below and the hundreds of volunteers who made our public documentation days a success: John D. Allen, Joy Bohanan, Helen Burkhart, Ann Eelman, Anne Fabbri, Winnie Friese, Elisabeth Gallagher, Courtney Ganz, Aleta Johnson, Lynn Kough, Janet Krache, June Lewin, Olive Loper, Charlotte Mackie, Sheila Marines, Susan Miles, Ronnie Mitchell, Lisa Mollé, Mary Lou Nichols, Leona Pancoast, Marti Porreca, Mae Pray, Anita Rhodes, Doris Rink, Peggy Sloan, Gwen Stokes, Dorothy Stratford, Leslie Tallaksen, Helen Tiger, Dr. James Turk. We also want to thank Nance Cruikshank, Diane Hill, and Merry Morton for their enthusiasm and participation at Quilt Discovery Days.

We thank the following people and their volunteers who made it possible to document private collections: Roxanne Carkhuff, Courtney Ganz, Kathy Jordan, Sheila Marines, Phyllis Mount, Jeanne Turner, Beverly Weidel, Kay Yeomans.

Very special thanks go to Helen Gould, President of the California Heritage Quilt Project, and Sheila Marines, Curator of History at The Morris Museum, for their on-going guidance and support.

We are especially grateful to Johnson & Johnson for its support.

We gratefully acknowledge grant awards from the Montclair Craft Guild, the National Quilting Association, and the Eastcoast Quilters Alliance.

We thank the many quilt guilds, historical societies, and individuals who supported our Project through monetary contributions.

We also want to thank the members of Bear's Paw Quilters for making our Oak Leaf Logo Quilt which was displayed at many Quilt Discovery Days.

We especially want to thank Chip Greenberg who cheerfully and generously gave his time and expertise to photograph all the quilts to make this book a reality.

We thank our families and friends for their continuing patience.

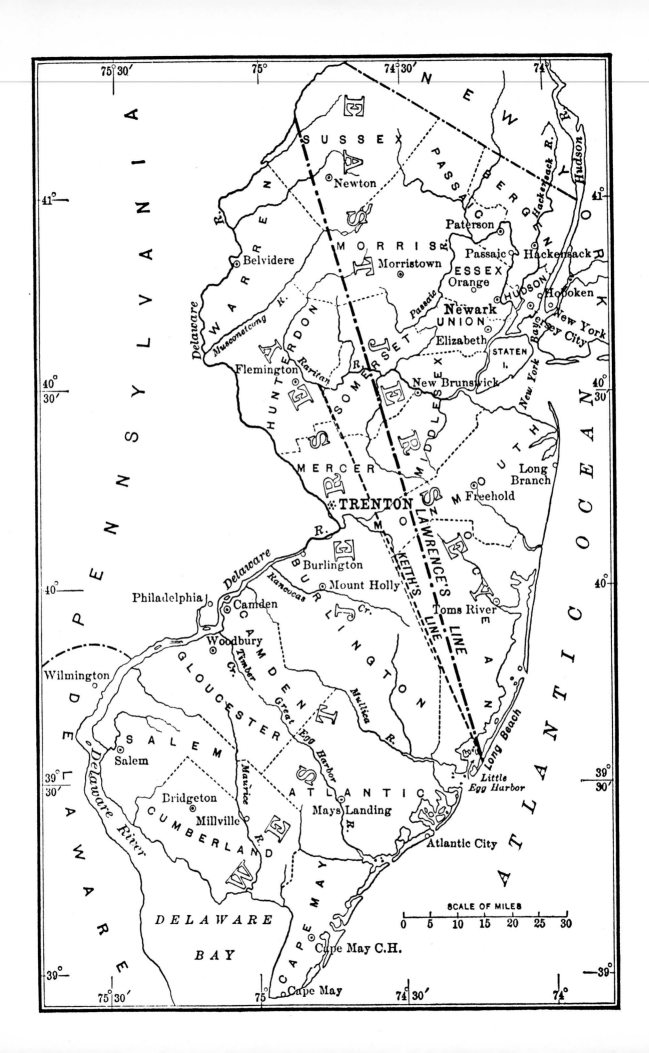

Preface

From the summer of 1988 to the spring of 1991, The Heritage Quilt Project of New Jersey conducted 32 Quilt Discovery Days throughout the state and recorded more than 2,100 quilts. This documentation effort was the result of the cooperation of local historical societies, quilt groups, museums, and historic houses and villages. These groups provided suitable locations, got the word out through local publicity, recruited essential volunteers, and rounded up the local quilts. We worked as an independent, non-profit organization of unpaid volunteers without statewide, university or museum affiliation. Our financial support came, not from large grants, but from private individuals, quilt guilds, and other local organizations. It was truly a "grassroots movement."

In our travels through our sometimes-maligned state, we were charmed by historic villages, white churches, misty mornings, and green hills that are unknown to those who pass through our state without leaving the industrial ribbon along the New Jersey Turnpike. The first snowflakes of the season fell during one of our early Quilt Days near the ski slopes in the northwest and a magnificent double rainbow appeared after one of our last Quilt Days near the beaches of the Atlantic in the southeast.

We were charmed by the people, both volunteers and quilt owners, who understood the reason for recording these fragile textiles and who took hours or sometimes days out of their own lives to make this documentation possible. We appreciated their good spirits and patience in the sometimes hectic atmosphere of busy Quilt Days.

Over the course of the documentation process, we saw everything from 1770's patchwork to 1940's appliqué. In addition to traditional cotton prints, we recorded quilts made from 1830's chintz, Quaker silks, turn-of-the-century cigar bands and wools, baseball uniform samples from the 1940's, and cuttings from lingerie and pajama factories. We heard stories of quilts made for grandparents' weddings, quilts hidden from Civil War battles, and quilts that came over from Europe with immigrant families. We discovered that our Garden State has an abundant quiltmaking tradition which has enriched all of America.

As we closed our series of Quilt Discovery Days, our regrets echoed those of other state projects: we know that the quilts we recorded are only a small sample of the New Jersey quilts that might be documented. We also know that we can print only a small number of the lovely and treasured quilts that were brought to us. We hope that all the quilt owners will enjoy seeing representative samples of our finds.

To represent the full range of the quilts we documented, we have selected those which photograph best. We wanted to show some interesting details as well as some striking overall views. We have identified some rarely published categories of quilts and have presented a few here so that others may be on the alert for them elsewhere. We have tried to show some ways in which New Jersey may have influenced quiltmaking throughout the United States and the ways that quiltmaking has been a part of New Jersey lives. Our thanks to all who helped along the way.

The Heritage Quilt Project of New Jersey

JUNE 1992

Table of Contents

***

Two Centuries of Quilts in New Jersey

While many Americans went West, small New Jersey towns grew into small cities and friends sat together in the afternoons exchanging patterns and completing quilts.

By Carter Houck

New Jersey has always been a prosperous state. It has farm land, waterways and ports, a fishing industry, and a few rugged and forbidding mountain areas. There has always been potential wealth and easy access to imported goods and to the large cities of New York and Philadelphia. As early as 1748, New Jersey Governor Jonathan Belcher is quoted as saying, "Take this province in the lump, it is the best country I have seen for men of middling fortunes, and for people who have to live by the sweat of their brows."[1] In comparing nineteenth century New Jersey life with that of other states, it appears prosperous, middle class, and small-town in contrast to the South, with its far larger farms, far wider ranging social scale, and greater emphasis on elegance. The nineteenth-century journey west that took so many Americans to the Midwest and on to California, Oregon, and Utah left New Jersey little affected. The small towns grew into small cities, mills sprang up along the great waterways, and friends sat together in the afternoons, exchanging block patterns and

completing quilts.

It is sometimes difficult for the outsider to think of a New Jersey beyond that great conglomeration of ships, refineries, trucks, and airplanes along the north end of the New Jersey Turnpike. In actuality this small state still has large farming areas, some of the best truck farms in the country, and an enormous percentage of state park land and wild area which includes everything from mountains to vast wetlands. Tucked between are towns and small cities where quilt guilds still meet and block patterns are still exchanged. In the north some towns are bedroom communities for the larger cities like Newark and New York, but in the south there are still small, often self-sufficient towns surrounded by farms and orchards. Along the coast there is a transient summer population, but many people go back year after year to the same cottage that their parents or grandparents had loved. The climate is mild enough to lure more and more people to settle year-round in the beach towns. After the summer people have left, the guilds often hold their quilt

shows and seminars, just like small-town people across the country.

Even the earliest New Jersey quilts show qualities that may distinguish them from quilts of other states. It is not surprising that the first New Jersey quilts were made with English fabric – as were those in the other coastal states – since the majority of early settlers were English. In New Jersey, block-style quilts seem to have prevailed over medallions, and piecing predominated over appliqué, making New Jersey quilts significantly different from Southern quilts. As early as 1841, fine signatures were being added to New Jersey quilts, giving researchers definite clues to their origins. At about the same time the first signed blocks appeared, a distinctively woven type of tape binding also came into use. Local quilt historians have named this tan-and-green cotton edging Trenton tape. It appears on quilts made in central New Jersey from a few decades before the Civil War to possibly just after. It is found on a variety of quilts, from utilitarian to elegant, from the lowliest print fabrics to the most elegant chintzes.

PLATE 1. SUNSHINE AND SHADE, c.1870, 83" x 86". Made by Anna Petersen Tice, Williamstown, Gloucester County, New Jersey. Sunshine and Shade and similar designs, such as Lend and Borrow, are frequently found in 19th century New Jersey quilts, but the quiltmaker's addition of appliqués over the pieced blocks is unique. The center flowers are appliquéd by hand while the stars are top stitched by machine. The result is a charming and original effort. The quilting design of parallel curved lines is sometimes called Clamshell by quilters along the Atlantic Coast although it may be known as Well Sweep or Baptist Fan elsewhere. Owned by Doris E. Havens, great-great-granddaughter of the maker.

Over the years women in New Jersey traded patterns and ideas not only among themselves but also across the borders with women in other parts of the country. Some of the same patterns that were used from the late nineteenth century to today throughout the nation are found among the quilts passed down in New Jersey families. Sunbonnet Sues and Dresden Plates abound here as in the South and the Midwest. Floral appliqués inspired by Marie Webster's patterns were favored in New Jersey as they were elsewhere.

So, we ask, what makes New Jersey quilts different from other American quilts? Actually, other than the Trenton tape binding of the 1840's and 1850's, the differences that emerge from the masses of nineteenth and twentieth century stitchery are subtle. For example, preferred block designs were sometimes set diagonally and sometimes straight, sometimes with sashes and sometimes without. In a number of quilts from the last half of the nineteenth century, the blocks are very effectively set edge-to-edge so that a

double design forms, making it hard to isolate the actual block. Many quilts have no borders to encompass the rather busy areas of repeating blocks, almost as though the block design was what interested the maker and at a certain point she decided there were enough blocks to cover the bed in question, and so put them together and bound the quilt. The quilts from the period of 1860 to 1920 are often dark, frequently made of small prints and random scraps. The total effect is rather cozy – quilts to be used for a pleasant effect in a pleasant middle-class house. By the mid-twentieth century, New Jersey quilts were not unlike those of the Midwest; it is easy to see the same middle-class values and small-town way of life reflected in quilts from both areas. The fabrics became lighter and brighter as the heavy furniture of an earlier era was exchanged for brass or white iron beds and skirted vanities. It is fairly obvious that the trends reflected in women's magazines and department store fabrics and patterns were influential among women in both New Jersey and the Midwest.

It remains for textile scholars to do far deeper research into the many cotton mills and their specific designs to see whether anything else as defining as the Trenton tape emerges. Perhaps the mills in the Trenton or Camden areas supplied very specific prints that can be found throughout quilts from central and southern New Jersey. It may be that the quilts from the north reflect the production of cotton prints in Paterson. In the era of the elaborate Victorian quilt it is certain that a number of those produced in the northern counties can be traced to the mills of Paterson, by then known as "The Silk City."

A state quilt project sometimes stirs up more questions than it can find answers for, but it does at least point the way for researchers who follow. New Jersey quilts now contain enough individual mysteries and puzzles to offer graduate students and social historians challenges for many years to come. ■

Carter Houck, editor of Lady's Circle Patchwork Quilts, *is a well-known author, editor, and quilt expert.*

The New Jersey Quilt Style

Rather than new or unusual features, the New Jersey quilt style often involves distinctive combinations – or sometimes simply an absence of the usual.

By Rita Erickson

As later state quilt projects complete their documentation efforts, they have the opportunity to compare the quilts they have recorded with those already published by other states. The nineteenth century New Jersey-made quilts documented by The Heritage Quilt Project of New Jersey are significantly different from the quilts published by earlier state projects, particularly by the Southern states stretching from North Carolina to Texas through Kentucky, Tennessee, Missouri, Arkansas, and Oklahoma. The most striking contrast is with the Texas quilts published in *Lone Stars, A Legacy of Texas Quilts, 1836-1936*, in which only about 18 of the 62 quilts shown would fit unobtrusively among the recorded New Jersey quilts.[1] The rest of these Texas quilts are conspicuously different in pattern, color, lattice or border treatment, or quilting design. Jonathan Holstein has suggested that the American quilting tradition became distinguishable from its British roots when American quiltmakers "discovered" the visual power of white background areas.[2] Only a few New Jersey quiltmakers seem to have acquired a taste for abundant white space and the accompanying opportunity for stencil-style quilting designs. This scarcity of white space often makes New Jersey quilts look darker or busier than the quilts published by the state projects in the South.

The Importance of Absent Features

Several features popular elsewhere before 1925 were rare or absent among the documented New Jersey-made quilts, including:
• Large areas of plain white fabric used as alternate blocks and lattice strips
• Stencil-style quilting
• Double or triple line quilting
• Stuffing of quilted designs
• Chintz appliqué medallion quilts
• Elaborate borders such as stairstep appliqué and three-strip borders with Nine Patch corners
• Quilts made of four large blocks (quadrant format)
• Particular color schemes including navy blue and plain white, pink appliquéd flowers, and the post-1870 bright Pennsylvania color scheme
• Several well known floral appliqué designs, usually with *rose* in their names
• Several of the more intricate pieced designs, especially those using sharp points within curved units such as Whig's Defeat, Rocky Road (New York Beauty), and Rattlesnake
• Colored quilting thread except in a few wool quilts and 1930's kit quilts

Bets Ramsey's observation that Log Cabin quilts were rather uncommon in the Tennessee sample[3] emphasizes the need for state projects to look for the characteristics that are absent or uncommon among the quilts made in their states. Identifying missing features is more difficult than summarizing those styles that are present. Yet, it is by recognizing quilt features that are absent in some locations that we will come to understand the national picture. For, as regional patterns are identified, one state's absence will come to be understood as another state's speciality.

FIG. 1. Rebecca and Eure Blackwell and a friend or relative.

PLATE 2. ORIGINAL APPLIQUÉ, c.1850, 86" x 103½". Made by Rebecca (1814-1895) and Eure (1822-1900) Blackwell, Hopewell, Mercer County, New Jersey. This stunning masterpiece of workmanship and design stands almost alone among nineteenth century New Jersey quilts in its use of alternate white blocks, its floral vine borders, and its heavy quilting in feathered wreath and double and triple rows of outline quilting. The unusual appliqué pattern may be an Oak Leaf variation. One similar design, called Friendship Leaf, can be seen in an album quilt owned by the Pennsylvania Farm Museum and published in American Quilts and How to Make Them by Carter Houck and Myron Miller. The quilt is bound with white twill tape and uses only four fabrics, probably indicating that the makers had the means to purchase fabric specifically for the quilt. It is thought that the Blackwell sisters made this quilt over a two-year period and then made an identical one. Rebecca was married to Samuel Dalrymple. Eure was married twice, the first time to Asa Titus, and the second time to James Hill. Fanny B. Drake, niece of the makers, gave the quilt to the current owner, the Hopewell Museum, Mercer County.

Common Threads: New Jersey Quilts to 1925

Although the features characteristic of New Jersey quilts are also sometimes found in quilts made elsewhere, taken as a group they may help to distinguish New Jersey quilts from those made in other states.

• Printed fabric used in place of white as alternate blocks or lattice strips
• Simple quilting designs such as a single straight line, outline, or laurel leaf shape
• Signatures and inscriptions in abundance, usually in ink or cross-stitch to the 1880's and in embroidery thereafter
• Diagonal emphasis, including diagonal set from the earliest recorded quilts and zigzag set after about 1870
• Central focus provided by a special central block, a center inscription, an enlarged central area, or a color change framing the center, very commonly seen before 1870 and occasionally seen thereafter
• A limited repertoire of pieced designs, including Uneven Nine Patch, Lone Star, various eight pointed stars, Album Cross and Album Block, Lady of the Lake, Lend and Borrow, several basket designs, Sunflower, Peony, Carolina Lily, and, after 1870, Log Cabin
• After 1900, a Split Nine Patch design that can be arranged in Log Cabin patterns
• An even more limited repertoire of familiar appliqué designs, primarily Oak Leaf and Reel blocks and swag borders
• A collection of unfamiliar appliqué designs (perhaps suggesting that New Jersey quilters were experimenting with designs that never gained wider popularity)
• Naturalistic leaves as appliqué motifs in blocks, lattice or borders
• Generally subdued color schemes, except for the red, green, and sometimes bright yellow of 1840 to 1890
• A tan-and-green cotton tape used as binding in the 1840's and 1850's (sometimes called Trenton tape)
• Silk quilts throughout the 1800's, often made by Quakers before 1870 and by the general population after

• Wool quilts in the late 1700's and again from the 1890's to the 1920's
• Embroidered cotton quilts beginning in the 1890's and continuing into the 1940's
• Printed backs in all periods, but most frequently from 1870 to 1925

New Jersey Joins the Mainstream (1925 - 1950)

In the decades after the Civil War, New Jersey quilts gradually became more like those of other states although throughout the nineteenth century they seemed to retain a characteristic subtlety of color and simplicity of design. By the 1930's New Jersey newspapers offered the same patterns as the newspapers in the rest of the country, quilters were using fabrics that were popular nationally, and many New Jersey quilts were identical to those being made elsewhere. In the 1930's and 1940's, New Jersey quilters occasionally even used stencil-style quilting designs, especially if they were provided in kits. But colored background fabrics remained common, pieced quilts were still sometimes rather "busy" for lack of solid fabrics, and the most elaborate floral appliqués of the period were not present among the New Jersey-made quilts recorded.

Local Themes and Variations

To those looking for regional variations within the state, New Jersey could be divided in several ways: north/south, urban/rural, lowland/upland, or Pennsylvania-focused/New York-focused. One real distinction goes back to the late 1600's when the state was divided into two parts – East Jersey and West Jersey – by a diagonal line running from the Atlantic Coast, near the present Atlantic City, to the northwest corner of the state at the Delaware River. West Jersey was acquired for the settlement of Quakers, and although these original settlers were eventually joined by English Anglicans (now Episcopalians), the area remained relatively homogeneous into the 1800's. On the other hand, East Jersey was settled by a variety of groups including English Presbyterians, Scottish Quakers, Dutch from

New York, Puritans from New England, Belgians, Finns, French, Germans, Irish, Swedes, Welsh, and forcibly imported Africans. Although the two halves of the state were united under the British crown in 1702, such groups as the Quakers and the Dutch retained separate customs of dress and speech for at least another century, and many of the differences found within the state today can be traced back to the original settlement patterns.[4]

The number of pre-Civil War quilts recorded in New Jersey is small enough to raise questions. Are apparent local differences really a reflection of regional ones or do they merely show better quilt preservation? Yet the following styles in quilts do seem to cluster in certain regions of the state:

• The few early medallion quilts documented were all recorded near the Atlantic Coast
• Many of the best and most characteristic 1840-1860 block-style quilts came from the southwestern counties originally settled by the Quakers (although signature quilts were recorded throughout the state)
• The unusual nineteenth century solid fabric appliqués that are almost Hawaiian in feeling came only from the northwest counties
• The early twentieth century Split Nine Patch quilts arranged in Log Cabin designs also came only from the northwest counties (more complex arrangements of this design have been reported in the adjacent state of Pennsylvania)[5]
• A tan-and-green cotton tape used as binding (Trenton tape) was recorded only on quilts made in the vicinity of Trenton

The quilts and quiltmakers recorded in New Jersey confirm the state's close and continuing ties with the adjacent states of Pennsylvania, New York, and Delaware. They also reflect the influx of northern Europeans into the state from the 1830's to the 1930's. Further, they document the migration into New Jersey from the South and the Midwest that became increasingly common in the 1930's. ∎

Rita Erickson is vice-president of The Heritage Quilt Project of New Jersey.

PLATE 3. SUNBURST WITH EIGHT POINTED STARS, c.1840, 94" x 97". Made in New Jersey. This exquisite quilt of early chintz done in the medallion style is a good illustration of the time period when American quiltmakers were beginning to turn away from the English medallion style of quilt in favor of making block-style quilts. Here the medallion center becomes smaller in relation to the surrounding blocks of Eight Pointed Stars. The alternate blocks made of light and dark triangles give the quilt a sense of motion. Descended in the family of Martha Tate Killey (1861-1931). Now owned by her granddaughter, Averill K. Tomlinson.

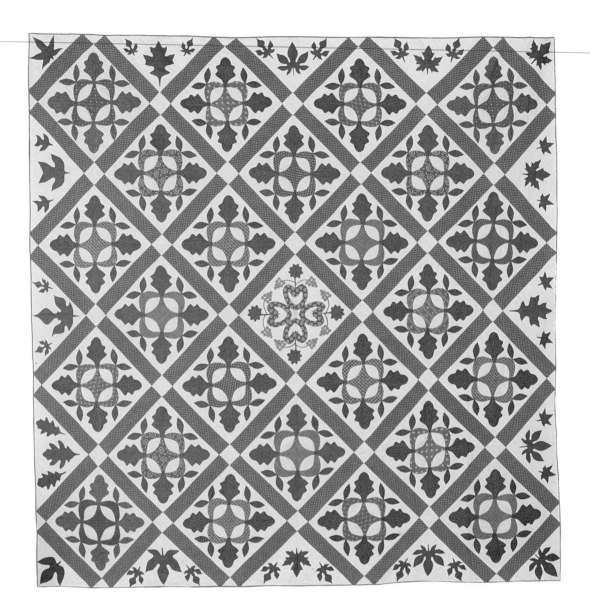

PLATE 4. OAK LEAF AND REEL, 1855-1856, 101" x 102". Made by Lydia S. Evans (1830-1882), Medford or Marlton, Burlington County, New Jersey. The Oak Leaf and Reel is one of the few familiar appliqué designs seen frequently in New Jersey quilts of the 1840's and 1850's. This large example has many of the classic features of New Jersey quilts of the period including a red, green, and white color scheme, a diagonal set, colored sashing, a center inscription, a distinctive block in the center, and even naturalistic leaves at the quilt's edge. The center block of hearts, grapes, and leaves is stamped with the maker's signature. The grapes are tiny circles cut from the same fabric as the hearts with small motifs perfectly centered in each one. The quilting is done with stencil designs as well as outline. The quilt-maker's sister, Rachel, made the lovely Rambler quilt in Plate 38. Owned by Lillian Rachel Braddock Gerber, great-niece of the maker.

PLATE 5. CRAZY QUILT, c.1890, silk, 54½" x 60". Made by Josephine Nicholas (b. 1862), Flanders (Mt. Olive Township), Morris County, New Jersey. The crazy quilt was one of the most frequently recorded styles in New Jersey. A foundation of diamonds gives this crazy quilt organization and order. Decorative herringbone stitching covers the seams, and five of the diamonds are heavily embroidered. This quilt was made by the owner's husband's grandmother, who belonged to the Missionary Society of the Presbyterian Church of Flanders that met once a week to quilt. Owned by Ruth M. Nicholas.

PLATE 6. SPLIT NINE PATCH, Barn Raising Variation, c.1930, 71½" x 85". Possibly made by Henzeney Marie Hanson Barnes (1880-1954), Knowlton Township, Warren County, New Jersey. This quilt is an example of a style frequently found in the northwestern counties of New Jersey. The basic block is a nine patch, divided in the center into light and dark colors. These blocks can be used to produce any set variation of the Log Cabin design. Most of these quilts were made from 1900 to 1930, and the makers were able to combine scraps of darker, earlier fabrics with the newer lighter colored prints. The maker came to this country from Denmark at the age of fourteen. She was the mother of six children and made many quilts. Owned by Andrew and Marilyn Barnes. Andrew is the grandson of the maker.

FIG. 2. Zena (Henzeney) Barnes

PLATE 7. FLOWERY FIELDS, c.1930, 89" x 105½". Made by Helen Alleman (1895-1967), Washington, Warren County, New Jersey. The quiltmaker used Alice Brooks pattern #624, but devised an original setting for this colorful scrap quilt. The fabrics were remnants from dresses she made for her four daughters. Winnie Friese, the daughter of the quiltmaker, quilted her mother's unfinished quilt in the early 1970's. Owned by Fred R. Alleman and Winnie Friese.

FIG. 3 (Left). Helen P. Alleman

Chapter One

Contributions To An

Here, between the Hudson and the Delaware, people of many nationalities came together...
for the most part in peaceful harmony, to lay the foundations of a colony whose
distinguishing mark was to be its heterogeneity.

Unlike New England, where the Puritan townsman typified the whole population,
or the South, where the tidewater English planter was predominant, New Jersey presented
a picture of infinite variety. Its founders spoke many tongues, belonged to many
religious denominations, and practiced their arts and crafts in many different ways.

Attracted by the promise of good land at a reasonable price, by favorable climate and
by a political environment that enhanced individual enterprise...the typical settler hoped
to find in New Jersey enhanced opportunities to provide himself and his family
with a satisfactory living.... Here there was no one-crop economy...he might be a farmer
growing any one of a dozen main crops, a cattle raiser, a lumberman, an iron miner,
a merchant or a ship owner, a craftsman, a fisherman or a tavern keeper.
Frequently he combined several occupations. Variety, then, rather than homogeneity,
characterized the economic scene.

– Richard P. McCormick

New Jersey from Colony to State 1609-1789

PLATE 8. Detail of OAK LEAF AND REEL, 1855-1856, 101" x 102" (Plate 4). Made by Lydia S. Evans, Medford or Marlton, Burlington County, New Jersey. The Oak Leaf and Reel is one of the few familiar appliqué designs frequently seen in New Jersey quilts of the 1840's and 1850's.

American Tradition

New Jersey: A Patchwork State

Diverse in its inhabitants and influences, New Jersey has contributed much to American life and traditions.

By John T. Cunningham

On my first major plane flight, as the propeller-driven craft lowered slowly across northern New Jersey in its glide toward Newark Airport, I gazed down on the fields and villages of Morris County, then saw the wooded hills of western Essex County and the towers of Newark. From the air, I saw varying, clear-cut patches of color and form, repeated again and again. What I saw, in essence, was a giant patchwork quilt laid gently across New Jersey's undulating terrain.

Years later, a fourth grade teacher proved to me that the same thought strikes anyone with the slightest bit of imagination. She and I were among thirty persons aboard a small plane chartered to carry us around the borders of New Jersey. We flew north from Newark Airport, over the Palisades, cut westward to High Point, then followed the Delaware River to Cape May before returning home along the Jersey Shore. We flew low; the objective was to show New Jersey's varied topography.

As we passed over the pasturelands of Sussex County, that long-remembered teacher gazed out at the neat fields, the carefully laid stone fences, and the intermittent clusters of woodland, all characteristic of the northern part of the state. Suddenly she exclaimed: "It looks like a patchwork quilt!" She warmed my heart. She understood!

We passed over the Delaware Water Gap, overlain with hardwood forests. We crossed Cumberland County's broad marshes, where the Mullica River twists and turns, for all the world like a blue-green ribbon carelessly tossed on a yellow-green bedspread. The mood lingered as we flew north along the Jersey Shore, above varied coastal towns set off by patches of white sand, white-tipped aqua ocean waves, and multi-hued sailboats challenging Barnegat Bay's winds. We soared high above our patchwork state.

Patchwork State! I like it, for all the same good emotions that an exquisitely fashioned quilt can evoke – a mixture of tones and patterns arranged in orderly sequence; a stitching together of bits and pieces to make the whole much more than merely the sum of its parts. Patchwork State – New Jersey fits that, whether the theme is geography or history, people or commerce.

Geography is a valid quilting theme for New Jersey or perhaps for anywhere. I have seen fourth grade children who have stitched together quilts using a state theme. They have learned geography painlessly as they cut and sewed, their handwork evoking awareness of simpler times.

No state has a greater diversity of landscapes than New Jersey. Geologists tell me the state's land structure represents every geological era except the carboniferous, or coal era. Prehistory shaped the land, a fact vividly demonstrated in the Watchung Mountains just west of the frenetic New York-Philadelphia corridor and in the majestic Palisades rising high above the Hudson River in Bergen County. Both were created more than one hundred million years ago in volcanic eruptions. Both endure in twentieth century beauty.

Moving southeastward from High Point on the north to Cape May on the south, 166 airline miles away, the terrain changes constantly – from Kittatinny Mountain's hardwood forest to rolling Highlands touched with lakes of blue; from dogwoods on the Piedmont slopes to evergreens in the Pine Barrens; from broad vegetable fields in the southwest to the sparkling Jersey Shore. Diversity in one small package is New Jersey's strength.

New Jersey history has been shaped by varied topography and by people moved along by the tides of time. Here we have known explorers, colonists, and revolutionists (against Great Britain, of course); railroad builders, inventors, and Victorian architects; shipyards, munitions plants, and two world wars. Every facet of American history is represented. Even the Westward Movement began here, as young families moved westward from Newark or Elizabethtown to Orange or The West Fields (Westfield) and beyond.

All who venture to new lands seek a better place. Our first immigrants, the American Indians, came here from what is now Siberia, sighting the Jersey Shore 10,000 years before Christopher Columbus "discovered" America. In turn, the early explorers in quest of a direct water route to Far Eastern gold, jewels, and spices earnestly hoped the Delaware or Hudson rivers might prove to be the long-sought passage.

The first European explorers represented four European nations. Giovanni daVerrazano, a hired Italian navigating a French ship, explored Newark Bay and the lower Hudson River in 1524 and claimed both for the King of France. Henry Hudson, an Englishman, sailed his Dutch-sponsored ship, the *Half Moon*, into the same waters in 1609 and gave Holland its first New World claim. Those voyages opened slightly what eventually would be called the Golden Door to America.

Dutch burgomasters settled both sides of the Hudson River before 1630, then followed Hackensack and Raritan riverbeds inland. Swedes and Finns founded New Sweden in the lower Delaware River Valley in 1639. England took over the land in 1664, bestowed the ultimate name – New Jersey – and offered generous terms to those already on the land. Dutch and Scandinavian families stayed in place, accepting land grants and in time marrying into English families, even as they kept their traditions. They cared little about who governed the land as long as they were able to farm it.

By the time of the American Revolution, New Jersey had the most diverse population in all the colonies, with settlers from Holland, Sweden, England, Ireland, Scotland, Wales, France, Germany, possibly a few from Italy or Spain, and many boatloads of cruelly imported African slaves. Religions further subdivided national groups: Dutch Reformed, Swedish Lutheran, Congregational, Puritan, Presbyterian, Episcopalian (Church of England), Baptist, Quaker, Methodist, and Universalist churches all were established before the Revolution.

New Jersey and the nation have grown on that varied ethnic base. Eventually the Golden Door opened wide. Between 1890 and 1915 millions of southern and eastern European immigrants flocked through Ellis Island – Italians, Greeks, Hungarians, Serbs, Slavs, Slovaks, Russians, Poles, as well as the traditional Anglo-Saxons. Ellis Island, once within New Jersey boundaries, sent the newcomers outward to supply the factories in need of their muscles and their skills. Ellis Island immigrants included such workers as the young Slovak women who became widely known as "the handkerchief girls" in one of the world's finest handkerchief factories, Acheson Harden & Company of Passaic, New Jersey. Elsewhere, Italian farmers made Vineland green and brought bloom to the estates of Morris County's newly rich. Hungarians made bricks in Middlesex County and dug iron ore in Morris.

This "nation of immigrants," as President Franklin D. Roosevelt so eloquently called us, found its hallmark in New Jersey. By 1920, the state had the highest percentage of foreign-born people in all the nation. The newcomers added zest and spice with their polyglot languages, tasty foods, lively dances, hard-earned skills, and delicate handcrafts. Late nineteenth-century Puritan-dominated America needed such leavening.

New Jersey industry helped smooth the way for those who would work with cloth in any form. As early as 1794, a Paterson mill powered by a bull on a treadmill (the "Bull Mill") manufactured cotton. That soon gave way to energy created by the Paterson falls. By 1840, only Lowell, Massachusetts, exceeded Paterson in the quantity and quality of cotton cloth it produced. Elsewhere in New Jersey, huge cotton mills prospered in Gloucester City and Millville before the Civil War. Woolen mills opened, too, but not in great abundance or size. It took a German, Eduard Stoehr, to establish a genuine woolen factory when he opened the Botany Mills in Passaic in 1889. Botany built one of the first complete woolen textile units, with all processes (spinning, weaving, finishing) under one roof. Wool remained the fabric of choice for men's suits; itchy males could protect parts of their anatomies with cotton shirts and long cotton underwear.

No fabric stirred imaginations like silk, considered for centuries the cloth of royalty alone. Paterson's first silk mill opened in 1838. The industry picked up pace in the 1850's, and by 1880 the city stood first among all American silk makers. Two-thirds of all raw silk imported into America in 1880 went to Paterson's ninety-three silk factories. Paterson well deserved its nickname, "The Silk City."

By 1870, bolts of quality American-made cloth first began to be within reach of an average person's purse.

Equally important, perhaps more important to the home seamstress, fine scissors and amazing sewing machines had become reality, both pushed to the fore by New Jersey entrepreneurs.

Scissors came first, as early as 1825, when Rochus Heinisch arrived from Austria to make surgical shears and tailor's scissors in Newark. His major contribution came by indirection in 1848, when young Jacob Wiss stopped in Newark on his way from Switzerland to Texas with his two St. Bernards. Wiss took "temporary" work with Heinisch to replenish his savings. In his spare time, using his dogs on a treadmill, the Swiss began making his own shears. In time, Heinisch and Wiss competed vigorously, bettering their shears and lowering prices for buyers. But neither saw the need for "ladies' sewing scissors" until Ebenezer Butterick of Massachusetts produced his first tissue paper patterns for ladies dresses in 1863. The demand for lightweight and sharp-cutting "ladies' scissors" accelerated.

As for the sewing machine, consider it a minor miracle, as nineteenth-century women certainly did. Elias Howe, a New Englander, developed the device in 1846, but it took promoter Isaac M. Singer to put sewing machines into living rooms and sewing rooms across the country. His company's "hire-purchase" plan allowed women to pay $5 down, $3 a month until the price of $125 had been paid. Ladies scrimped to get $5 and waited in line to buy the Singer model.

The Singer Company stood the world of stitching on its collective ear in 1873 by opening a huge new factory in Elizabethport, hiring 3,000 workers for its revolutionary new assembly lines. By 1879, the company was selling two million machines yearly. Some of its salesmen threw a double punch – first selling the machine, then selling cloth to feed the machine. It was effective, however dubious ethically.

Beginning in the 1860's two New Jersey factories supplied most of the thread for the nation's needles and sewing machine bobbins. In 1864, George A. Clark opened a massive plant on the east side of the Passaic River in Newark, spinning millions upon millions of miles of fine thread. Every spool carried one of the world's best-known trademarks, "O.N.T." (Our New Thread). Clark's main competition came from the Barbour Flax Spinning Company of Paterson.

Thus American women cut cloth with Newark shears, ran the materials up on Elizabethport machines, used Newark thread, and if they did not credit New Jersey for the help, it was probably because they were too busy using the products to notice their origins. If modern quilters doubt those sewing boons affected their craft, they do not know of a time when merely getting scraps of material took ingenuity. If nothing else, the astronomical increase in home-sewn clothing created mounds of potential patches.

I think of early settlers and latter-day counterparts as being stitched together with common bonds – saving, conserving, dreaming of better things. New clothing became hand-me-downs, then cut-me-downs, then patches. Remnants quite naturally became snippets for the skilled fingers and imaginative minds of quiltmakers.

Wouldn't it be wonderful if a quiltmaker could actually combine all of New Jersey's diverse elements – the terrain, the people, the history – into a modern "New Jersey Quilt"?

I think of a quilt that would feature soft, warm earth tones to stand for the light green fields, the dark greens of cedar swamps, the multifold hues of autumn foliage. It would have highlights of red for cranberries, blue for blueberries, yellow or green for snap beans, black and white for Holstein cows, a pink blush for peaches, and purple for grapes.

More colors would represent our many kinds of forebears: crimson for the blood of European wars, blue for the Mediterranean Sea, black for the forests of Germany, white for Switzerland's Alpine peaks, green for the slopes of Greece, purple for England's royalty, gold for the spires of Eastern Europe, fiery red for the dragons of China, a multitude of colors for the tulip fields of Holland, and every color in the rainbow for the more than 100 different nations now identified in New Jersey.

This quilt would be something for future generations to recognize immediately; something for future fingers to seize upon as a dependable standard. Let me know if this quilt is ever created. I will be the first customer in line. It will be my security blanket whenever I venture away from this Patchwork State. ∎

John T. Cunningham, a life-long resident of New Jersey, is the well-known author of 25 books on New Jersey life and history.

Early Calico Manufacturing

Though almost no records or samples remain, in the nineteenth century millions of yards of calico were printed in southern New Jersey.

By Phyllis Mount

When Britain founded the American colonies, they were viewed as a source of raw material and a market for British goods. Continuous repressive measures, including the prohibiting of emigration by textile workers, were levied against American manufacture.[1] After the Revolution, what had once been regulated by the Crown was maintained by British manufacturers who wanted to keep their export business. Plans and models of textile processes and machinery were jealously guarded. In 1782, one year after the end of the American Revolution, Parliament enacted a law prohibiting the exportation of blocks, plates, machines, tools, or utensils used in the preparation or finishing of calico, cotton, or linen printing manufacture. There was a penalty of five hundred pounds sterling for those who defied this prohibition.[2] Yet some individuals, like the well-known Samuel Slater, eluded the prohibitions. Slater's re-creation, entirely from memory, of the complicated-for-its-time Arkwright machinery for the Rhode Island firm of Almy & Brown brought growth to the early American textile industry and earned him the name "Father of American Manufacturers."

While New Jersey's earliest cloth manufactory was in operation in 1697,[3] calico printers from 1625 to the Revolution and from the war to about 1800 are known, if at all, through advertisements or town records rather than historical accounts. But because of the fierce competition from British imports and trade restrictions, early calico printing in America seems to have been a "comparatively obscure profession."[4] In a list of eighteenth century American calico printers and dyers, three New Jerseyans are included: Stephen Addington, Springfield, 1792; Edward Harper & Co., Paterson, 1794; and "Unknown," Pompton, 1796.[5] As the others are primarily from Boston, Philadelphia, Providence, Wilmington, and New York, New Jersey would appear to be ideally situated in the middle of any activity. An advertisement in *The Diary or Louden's Register* of September 20, 1792, reads: "CALICO PRINTING AND DYEING. Stephen Addington Respectfully informs the public he has established a Manufactory at Springfield, Essex County, New Jersey for printing Muslins, Muslinettes, Calicoes and Linen and the Dyeing of Brown Cloth."[6] In his book, *An Excursion to the United States of North America in the Summer of 1794*, Henry Wansey wrote that Addington "has a considerable business in printing callicoes [sic], muslins, and linens, and an excellent bleaching ground; but it is as yet quite an infant undertaking, and will hardly succeed for want of a larger command of capital. The difficulty of making returns of money will for many years operate against establishing such concerns."[7] However, the British prohibition of 1782 would suggest that this profession was becoming more successful than might be supposed from other evidence. By 1836, 120 million yards of calico were printed in the United States,[8] and by 1840, there were 36 cotton printing establishments in the country.[9] Unfortunately, almost no records and few samples of the work from all these manufactories remain.[10]

While New England is often associated with textile manufacturing, southwestern New Jersey is rarely mentioned in connection with manufacture of the printed cottons documented in early quilts. However, evidence indicates that, in fact, there were several firms in the counties along the Delaware that were printing large amounts of calico or chintz.

The Eagle Factory

Cotton manufacturing around Trenton, in what is now Mercer County, appears to have begun early in the nineteenth century. This area had already been recognized for its abundant water-power opportunities. Dye houses and fulling and carding mills were already located there.[11] In 1812 Joseph Fithian was listed as having a cotton mill near Stacy Potts' steelworks, behind the Old Barracks – about where New Jersey's statehouse is now located, but little is known about that operation.

A more extensive record has been established for the cotton factory which Robert Waln and his brother-in-law Gideon H. Wells began planning in March of 1814 and built by 1815. Initially, they speculated that they could compete with Great Britain if they limited their efforts to less refined goods such as girths (straps or beltings) and tapes.[12] It was decided to build the factory on the Wells' estate, which had belonged to Waln's father. This is said to have been the site of Mahlon Stacy's gristmill built in 1680,[13] and is currently called the Mill Hill Historic District. By 1815, this district as well as the area adjoining Trenton known as Bloomsbury was undergoing extensive development. In an advertisement for carpenters and masons which Daniel W. Coxe placed in the *Trenton Federalist* on April 17, 1815, he described the Bloomsbury district as being "at the head of navigation, where extensive Cotton Factories are now established."[14] Descriptions vary about the

actual construction of the mill building, but accounts refer to it being about 60 feet long, 36-40 feet wide, and either four or five stories high.[15] It was designed with a unique central heating system, instead of the more commonly used stoves.

Throughout 1814, Waln corresponded with several cotton mill owners in New England, in particular the Brown family in Rhode Island, who had been involved in establishing Samuel Slater in the 1790's. The New England mill owners were not forthcoming with information which would assist a competitor, and when he canvassed those working in local factories, Waln found that they knew little about the engineering of the larger, more sophisticated operation he was planning. The best information came from mill owners in Paterson, New Jersey, who were developing their mills at the same time. After an extensive but unsuccessful search throughout New England for a superintendent, Waln and Wells hired a local man, a Mr.

Longstroth, possibly John Longstroth. The Longstroth family had operated various types of mills in the Trenton area and in nearby Groveville, so it would be reasonable to assume he had had experience in the mechanics of milling.

The Eagle Factory, as Waln and Wells named their enterprise, produced muslins, sheeting, ginghams, and stripes.[16] In addition, Waln and Wells leased excess floor space to Wilkenson and Howe, builders of textile machinery. By 1819 advertisements announced that Arnold and Company of Rhode Island was also supplying cotton machinery from this building. In the 1820 Federal Census of Manufactories, Gideon Wells declared that the production of cotton fabric manufactured during the year would not fall short of 480,000 yards. The Eagle Factory continued to be operated by various members of the Waln and Wells families until it was damaged by flood in 1843 and destroyed by fire in 1845.

FIG. 4. Gideon Wells' signed statement to the 1820 Federal Census of Manufactories about production at the Eagle Factory. Courtesy: New Jersey State Library.

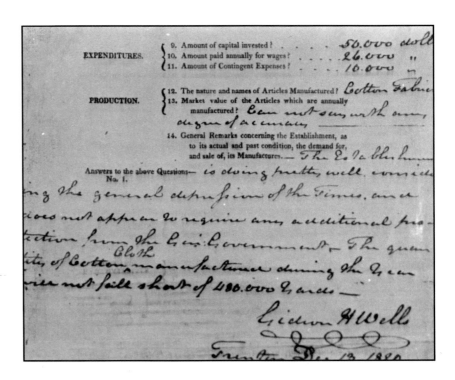

The Trenton Calico Printing Manufactory

Trenton in the 1820's was one of the young nation's urbane, intellectual centers. Joseph Bonaparte, brother of Napoleon and former King of Spain, chose nearby Bordentown for his home when in exile from Europe, and many of the leading contributors to the philosophical thought of the New Republic resided in the vicinity of Trenton. This, plus the extensive textile activity taking place in the area, may have encouraged Giovanni Battista Sartori, Roman Consul from the Pope to the United States, to build a calico printing factory in Trenton at the foot of Federal Street on the Delaware River.[17] Sartori is perhaps better known for organizing the first Catholic service given in Trenton (in the printing shop of Isaac Collins) and for establishing the first spaghetti factory in the country.[18] Except for vague statements in local histories and legal records, little is known about the fabric that Sartori's firm produced. It has been suggested that he may have attempted to produce a product similar to late eighteenth century Italian *mezzaro*, a colorful cotton printed near Genoa and well known in his native Italy. (John Hewson of Philadelphia, considered America's foremost eighteenth century fabric printer, left in his estate a bed quilt of similar material which he termed "India Chintz" that is now thought to be an example of *mezzaro*.)[19]

Some references to Sartori and the Trenton Calico Printing Manufactory have, however, been found in various records of the time. *The Trenton Emporium* of May 2, 1829, announced the marriage of Eugenia Sartori to a Peter Hargous, possibly the son of Peter A. Hargous, director of the calico works and evidently a partner of Sartori. In that same year, Stacy A. Paxsou and P. A. Hargous are listed as directors, William Potts as president, and S. L. Shreve as treasurer of the Trenton Calico Printing Manufactory in a Judgement by Confession in the New Jersey State Archives. The records show a settlement between Jonathan L. Shreve and George Potts against the Manufactory.[20] The Manufactory was

determined to be heldbound to Shreve and Potts for $6,000, half to be paid by April 13, 1829.

The outcome of this settlement may have persuaded Sartori to dissolve his interest in the Manufactory. In 1832 he returned to his native Tuscany, where he died in 1854 at the age of 86.[21] His New Jersey home, "Rosey Hill," on the bluff overlooking the Delaware, was near the calico factory. In 1856 it was acquired by the Cooper & Hewitt Company, which established an iron rolling mill there.

It is difficult to know whether the Trenton Calico Printing Manufactory had any connection to a company called the Trenton Manufactory which was sold by Sheriff's sale on January 23, 1826. According to a notice published in *The True American*, this was "siezed [sic] as the property of Jno. Greiner and John Groves, and taken in execution at the suit of the President and Directors of the Mechanic's Bank of the city and county of Philadelphia." The notice described a brick building three stories high, 80 x 40 feet, which included a dye house and blacksmith shop. The equipment also in the sale included four "throstle frames" (machines which spun thread and had evolved from Arkwright's famous water-frame), stretchers, carding engines, eight power looms, two wrapping mills, and two mules with 258 spindles.[22] These last two types of machinery may have played a large part in the reason for the sale; in 1825 Richard Roberts in Manchester, England, had invented a self-activating mule in response to the legalization of trade unions there. Soon after this major technological innovation a number of textile manufacturers were quickly affected by their inability to compete. No doubt, the Trenton Manufactory had been established at considerable cost, and had probably operated for only about ten years.

The Shreveville Manufactory

Brothers Jonathan L. and Samuel L. Shreve were parties to the settlement with the Trenton Calico Printing Manufactory; while Samuel served as the company's treasurer, Jonathan had evi-

dently been an investor. As early as 1820 they operated a store in Columbus (then called Black Horse), Burlington County, New Jersey,[23] where they are said to have sold dry goods. Evidence of the Shreves' early involvement in the sale of calico has been documented by a paperbound account book from 1825 recently discovered in a home a few doors down from the Shreve's store.[24] Zilpah Burtis and Agnes Tallman, an occasional boarder, appear to have been partners in two separate businesses: a tailoring business and an apothecary business, each with records entered in separate ledgers. On April 1, 1826, Zilpah Burtis recorded the payment of a bill to "J. and S. Shrieve" [sic] for $12.14. On September 11, 1826, she again paid a bill from "Shrieves" [sic] and also spent an additional $8.68 for seven yards of "callico" [sic]. The same book records a payment Agnes Tallman made in May 1825 to Zilpah's husband, Daniel, for room and board in which a quilt served as payment. The names of Zilpah Burtis, Daniel Burtis, the Burtis children, and Agnes Tallman appear on several New Jersey signature quilts now in New Jersey museums. A dramatic example owned by the Burlington County Historical Society was shown in a 1983 issue of *Lady's Circle Patchwork Quilts*.[25] This quilt was apparently made in 1853, the year after Daniel's death, as a memorial or symbol of family unity, as was the Quaker custom.[26]

In 1831, Jonathan and Samuel Shreve applied the money they received from the Trenton Calico Printing Manufactory toward the purchase for $14,000 of a complex of grist and sawmills several miles from their store and about six miles from Mount Holly, Burlington County. Their enterprise, known as Shreveville, provided moderate success until they suffered a setback in June 1839 – a fire destroyed uninsured property valued at $15,000 to $20,000. They immediately began rebuilding and with an investment of approximately $250,000 throughout its operating years, the village of Shreveville grew to include a mansion, workers' housing, a cotton spinning

FIG. 5. *Shreveville label from an 1850 engraving. Courtesy: Burlington County Cultural and Heritage Commission*

and weaving factory, a spool cotton manufactory, a calico printworks, and a machine shop, in addition to the original gristmill, sawmill, and general store. The Shreves employed 209 workers while 420 people resided in the village's 60 houses.

During its peak years in the 1840's, the business returned an annual 20% profit. Two separate complexes divided the activities between the spinning and weaving operation and the finishing, dyeing, and printing operation. In the first complex, 101 looms were in use as well as 2,786 spindles. According to the 1850 census, the annual production was 181,000 pounds of cotton yarn and 546,000 yards of muslin. The annual return profit was $4,000 on an investment of $85,000. The second complex contained the calico printing works. Here, 165,000 yards of muslin sent from the first complex were washed, bleached, starched,

printed, dried, and packaged. The annual profit was $17,000 on an investment of $60,000.[27] Even more financially successful was the spool cotton operation which was developed by Samuel Semple. After his arrival from Scotland in 1846, he established in Shreveville one of the country's first spool cotton thread manufacturing operations. It had taken an initial investment of $40,000, but yielded an annual profit of over $25,000 and produced 400,000 dozen spools of cotton thread annually.

After nearly twenty years of successful growth, the company began to lose money. This resulted primarily from the protective import tariffs which caused a general depression in the 1850's in the American textile industry.[28] And if the Shreve brothers were obtaining their raw cotton from their cousin, Henry Miller Shreve of Shreveport, Louisiana, they may not

have been able to find another profitable source of supply after his death in 1851.[29] Desperately struggling for capital, the Shreves began to mortgage their property to relatives and friends. In 1854 they borrowed $48,012 from their brother Benjamin of Medford, and another $9,790 from their sisters Mary Ann, Phebe, and Rebecca. The same year they borrowed another $41,339 from 31 separate investors.[30] In 1856, with the mortgages long overdue, and another fire having caused extensive damage, Samuel Shreve died from apoplexy. An attempt was made to auction the property at the Philadelphia Exchange, but no serious buyer was found. Jonathan Shreve died in May of 1857,[31] and the sheriff foreclosed on the property, selling it to Benjamin Shreve. The property was later sold to H.B. Smith who, after renaming the town Smithville, became the successful manufacturer of the renowned Star bicycle. For his part of the settlement, Samuel Semple accepted the machinery he had bought abroad and established the S.F.T. (Soft Finished Thread) Mills in Mount Holly, which developed into a successful business and established him as a pillar of Mount Holly society.

Despite an extensive search to identify fabrics which may have been manufactured at Shreveville, no documented examples have been found. One approach has been to cross reference names on the list of mortgages with those on album quilts, to thus provide a clue to what may have been Shreve calico. Names such as Shreve, Budd, Lippincott, Shinn, West, De Cou, Doran, and Bishop, as well as Semple, are significant when found on quilts made before 1856 because they suggest that the fabrics may have been manufactured at Shreveville.

The Washington Manufacturing Co. & the Gloucester Manufacturing Co.

In 1844 David S. Brown established the Washington Manufacturing Company in Gloucester City, Camden County, New Jersey. Brown was born near Dover, New Hampshire, in 1800, to parents who became Quakers soon after their marriage. Educated in Boston, Brown joined his brothers in business in Philadelphia between 1817 and 1821. In 1821 he became a member of the firm of Hacker, Brown, and Company, dry goods commissioners. Throughout the 1820's, advertisements in the Philadelphia newspapers for Hacker, Brown, and Company offered the public Merrimack goods (fabric manufactured in the Merrimack Mills at Lowell, Massachusetts), in indigo and printed cottons.

By the end of the 1830's, Brown's home town of Dover had developed into an enormous center for the production of calico. The most important company in town was the Dover Cotton Factory which had been established in 1812, ironically, by using models for its bleaching and printing operation originally seen in Philadelphia and Baltimore. Despite continuous experiments in cylinder printing, the Dover factory appears to have been

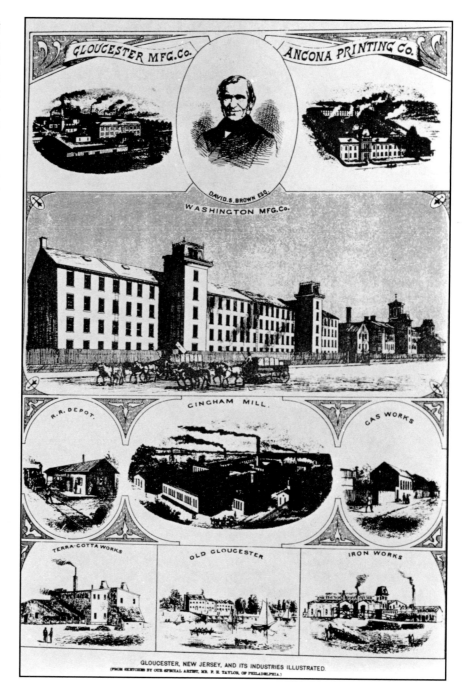

FIG. 6. The Gloucester Manufacturing Company and Ancona Printing Company. Courtesy: Gloucester County Historical Society.

a hand printing operation. Skilled mechanics and chemists were brought over from England, as was the case with most early attempts at textile manufacturing in America. But by the end of the 1820's financial difficulties forced the Dover company to restructure, isolating the printworks which was renamed the Cocheco Manufactur-

ing Company and remained so into the twentieth century.[32]

It is quite reasonable to assume that Brown kept abreast of these developments, as well as similar activities in the textile industry throughout the country. By 1830 he had acquired the controlling interest of the dry goods firm, which he renamed David S.

Brown and Company. While Brown continued to serve as a commissioner of textiles, he aggressively studied the manufacturing process of cotton goods, and finally, in 1844 founded the Washington Manufacturing Company in Gloucester City, New Jersey, just across the Delaware River from Philadelphia. These cotton mills were established with $260,000, which was acquired by the sale of stock. Within a year, he and a number of other investors incorporated the Gloucester Manufacturing Company, which carried out the bleaching, dyeing, printing, and finishing of cotton goods. The main purpose of this new firm was to print the yardage of the Washington Mills. The printworks were finally complete in 1850 and evidently still used the block printing process until 1855 when the facilities were enlarged to accommodate the introduction of roller-plate printing machinery.

As with the case of Shreveville, the Washington Mills suffered severely in the panic of 1857. Brown proposed to pay his creditors 75% of his loans in cash payments with interest over the next twelve months, and offered the remaining 25% in the stock of the Gloucester Land Company and the Gloucester Manufacturing Company.[33] Through this clever arrangement all debts were paid back with interest at the end of three years.

In 1860 Samuel Raby, the first superintendent of the Washington Mills, built another factory in town for the manufacturing of cotton-ades (utilitarian cottons) and coarse ginghams. Although a capable superintendent at the Washington Mills, he had alienated himself with the workers during a strike in 1848 and had been forced out. In 1872 the Gloucester Gingham Mills Company was incorporated with Brown as president, Samuel Chew as secretary,[34] and Henry F. West as treasurer, and expanded to include improved machinery to manufacture a finer grade gingham. By 1886 this operation had expanded so rapidly that its six principal buildings covered seven acres and 500 employees turned out six million yards annually.

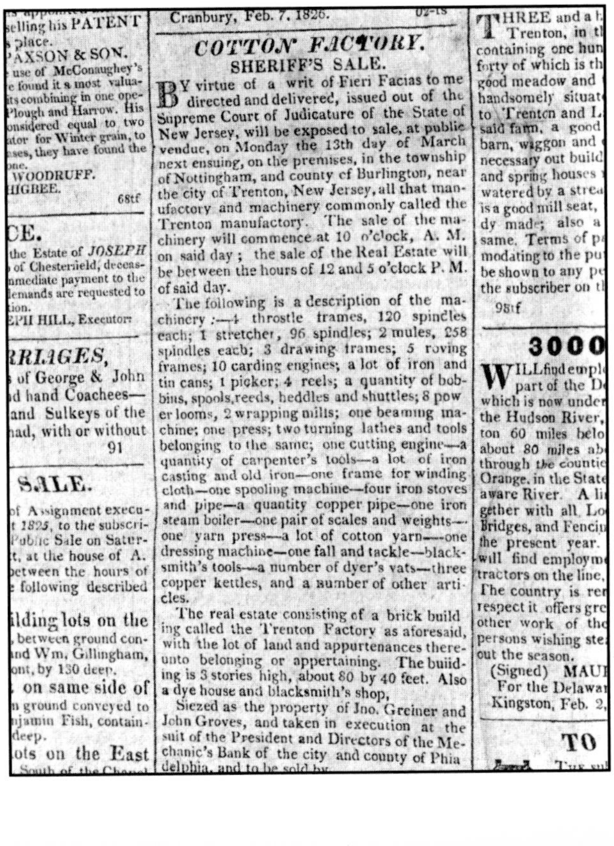

At the same time he was involved in the Gloucester Gingham Mills, Brown was also working on the incorporation of the Ancona Printing Company. The purpose of this new works was to introduce new discoveries in the application of colors which, although successful in Europe, were still untried in this country. Ancona's production included such popular designs described in literature of the time as "Dolly Vardens," "Japanese Stripes," "Oil Colors," "London Smokes," and "Scotch Clan Plaids." These fabrics kept the company operating to full capacity so that by 1875 it employed 300 persons and turned out six hundred thousand pieces or 27 million yards of printed muslin annually.[35]

FIG. 7 (Left). Clipping from the Trenton Federalist, *1815, advertising cotton machinery available for purchase at the Eagle Cotton Manufactory. Photo courtesy: Monmouth County Park System.*

FIG. 8 (Right). Clipping from the January 25, 1826 Trenton Federalist, *advertising a sheriff's sale of the equipment of the Trenton Factory. Photo courtesy: Monmouth County Park System.*

Cotton Machinery.

THOSE who are in want of Cotton Machinery are respectfully informed that the Firm of Hines, Arnold & Co. of Rhode-Island, will supply them with any quantity of COTTON MACHINERY, built of the best of materials, warranted to operate as well as any now in operation. For particulars enquire of Thomas Dearth, at Trenton, New-Jersey; he may be found at the Eagle Cotton Manufactory.

October 28, 1815. 71-3wpd.

Cranbury, Feb. 7, 1826.

COTTON FACTORY.

SHERIFF'S SALE.

BY virtue of a writ of Fieri Facias to me directed and delivered, issued out of the Supreme Court of Judicature of the State of New Jersey, will be exposed to sale, at public vendue, on Monday the 13th day of March next ensuing, on the premises, in the township of Nottingham, and county of Burlington, near the city of Trenton, New Jersey, all that manufactory and machinery commonly called the Trenton manufactory. The sale of the machinery will commence at 10 o'clock, A. M. on said day; the sale of the Real Estate will be between the hours of 12 and 5 o'clock P. M. of said day.

The following is a description of the machinery:—4 throstle frames, 120 spindles each; 1 stretcher, 96 spindles; 2 mules, 258 spindles each; 3 drawing frames; 5 roving frames; 10 carding engines; a lot of iron and tin cans; 1 picker; 4 reels; a quantity of bobbins, spools, reeds, heddles and shuttles; 8 power looms, 2 wrapping mills; one beaming machine; one press; two turning lathes and tools belonging to the same; one cutting engine—a quantity of carpenter's tools—a lot of iron casting and old iron—one frame for winding cloth—one spooling machine—four iron stoves and pipe—a quantity copper pipe—one iron steam boiler—one pair of scales and weights—one yarn press—a lot of cotton yarn—one dressing machine—one fall and tackle—blacksmith's tools—a number of dyer's vats—three copper kettles, and a number of other articles.

The real estate consisting of a brick building called the Trenton Factory as aforesaid, with the lot of land and appurtenances thereunto belonging or appertaining. The building is 3 stories high, about 80 by 40 feet. Also a dye house and blacksmith's shop,

Siezed as the property of Jno. Greiner and John Groves, and taken in execution at the suit of the President and Directors of the Mechanic's Bank of the city and county of Phiadelphia, and to be sold by

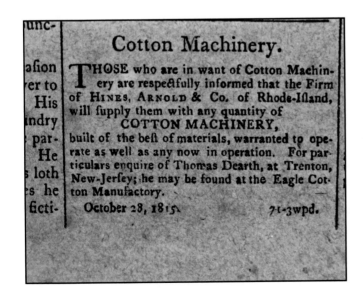

When David S. Brown died in 1877, he was recognized in both Trenton and Philadelphia as a champion of domestic industry and, therefore, instrumental in breaking up foreign control of the American market. In addition to his involvement in textiles, he incorporated the Gloucester Iron Works; the Gloucester City Gas Works; and the Camden, Gloucester, Mount Ephraim Railroad. He was also an innovator in education, founding in 1848 along with Mrs. Sarah Worthington Peter, the wife of the British Consul, the School of Design for Women in Philadelphia.[36] During the Centennial in Philadelphia, American manufacturers were astounded by the complexity and skill of the European textiles displayed and realized the need to establish trade schools in order to stay competitive with foreign countries. The school Brown and Peter founded is now known as Moore College of Art and Design and continues to train women to be self-supporting.[37] Once again, Brown, even in his final years, exhibited the foresight so basic to his success.

Despite the size and impact of these mills on their regions, the innovators of the textile industry are rarely known today, even to local historians. Currently, no swatch books have been found from any of these companies and no examples of fabric can be definitively attributed to them. The availability of these locally produced fabrics may account for the beauty of quilts made in the 1840's in New Jersey and for Mount Holly's seeming to have been a center for quiltmaking. A further study of album quilts may yield some clues. As more names are gathered and a better recognition of printed patterns and processes is developed, there will be a renewed appreciation of New Jersey's nineteenth century artisans; not only those who made the quilts, but also those who produced the fabric for them. ■

Phyllis Mount is a Preservation Specialist for the Monmouth County Park System.

FIG. 9 (Left). Clipping from the Trenton Federalist, *1815, calling for workers to relocate near the cotton mills. Photo courtesy: Monmouth County Park System.*

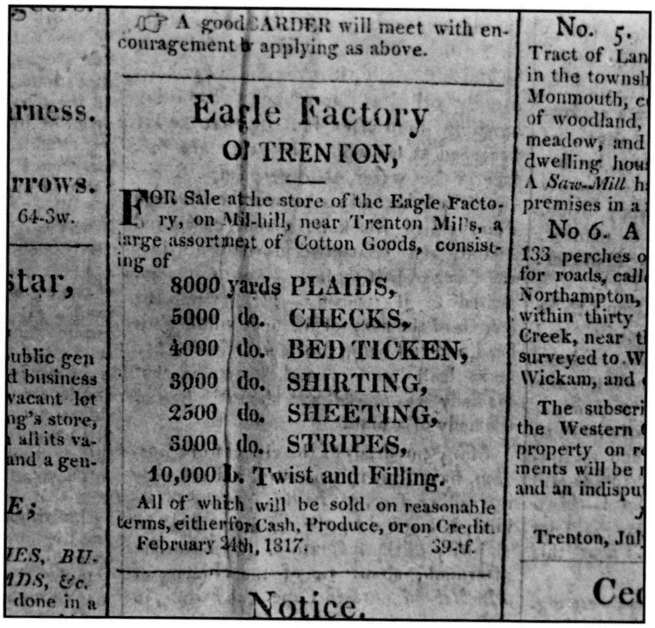

FIG. 10 (Right). Clipping from the Trenton Federalist, *1817, advertising fabrics for sale at the Eagle Factory. Photo courtesy: Monmouth County Park System.*

JOHN CARR, } Ex'rs.
JOHN LEQUEAR. }
April 3d, 1815. 41-3w.

To Carpenters, Masons, and other Mechanicks.

THE subscriber being desirous of encouraging the improvement of Bloomsbury, a growing Village, adjoining Trenton, at the head of Sloop navigation, where extensive Cotton Factories are now established; hereby offers to accommodate industrious Mechanicks and Labourers, with Building-Lots on a credit of several years, provided they will erect Houses, Shops or other sufficient Buildings thereon.

The prices will be moderate, and not more than one tenth to one twentieth of the prices asked for ground in Trenton, within a few steps of Bloomsbury. For terms apply to

DANIEL W. COXE,
No. 37, Dock-Street, Philadelphia,
or to his Agent, JOHN McMAKIN,
on the premises.
April 8, 1815. 41-3w.

For Sale,

A Tract of Land situated on both sides of Delaware river, and adjoining the city of

A good CARDER will meet with encouragement by applying as above.

Eagle Factory
OF TRENTON,

FOR Sale at the store of the Eagle Factory, on Mill-hill, near Trenton Mills, a large assortment of Cotton Goods, consisting of

8000 yards PLAIDS,
5000 do. CHECKS,
4000 do. BED TICKEN,
3000 do. SHIRTING,
2500 do. SHEETING,
3000 do. STRIPES,
10,000 lb. Twist and Filling.

All of which will be sold on reasonable terms, either for Cash, Produce, or on Credit.
February 24th, 1817. 39-tf.

Notice.

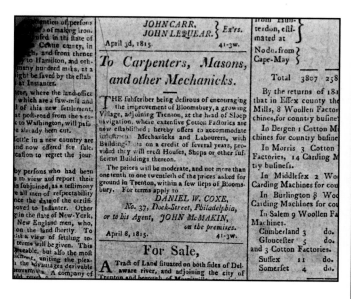

Great-Grandmother's Sewing Supplies

In the last half of the 1800's, New Jersey was prepared to provide nearly everything American home sewers needed, whether they lived in Clinton, New Jersey, or Clinton, Iowa.

"Ladies of the Gay Nineties knew New Jersey as they stitched away in their homes. They read their fashion magazines, bought Butterick patterns, cut Paterson silk with Newark shears, sewed pieces together on Elizabeth machines, using Newark or Paterson thread...unaware of their dependence on New Jersey."[38]

Fabric

Although most American pioneer women probably went West in clothing they had made for themselves, the fabric used in that clothing may well have been manufactured commercially rather than made at home. In 1800, even before the great westward migration was underway, the United States, with a population of less than 5½ million people, imported 3,710,471 yards of printed linen and cotton fabric from Great Britain.[39] By the late 1700's, enterprising new Americans were well aware of the potential profit in the manufacture and printing of fabric, and a few were struggling to establish weaving and cloth printing factories whose goods could compete with the British imports. As the 1800's progressed, American textile manufacturers became more successful at producing attractive printed cottons at a price that could compete with imported fabrics. Yet between 1830 and 1840, the city of Baltimore alone imported more than 10 million dollars' worth of foreign cloth every year from England, France, Germany, Switzerland, and the Near and Far East.[40]

Although few American swatch books exist to distinguish American-made cloth from foreign prototypes, written records show a vast increase in the quantity and quality of printed cottons being manufactured in America from New Hampshire to the Carolinas by the 1800's. In New Jersey, early calico printers were operating in Springfield (Essex County) in 1792, in Paterson in 1794, and in Pompton in 1796 (both in Passaic County). All of these early locations were in the northern part of the state, west of New York City. In the 1820's other companies were established in Trenton, Mercer County, and in Shreveville, Burlington County, east and south of Philadelphia.[41]

In the 1840's and 1850's, at the same time American women were struggling across the prairie to establish homes in territories not yet states, railroads were being built to link the cities of the East together, and by 1869 a rail line connected both shores of the continent. These new cross country railroad links meant that the products of the Eastern seaboard would soon follow the pioneer women west and, as their families replaced their original log cabins or sod houses with classic American farm houses, the few possessions that these women had brought with them would soon be supplemented by the new "necessities" being manufactured on the East Coast. In the last half of the 1800's all American women, except perhaps the very rich, were home sewers, and New Jersey was prepared to provide nearly everything that American home sewers needed whether they lived in Clinton, New Jersey, or Clinton, Iowa.

Thread

In the 1790's as Samuel Slater, the creator of the first successful American cotton mill, struggled to devise a cotton thread strong enough to serve as the warp for his mechanized looms, his wife Hannah spun the first cotton thread for hand sewing on her hand spinning wheel.[42] As the American textile industry developed, the production of cotton thread for hand sewing was sometimes a by-product of textile manufacturing, as can be seen by the spool cotton operation developed by Samuel Semple in conjunction with the Shreve textile factory in Burlington County.

However, the two most successful manufacturing operations for cotton sewing thread began in Paisley, Scotland. Because of its strength, silk thread was preferred for sewing until Napoleon's blockade cut off Britain's supply of silk thread in 1812. The first Scottish thread company was founded by James and Patrick Clark; three years later, a second thread company was begun by James Coats, a former employee of the Clark Company. In the first half of the 1800's, the problem of strengthening the normally soft cotton thread was met by twisting, or plying, three strands together like a miniature rope. By 1840, a six-ply thread was being produced, but even early six-ply was not strong enough to be used efficiently in the sewing machines that came into production in the early 1850's.[43]

In the mid-1860's, two grandsons of the Scottish Clark family established a huge thread manufacturing complex in Newark, Essex County, New Jersey.[44] The George A. Clark factory was set up to make a new type of thread that met the needs of machine sewers and was to become the standard of the industry. It was made of six strands that were first twined as pairs and was known as "cabled six-cord." The Clarks labelled their new product O.N.T. – Our New Thread – and its initials became well-known to sewers throughout the United States.[45] By the 1870's the Clark thread mills occupied two dozen buildings in Newark and East Newark.[46]

In addition to cotton thread, silk and linen thread was also being produced in New Jersey. In the 1840's, John Ryle of Paterson was the first person in America to make sewing silk and the first to wind it on a spool.[47] In the 1860's, the Barbour Flax Spinning Company, later known as the Linen Thread Company, was established in Paterson.[48]

Scissors

Just as Newark, New Jersey, was a great manufacturing center for Clark thread in the 1800's, it was also the home of two competing manufacturers of sewing scissors. Austrian Rochus Heinisch established his cutlery company there in 1825. Jacob Wiss worked in Heinisch's company when he first arrived from Switzerland, but by 1858 Wiss had established his own company. By the Civil War the two firms had put New Jersey in a leading position in the manufacturing of scissors and shears. The two Newark firms were eventually taken over by the founders' sons, and maintained a friendly rivalry until 1914 when the Wiss firm absorbed the Heinisch com-

pany, making Wiss the dominant name in American scissors.

Tapes and Bindings

Before the Civil War, the Trenton area of New Jersey manufactured a tape that was used locally as a binding for quilts. Other companies, largely in the northern part of the state, specialized in laces and trims. At one time, North Hudson made 90% of both the country's machine-made lace and embroidery.[49]

One tape and trim company associated with New Jersey that is still well-known to home sewers is the Wm. E. Wright Company, which had its operations in Orange, Essex County, New Jersey, in the 1920's and 1930's. While New Jersey thread and scissors firms were established by recent immigrants from Europe, William E. Wright, the company's founder, began his career as a clerk in a country store in Iowa. A few years later, he became a traveling salesman for a wholesale notions firm and worked for this firm for twenty years. In 1895 he came to New York to head a wholesale notions company and three years later left to establish his own firm with his five sons and two sons-in-law. One part of the success of Wright's new business lay in the fact that it offered bias tape and other notions that were prepackaged rather than cut from a spool at the local store. In 1922 Wright began offering a guarantee that its trims were washable and colorfast, another factor in its success.[50] Although Wright's, like some other manufacturers, has transferred its operations elsewhere, for a time it took its place among the New Jersey companies that have provided thread, scissors, fabrics, binding materials, and sewing machines to serve the needs of a nation of quiltmakers and home sewers. ∎

The Sewing Machine

Perhaps nothing changed home sewing to the degree that the sewing machine did. Suddenly, a woman could sew in one hour what would otherwise have taken 14 hours.

"The sewing machine became the first widely advertised consumer appliance, pioneered installment buying and patent pooling, and revolutionized the ready-made clothing industry. It also weathered the protests of those who feared the new machine was a threat to their livelihood."[51]

By 1800 an increasing amount of cloth was being produced because of the development of machines that could spin thread, weave cloth, and remove seeds from raw cotton. Many inventors and potential entrepreneurs saw that vast profits could be made from a machine that sewed cloth efficiently. Machines capable of some type of sewing had been patented in England in 1790, in France in 1804, and in Austria in 1814, but apparently none were good enough to be practical. Early attempts to duplicate the hand sewing stitch were not destined to be successful, partially because of the frequent need to re-thread the needle.

The first machine used to sew clothing commercially was produced in France. It used a chain stitch and took thread continuously from a spool, but it had no automatic means of moving the fabric so the evenness of the stitches depended on the operator's skill in feeding the fabric. Tailor Barthelomy Thimmoniers received this French patent in 1830, and by 1841 he had 80 machines operating in Paris to produce army clothing. But local tailors quickly saw that the machines were a threat to their employment. They broke into the shop and destroyed the machines.[52]

In the 1840's the search for a practical sewing machine shifted to America. In 1846 Elias Howe patented a machine that used two sources of thread to produce a lock stitch. Although he claimed to have seen the lock stitch mechanism in a dream, some speculate that he had somehow learned of a similar unpatented machine designed by Walter Hunt in the 1830's. Howe did not intend to manufacture his machine himself. Instead, he hoped to make his fortune by licensing the design to others who would produce and market the machine. He proved the speed of his machine by sewing more than the combined output of the five fastest seamstresses at the Quincy Hall Clothing Manufactory in Massachusetts. But Howe's machine still had major flaws. Since it held the fabric vertically, it could sew only in straight lines and had to have the fabric repositioned frequently. Potential manufacturers were deterred by the protests of American tailors and by concern that the machines would be too expensive to produce.[53]

Although Howe could not, at first, interest American manufacturers in producing his machine, he did seem to spur other inventors to try to correct its flaws. The sewing machine as we know it requires several different devices. It needs a special type of needle, a pressure mechanism for holding the fabric in place (now the presser foot), a feed mechanism for moving the fabric (now the feed dogs), mechanisms to position two separate threads to create the lock stitch, tension mechanisms to keep each thread from knotting or breaking, and a timing mechanism to coordinate all of these elements. From 1848 through 1853, 14 U. S. patents for sewing machines were issued, offering various solutions in addressing these needs.[54]

Some of these patent holders had better luck than Howe at getting their models into production. The history of the sewing machine in the early 1850's is a complicated web of partnerships formed and dissolved, and patents bought and sold. By 1851 several companies were offering sewing machines for sale. One of these was the Wheeler and Wilson Manufactory Company. It used the patents of inventor Allen Wilson, who introduced the feed dog system for moving the cloth. Issac Singer began producing machines in August, 1851, although his patent was not granted until 1852. His model held the cloth horizontally, used a presser foot, and had tension systems for the thread. He soon bought the patents of John Bachelder and Sherburne Blodgett, whose ideas his machines incorporated. In 1853, two companies, Wheeler and Wilson and Singer, each produced about 800 machines. A third company, Grover and Baker, whose machines did not use the lock stitch, produced about 700 machines that year.

By 1853 the battle to reap profits from the sewing machine shifted from the inventors' workshops to courtrooms and lawyers' offices. Elias Howe saw that two of the three major companies producing sewing machines were using a lock stitch mechanism, and he was determined to profit from his 1846 patent. He persuaded his father to mortgage his farm to help pay the legal fees needed for a patent fight. He got a court order requiring anyone selling or using machines incorporating his designs to set aside part of their profits until his claim could be resolved. To avoid this legal entanglement, seven sewing machine manufacturers bought licenses from Howe in 1853. But Singer resisted, citing Hunt's earlier unpatented lock stitch machine. When Singer lost in court, he finally capitulated and took out a license from Howe for $15,000.[55]

But the sewing machine wars were not yet over. From 1853 to 1856 suits and countersuits continued among the sewing machine manufacturers because the patents needed to produce a practical machine were scattered among several holders. Finally, in 1856 lawyer Orlando Potter, a partner in Grover and Baker, proposed that the three major manufacturers and Howe form the Sewing Machine Combination

or Trust, the first patent pool, which would allow them to use each other's patents, share in the distribution of each other's profits, and allow smaller manufacturers to use the pooled patents for a licensing fee. This time Howe was the holdout until he was granted $5 for every machine sold under the agreement.[56]

In 1867 Howe stated that he had received $1,185,000 from his patent, and his renewal application was denied on the grounds that he had received sufficient compensation. (As a sidelight, Howe served as a private in a volunteer regiment in the Civil War, and on one occasion, when government pay was delayed, Howe lent the money needed to pay the whole regiment.)[57]

Once the patent disputes were resolved, the production and marketing of sewing machines began in earnest. The advantages of the sewing machine were quickly evident. With the sewing machine a person could sew in one hour a man's shirt that would have taken 14 hours by hand. From 1861 to 1865 the Civil War created a massive need for uniforms and blankets, and the sewing machine was quickly adopted on both sides to meet these needs.[58] In 1859 over 40,000 machines were sold, and in 1866 80,000 machines were sold. From 1871 to 1876 at least 500,000 machines were sold each year, so that by 1876 over 2.5 million sewing machines had been produced, many of which were sold outside the United States. As manufacturers turned their attention from commercial machines to those for the home and as patents ran out and royalty payments declined, the price of a sewing machine eventually fell from $75 in 1860 to $25 in 1871. Until 1876 Wheeler and Wilson led in sewing machine sales. In that year Singer took the lead and eventually absorbed many other competitors.

Singer took the lead in sales of

sewing machines for several reasons. First, as early as 1856 Edward Clark, Isaac Singer's partner, pioneered the idea of installment buying which allowed the purchaser to pay $5 down and the rest in monthly installments. Second, Singer accepted other companies' machines as trade-ins and then destroyed them to prevent the development of a market in used machines. Third, the Singer Company indirectly addressed social obstacles to the acceptance of the machine for home sewing. To combat the idea that women couldn't use machinery the Company paid its salesmen $6 extra per month if their wives would come to the company's showrooms to demonstrate the machines.[59] It also used advertisements showing children operating the machines to stress their simplicity. To combat husbands' fears that, freed from hours of tedious production of family clothing, women would enjoy a dangerous amount of free time, advertising stressed that women with sewing machines would have more time for their husbands and children.[60]

In addition to taking several clever steps to market their machines, the Singer Company took an innovative step to produce its machines. In 1872 the company consolidated its widely separated operations into a single vast plant in Elizabethport, Hudson County, New Jersey, that would employ 3,000 workers. The innovative nature of this factory lay in the fact that it was one of the first to be powered by steam rather than water power. Its location next to the Jersey Central Railroad allowed for the efficient delivery of coal to provide the steam power and shipping out of the finished sewing machines.[61] The wisdom of the Singer Company's marketing and production decisions can be seen in the fact that it took the lead in sewing machine sales in 1877 and dominated the industry for the next 100 years. ■

The Quilts Of One New Jersey Family

The Dunlap/Clegg quilts represent one hundred years of rural and urban traditions in New Jersey.

The quilts inherited by Harold Dunlap, his wife Edna Smith Dunlap, and her cousin, Gladys Clegg, were made over a period of 100 years. Together they illustrate many facets of New Jersey life and provide insight into both the rural and urban aspects of the New Jersey scene.

The Dunlap Family Quilts

Harold Dunlap's family quilts represent the rural tradition in New Jersey. His father, Theodore Dunlap (1857-1935), lived in western Morris County and married twice. In 1883 he married Mary S. Keen (1865 -1892), the great-granddaughter of Joseph Huff, a Dutchman who settled in Sussex County with his four brothers in 1776. Sussex County, in the northwest corner of the state, remains one of New Jersey's more rural regions, now serving as a popular vacation area because of its lakes, ski slopes, and hiking trails, including a section of the Appalachian Trail. The lovely Sunburst and Swag quilt (Plate 9) that Mary Keen brought to her marriage to Theodore is not believed to have been made by Mary herself. It is more likely to have been made by Mary's mother, Catherine

Huff Keen, who was born in 1838 and married in 1858. Mary was always considered frail and died of consumption at 27, leaving two small children.

In 1895 Theodore married Mary Elizabeth Hiler (1870-1968), sometimes called Lizzie. She was the daughter of William Hiler, a professional wood worker who carved and fitted wooden handles for tools. As a child, Lizzie helped her father by smoothing the

FIG. 11. Mary Elizabeth "Lizzie" Hiler Dunlap

wooden handles with pieces of broken glass, since sandpaper was not yet available. Lizzie had been a good friend of Theodore's first wife. The relationship between the two women can be seen in the fact that Lizzie kept her predecessor's photograph on the wall of the family dining room for decades, perhaps in deference to Mary's children, whom Lizzie raised as her own. In 1910 Theodore and Lizzie moved to West Orange, Essex County, in the more urban eastern part of the state, where Theodore eventually became a foreman in a lumber yard.

Lizzie was a skillful seamstress by the age of 14. She is believed to have made the Courthouse Steps quilt (Plate 10) and a companion Log Cabin quilt in the years before her marriage. In her late twenties Lizzie gradually became deaf, a process that accelerated with each child she bore. Her condition was genetic, and her aunt Martha Minard went deaf about the same time. The family recalls these two very hard-of-hearing women meeting each Sunday for tea and shouting at each other through their ear trumpets as long as they had the slightest remaining ability to hear.

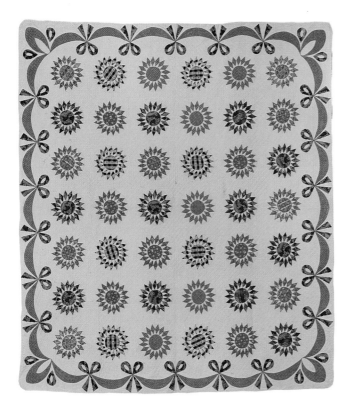

PLATE 9 (Left). SUNBURST AND SWAG, c.1850, 83" x 96". *Probably made by Catherine Huff Keen (b. 1838), Sussex County, New Jersey. The Sunburst block is one of the more intricate pieced blocks to appear in documented New Jersey quilts and the Swag border is one of the few elaborate border treatments seen with any frequency. Although this beautifully made quilt has a larger area of white than many New Jersey-made quilts, the white area is quilted in the typical New Jersey outline and crosshatch design. Owned by Harold Dunlap and Edna Smith Dunlap.*

PLATE 10 (Right). COURTHOUSE STEPS, c.1890, 80"x 94". *Probably made by Mary Hiler Dunlap (1870-1968), Beach Glen, Morris County, New Jersey. This classic quilt displays a lovely assortment of fabrics of the period. It also represents a continuing New Jersey tendency to set blocks on the diagonal rather than on the square, an arrangement not commonly seen in Courthouse Steps quilts. The quilt is believed to have been made by the same quiltmaker who made the 1930's Starflower quilt (Plate 11) in her later years, thus illustrating the work of a single quiltmaker at widely separated times of her life. Owned by Harold Dunlap and Edna Smith Dunlap.*

Lizzie learned to read lips very well and had a trained dog to let her know when someone was at the door. As her hearing loss increased, she immersed herself in needlework, often spending six hours a day making clothing, crocheted bedspreads, quilts, and other items for family members. Although her Starflower quilt made in the 1930's (Plate 11) uses a design long available as a commercial pattern, Lizzie had no need to purchase a pattern as she drafted the design from memory after seeing the quilt in someone else's home.

The Clegg Family Quilts

Edna Smith Dunlap, wife of Theodore Dunlap's son, Harold, is a part of the Clegg family through her mother Frances Smith (1888-1950), whose maiden name was Clegg. Edna inherited the Lone Star quilt (Plate 12) from her mother's sister, Caroline (Carry) Clegg (1875-1950). Just as the Dunlaps represent the more rural side of New Jersey life, the Cleggs are associated with its more urban aspects. The family owned a florist business in West Orange, Essex County, for many years. This town was both residential and

industrial; Thomas Edison had both a Victorian mansion and a laboratory a few blocks from the Clegg's florist business.

Although Carry Clegg and Lizzie Dunlap were contemporaries, their lives were very different. Carry never married and, for a time, commuted to work in New York City, for an import/export business. Family tradition says that Carry had "an eye for the finer things." She collected Tiffany silver and Oriental art works, which have been passed down to family members. The family does not know how she

PLATE 11. STARFLOWER, 1931, 82" x 90". Made by Mary Hiler Dunlap (1870-1968), Cedar Grove, Essex County, New Jersey. Although this quilt is clearly part of the 1930's fashion for floral quilts, this particular design is not seen as often as others. The quilt was one of a pair made at nearly the same time. The color of the flowers in each quilt was selected by the person for whom the quilt was being made. The pattern was drafted by the quiltmaker from her memory of a quilt seen earlier. The use of a stencil-type quilting design in the white areas illustrates a New Jerseyan's use of this style of quilting even when such a design was not provided by a kit. The fact that the quiltmaker is also believed to have made the Courthouse Steps quilt (Plate 10) before her marriage illustrates the range of quilts that a single quiltmaker might have made in her lifetime. Owned by Gail Dunlap Reuben, daughter of Harold Dunlap and Edna Smith Dunlap.

PLATE 12. LONE STAR WITH BRODERIE PERSE, c.1850, 84" x 85". Much of the broderie perse on this lovely Lone Star quilt is finished with a closely worked buttonhole stitch in red thread. The center of the Lone Star is made of a single blue circle of fabric. The gold sunburst is appliquéd to the center circle and is accented with gold chain stitching representing the sun's rays. The inner ring of light green diamonds is also appliquéd to the center blue circle, which was not cut away under the diamonds and can be faintly seen in certain lighting. Owned by Hilary Elizabeth Reuben, a grand-daughter of Harold Dunlap and Edna Smith Dunlap.

came to own the impressive mid-1800 Lone Star quilt, but she valued it highly and sometimes reminded family members that "The Quilt" was kept in a trunk in the front hall.

Frances and Carry Clegg had several other brothers and sisters. One sister, Laura, married Charles Wright, a member of the family that owned the Wm. E. Wright Company. The Wrights pioneered the idea of seam bindings and tapes that came in packages rather than on a spool to be measured and cut at the store at the time of purchase. For more than a decade in the early 1900's, the Wrights' manufacturing operation was in Orange, Essex County, not far from the homes of various family members. The Wrights add a major manufacturing component to this diverse family history, and, until 1972, Charles Wright's father's photograph could be seen on packages of seam binding sold throughout the country.

Other members of the Clegg family with interesting quilts to contribute to the family story are Frances Clegg's cousins, Amelia (Millie) (1890-1965) and Gladys Clegg. From 1942 to 1951 Millie Clegg made six complete quilts and a top, with some assistance from her sister Gladys, who now owns all of these quilts.

Generally, Millie made the tops and Gladys helped with the quilting. In the case of the Summer Garden quilt (Plate 13), Gladys also helped with an adaptation of the design. A seventh quilt which Millie had in progress at the time of her death was completed by her niece, Doris Larsen. This Peony quilt, plus three others can be seen as a group in Plate 127. Around 1950, Millie's quilts were exhibited in the sisters' home as a fund-raiser for the Evening Circle of the Central Presbyterian Church of Montclair in Essex County. The quilts were displayed draped on banisters and pieces of furniture. An admission of 25 cents was charged to view the quilts.

The stories associated with the quilts of the Dunlap and Clegg families introduce several themes that will be explored in this book. They represent the lives of diverse New Jerseyans from original settlers to New York commuters and from rural craftspeople to urban manufacturers. They present many facets of women's lives from the nurturing of children to the raising of funds for community organizations. And in these families we see inheritors who valued these quilts enough to preserve them, along with the family histories that they represent. ∎

From information provided by Gail Dunlap Reuben, daughter of Harold and Edna Dunlap. She compiled these accounts with the help of many family members including her parents and Gladys Clegg and Doris Larsen.

PLATE 13. SUMMER GARDEN, 1943, 75" x 87". Made by Amelia Estelle Clegg (1890-1965), Montclair, Essex County, New Jersey. This lovely medallion quilt was redesigned by Gladys Clegg because her sister, Amelia, did not like the original which was from a kit. Typical of the work of Amelia is the swag border with its scalloped inner and outer edges. Another distinguishing feature of her quilts is the embroidered inscription of the quilt title, maker, date, and place. Owned by Gladys Clegg, sister of the maker.

Florence Peto: Historian & Collector

An innovator in the preservation of quilts and quilt history, Florence Peto led the way for future generations of quilt enthusiasts.

Florence Peto, a New Jerseyan by marriage, might have been a quilt historian of the 1970's and 1980's because of the importance she placed on historical accuracy. In the Depression and World War II years, while some of her fellow authors were describing quilt history based on fantasy and hypothesis, she printed quilters' diaries, put together a collection of 100-year-old quilts, did extensive research on the histories of the families associated with her quilts, and wrote books on quilt history. She lectured at national events, organized museum exhibits, and was instrumental in getting wonderful old quilts into museum collections.

Mrs. Peto learned sewing skills from her grandmother, and her interest in old textiles came from her familiarity with sample books from the cotton mill her husband once owned. She won prizes with the quilts that she herself made. Her works were often revivals of the styles of the 1830's quilts that she collected. Her quilts included chintz appliqué, the medallion format, and the use of historic fabrics. Although she often worked in styles popular 100 years earlier, in some of the techniques she preferred

she was quite ahead of her time. She quilted her pieces block-by-block in an era when quilting without a frame was relatively unknown.[62]

Many of the details of her life, both important and trivial, are known from her correspondence with quilting "pen pal" Emma Andres. In her first letter to Miss Andres in 1939, she wrote "my photographs of American-made quilts, spreads and woven coverlets number over three hundred – all have authentic histories verified by family records and papers. What I desire to do in gathering this material [is to] preserve the memory and identity of the quiltmaker as well as her needle work."[63] Amidst details of getting a new hairdo and making pudding for dinner, she tells Miss Andres about her lecture at the New York World's Fair of 1939 where she represented the Index of American Design, a vast, federally sponsored compilation of objects of American design and craftsmanship made from the colonial period to the close of the nineteenth century. A major event in her life was an invitation to the White House during the Eisenhower administration to present the winning quilt from a Vermont show she had judged.

Quilts from Mrs. Peto's collection of antiques were frequently displayed in museum settings. In 1948 the New York Historical Society displayed her collection of 50 quilts. The Henry Ford Museum in Michigan had an exhibit of her quilts in 1955, and on December 12, 1967, she wrote to a friend, "Now I am getting ready for the big exhibition of my whole quilt collection in the Suffolk County Museum in Stony Brook Long Island....This will be the last time I will show quilts as a collection for, after the show, I mean to offer many of them for sale."[64]

Mrs. Peto's collecting of fine quilts partially explains why quilts from New Jersey and adjacent areas are so well represented in museum collections. Among the outstanding works from her collection now in museums are the Mary Totten Rising Sun at the Smithsonian Institution, the Sophonisba Peale Star Medallion at the Philadelphia Museum of Art, three quilts in the Newark Museum, and 17 quilts that form the nucleus of the Shelburne Museum collection. When the world went looking for quilts in the 1970's, Mrs. Peto's finds were preserved and catalogued in major museums for new quilt lovers to enjoy and study. ∎

The Newark Museum: A Pioneer

**Under the leadership of its founder, John Cotton Dana,
the Newark Museum began collecting and exhibiting quilts in the 1900's.**

Since its opening in 1909, the Newark Museum, located in Essex County, New Jersey, has been a pioneer in exhibiting and collecting American quilts. According to the 1959 museum publication *A Survey: 50 years of the Newark Museum*, "Its collection of pieced and appliquéd quilts is one of the best, if not the best, to be found along the Atlantic Seaboard."[65]

Museum founder John Cotton Dana envisioned the museum as "an institution of and for active service to the people of the community."[66] His idea, though radical at the time, emphasized the importance of ordinary objects. By recognizing and exhibiting the "living arts of everyday people,"[67] he was able to combine the practical with the artistic.

The museum's first quilt exhibit was held in 1914 and was entitled, "Textiles: Antique & Modern." The exhibit ran from November 26 to December 27, 1914.[68] Four years later, in 1918, the museum acquired the first quilt for its permanent collection, for

which Dana had established the following criteria: uniqueness of design, quality of stitching, materials, condition, and provenance. In *American Quilts in the Newark Museum Collection*, Philip Curtis describes the quilt: "Wild Goose Chase, 72" x 91½", United States, c.1800-1830. Red homespun wool top with pieced parallel rows of blue wool triangles. Tan wool backing; lined with a thick wool batting, edges bound with cotton twill tape. The blue triangles, measuring 11" across and 5" from base to apex, were produced by cutting a square or rectangle in half. The three-corner patch was a recognized bird symbol."[69]

In 1919, a New Jersey-made quilt, "Delectable Mountains," c.1840-1860, was added to the permanent collection and, according to Curtis, "Quilting legends suggest that the design originated in New Jersey and was first made by the invalid wife of a New Jersey clergyman."[70]

During the period 1920-1929, 28 quilts were added to the permanent collection, 15 of which had New Jersey

provenance. Gifts to the museum in 1925 included two quilts from John Cotton Dana. Both were given the design names of "Patchwork" even though one was a quilt dating from 1815-1830, and the other a quilt top c.1850-1870. It is no surprise to see that both quilts originated in Vermont for Dana maintained homes in both Newark, New Jersey, and Woodbury, Vermont.

Curtis mentions additional quilt exhibits in 1920, 1927, and 1929. However, of these three dates, current museum records show only one exhibit from January 1 to January 31, 1927, entitled "Needlework."[71] During that year the museum was presented with its first appliqué quilt, a quilt known as the "Masonic Quilt." It was made in Newark, New Jersey, in 1856 by Mrs. Rose Van Wart. Her husband, who was evidently a member of the Fraternal Order of Free and Accepted Masons, designed and cut the symbols which included builders' and masons' tools, anchors, and stars. The red, green, and yellow calico pieces were appliquéd with a buttonhole stitch in matching thread to a white cotton background. It was machine quilted in the Fan and Orange Peel patterns.[72]

During the years 1930-1939, thirteen quilts were added to the permanent collection, eight of them from New Jersey. The museum was the first to hold exhibitions of American folk art, with its landmark shows of 1930 and 1931. In the January 1930 issue of *The Museum*, an article on American patchwork quilts said, "Though they belong essentially with furniture of colonial America, their angular design and crude colors fit sympathetically with modern decoration. For this reason machine made patchwork quilts may now be purchased in department stores – the first time such quilts have been merchandised." The article goes on to say, "Quilt making is once more a popular diversion, though it is not so much a cause for hospitable gatherings as in the old days." And, in comparing old-time quilting bees to present day social events, the article added, "the woman who was socially ambitious must excel with her needle, as today one must play a good game of bridge."[73]

The Art Department of the Contemporary Club of Newark held an exhibit of "creative art work" by its members from January 20 to February 2, 1930. Examples of applied art, and how it had changed over the past 50 years, gave visitors to the museum a chance to review objects ranging from the 1880's to 1929. Earlier examples were mostly paintings, crewel-work, china painting, drawn-work, and embroidery; more recent ones included wood carving, metal-work, jewelry, and those revived crafts of an earlier day such as hooked rugs, patchwork quilts, and [cross stitch] samplers.[74]

Eight out of the 21 quilts added to the permanent collection between 1940 and 1950 were from New Jersey. A quilt exhibit in 1943 was entitled, "Quilts (3 High)." It is unclear what the title implied, but the exhibit ran from December 11, 1943, to March 22, 1944.[75] In 1947, New Jerseyan Florence Peto – author, quilt historian, and collector – donated a fragment of printed cotton (4½" x 5⅛") to the museum collection.[76] The piece is familiar to us today as a commemorative because it features a small stripe, and the hat and glasses of Horace Greeley along with a hammer and a sickle. It commemorates Greeley's acceptance of the nomination for the presidency when he ran against Ulysses S. Grant in 1872.

A review of the 1947 quilt exhibition "Early American Quilts and Coverlets" appeared in the May issue of *Antiques*. The review seems unusually mild to us now as it mentions only that the exhibit would continue through the summer and that it included quilts and coverlets from the museum's own collection. In giving readers an idea of what to expect, the review stated, "The display includes many patterns and designs familiar to collectors."[77] It then listed such patterns as Delectable Mountains, Star of LeMoyne, and Wheel of Fortune, and briefly discussed their history. The exhibit was initially installed from March 1 to March 16, 1947, but museum records indicate that it was reinstalled in another gallery and ran from March 18 to September 21, 1947.[78]

Because more than 50 examples of quilts had been acquired by 1948, it became apparent that a catalog of the collection was needed. The Newark Museum published *Quilts and Counterpanes in the Newark Museum*, written by Margaret E. White, Curator of Decorative Arts. Acknowledgments were given to Mrs. Florence Peto and Miss Marie D. Webster for permission to quote from their books, *Historic Quilts* and *Quilts: Their Story and How To Make Them*, respectively.

In 1949, Florence Peto donated to the museum an elaborately stitched and stuffed all-white quilt known as the Voorhees Quilt. It originally belonged to a Dutch family in Long Island, New York, and exhibits the finest of workmanship in intricate vines, flowers, leaves, and a central oval feather-wreath medallion. It is signed in French knots with the name Jane Voorhees and dated 1830/1831.[79]

In the years following 1950, the Newark Museum maintained its well-deserved reputation as an esteemed collector of American quilts. It acquired not only antique quilts but also contemporary ones from living artists. To this day, the museum continues to add to its collection with an eye to preserving the past for the future. ∎

Chapter Two

New Jersey Beginnings

1 August. The last week I was a Quilting at Peggy Cox for Ellen. I quilted 4 days.

September 22, 1837. Margaret Cox Paid me 5 Dollars. She owes me 5 yet. She paid Dow 2 dollars....

March 19, 1837 [sic]. I was at Mr. Timbrooks 3 day a Quilting and at Mrs. Farratts 3 days....

May 1, 1838. [?] settled with Margaret Ten Eyk all accounts to this day by me. I paid my Brother James 48 for my Board. James Ten Eyk 30 dollars interest he owed me.... I was abroad 24 weaks out of the year in 1837....

I eat Breakfast at home. I spun my woll. Was at home till the 19 of June. I went to Mr. Elmondorf. I was there till the 9 of July sowing. I et dinner at Jimmeys. I was at Mr. Emmondorfs 2 weaks and 4 days. I was at Giddeon Cox's 3 days a sowing and I was a sowing at Onsh Van Pelts 3 days and the next weak I was at Onsh Van Pelts 4 days and I went to old Mrs. Stulls and was their 2 a sowing for our Peter.

The 26 of July I was at our Peters a sowing for him 1 day and the weak at home....

August 15. I sowed for Easter 2 weaks and 5 days and mended stockings 2 days.

October 22. I nit one pare of stockings for Tunis. 6 shillings....

Feb. 8. I maid 2 Linnen Shirts for my Brother James. 6 shillings....

– From the diary of Margaret Ten Eyck, an unmarried woman of Dutch descent,
whose family lived in the Raritan River Valley, New Jersey

from *The Folklore and Folklife of New Jersey* by David S. Cohen

PLATE 14 (Below, Detail). SAWTOOTH STAR, 1829, 106" x 106". Made by Mary Burns Joy, Bordentown, Burlington County, New Jersey. Star patterns have always been popular with quilters, and they are frequently found in the earlier New Jersey quilts. The stars in this quilt are made of a variety of polished chintzes and the fabric in the alternate blocks incorporates palm trees. The date "1829" and initials "M.B." are cross-stitched on the back. The maker lived into her 90's and was well-known by the current owner, her cousin, Caroline Armstrong.

PLATE 15 (Right). Another detail of blocks from SAWTOOTH STAR (Plate 14, Below) with section of the back folded over to reveal date.

1777 to 1840

Pieced Blocks & Floral Prints

Quilts made in New Jersey before 1840 often show a distinctive preference for certain styles.

The quilts made before 1840 in New Jersey can best be understood by comparing them to published early quilts from the original Southern states, such as Virginia and North Carolina.[1] These early quilts from the coastal Southern states are almost always medallions with large areas of white space. Some examples are finished as unquilted counterpanes, but those that are quilted have lovely and often elaborate quilting. The earliest of these medallions, dated from about 1780 to 1800, are almost exclusively pieced. After that date, chintz appliqué comes to dominate these medallions, with pieced designs being relegated to the borders. Of the quilts in Gloria Seaman Allen's book *First Flowerings, Early Virginia Quilts*, the earliest medallions date from 1780 to 1800 while the earliest block-style quilts appear about 1840.[2]

Among the New Jersey quilts recorded, the situation is rather reversed. Cotton block-style quilts were recorded with family-attributed dates as early as 1778 and 1797 (Plate 17). In addition, two early wool quilts constructed of star patterns in alternate blocks are owned by Historic Allaire Village in Monmouth County (Plate 16) and the Tempe Wick House in Morris County.[3] The New Jersey Project did record four medallion quilts

dated before 1840, but all are primarily pieced with little or no open white space. Appliqué on these quilts is a rather limited part of the total design and does not closely follow the outlines of the printed figures. A particularly interesting medallion quilt (Plate 163) has a miniature Irish Chain as the center medallion and features portraits of the first six presidents cut from English or French commemorative fabric. Although floral fabric is also appliquéd on this quilt, the flower motifs are cut in clamshell shapes to include some of the original background, rather than following the outline of the flowers. While glorious chintz appliqué quilts were eventually made in New Jersey, they seem to have been made after 1840 and with a block style, rather than a medallion format.

All-white quilts do not seem to have been of major interest to New Jersey quiltmakers in the period before 1840. A lovely example with some candlewicking and a worked date of 1807 was recorded by the Project, but it was made in neighboring Pennsylvania. The only other all-white quilt recorded by the Project was attributed by the family to about 1860. While this is a rather late date for all-white quilts, two others made in Newark and owned by the Newark Museum bear similar dates of 1850 and 1870,[4] perhaps indi-

cating New Jersey's rather late interest in the possibilities of white spaces in quilts.

A single Stencil quilt (Plate 18) was recorded in New Jersey. It has no firmly attributed date, but it appears to have been a totally hand-crafted effort with red and blue pigments applied to possibly hand-woven linen.

Interestingly, the tape bindings often ascribed in other publications to the earliest quilts seem relatively uncommon in early New Jersey quilts. Instead, edges are frequently turned in and reinforced with a double row of quilting. Tape bindings on New Jersey quilts are most common from about 1830 to 1870, with tan tape being seen relatively frequently, as described further in the section on Trenton tape, and white tape appearing less often.

If the themes of early Southern quilts can be said to be the medallion format, large areas of white space, and lovely quilting; the themes repeated in early New Jersey quilts can be said to be the use of blocks and large areas of floral prints. These sometimes-glazed, large-scale florals are seen uncut as whole cloth quilts, incorporated into strip quilts, used as borders, alternated with pieced blocks, and used in large triangles to finish rows for diagonally set quilts. ∎

PLATE 16. SAWTOOTH STAR, c.1800, wool, 105½" x 105½". Simple wool stars against an indigo background give a dramatic beauty to this quilt. The large size is typical of its time, as is the cut-out at the lower edge to accommodate a four poster bed. The quilting is done with dark thread in classic quilting motifs that include leaf and vine patterns and laurel leaves between the stars. Owned by Allaire Village, Inc., Monmouth County.

PLATE 17 (Left, Folded). OHIO STAR WITH SASHING, 1797, 87" x 105". Made in Cape May, Cape May County, New Jersey. This Ohio Star pattern is surrounded by an unusual sashing, similar to the Irish Chain design. The former owner was Clara Bohm, a Cape May City school principal. She received it from a descendant of the original family, along with a note attributing it with a date of 1797. A faint signature on the back may say, "Diane F...Wood." In good condition for its age, it appears to have been repaired at the edge with 1840-era fabrics. Owned by Ruth Toft.

(Right, Folded). UNEVEN NINE PATCH, 1778, 79" x 81". Made by Abigail Rodgers, New Jersey or New York. Nine Patch blocks alternate with floral print squares in this timeless beauty. Two slashes at the lower edge are designed to fit a four poster bed. The quilting is done in both blue and off-white thread, and includes straight lines, hearts, and daisies. The back of the quilt is signed and dated. This quilt was passed down to the present owner through the family of Clement C. Moore, a family that had been in the cotton business since 1848. Owned by H. Justine Spaulding.

PLATE 18. WHOLE-CLOTH STENCILED QUILT, c.1820, linen, 74″ x 88″. This is a rare quilt, hand stenciled in blue and red on a sturdy tan background material that is probably hand woven. It is faded, but otherwise in excellent condition. A medallion center design is surrounded with paisley shapes, circles, half-circles, and pots of flowers. The heavy quilting follows the stenciled designs. Owned by the Hopewell Museum, Mercer County.

PLATE 19. MEDALLION, c.1820, linen and cotton, 77½" x 94½". Probably made in New Jersey. This is a center-medallion-style quilt, but as the medallion is a square of a single fabric, the main emphasis is on the pieced work surrounding it, a lively and endlessly fascinating collection of fabrics. The pale azure watery blue is a definitive color of 1820's fabrics. A seam visible in the coarsely woven fabric of the back shows that the quilt was originally larger. The name "Leewin" is written on the back. Privately owned.

PLATE 20. MEDALLION, c.1820, 94" x 97". Made in New Jersey. This medallion-style quilt is beautifully designed with many borders surrounding and echoing the center motif. Both piecing and appliqué techniques have been used. While some of the early chintz fabrics have deteriorated, others are still in fine condition and give a good idea of what the quilt looked like when it was new. Floral chintz, shown here in the border triangles, appears frequently in New Jersey quilts of this era. This quilt was purchased from Fred Noyes, founder of the Noyes Museum and the Smithville Restoration, both in Atlantic County. Owned by Gary and Niki Giberson.

PLATE 21. OHIO STAR, c.1820, 82" x 101". The Ohio Stars set side-by-side with squares of floral fabric create a shaded look in this quilt. The repeated use of floral print fabric is common in early New Jersey quilts. This particular print differs in that it is coarsely woven in contrast to the more usual chintz. There has been some replacement of deteriorated fabric at the edges. A stamp on the back is of faded blue lettering, now illegible, in an oval shape. The quilitng is done in diagonal parallel lines. Owned by the Hopewell Museum, Mercer County.

PLATE 22. MEDALLION, c.1835, unquilted, 85" x 100". Made in Rochester, New York. This early quilt top uses the medallion style of construction: a central focus with several surrounding borders. The sewing is done using the English paper piecing method: patches have been joined to one another after having been lined with paper templates. Among the paper fragments showing on the reverse side is one with a handwritten date of 1834. The piece presents a stunning array of early fabrics including chintz and linen with a myriad of appliqué details including cherubs, realistic animals, mythical creatures in broderie perse, stars, plants, and decorative bows. Much of the appliqué is done with a herringbone stitch. The diamond appliqué borders are made of one continuous piece of fabric. Pieced patchwork borders as well as the diamond appliqué borders enclose the varied delights of this masterpiece. Owned by The Morris Museum, Morris County.

The British Heritage

The traditions and textiles of the British Isles contributed much to early quiltmaking in America.

At the time of the American Bicentennial, quiltmaking was touted as a uniquely American art form, yet the roots of the American tradition clearly lie in Europe, primarily in the British Isles.

Written records indicate that whole-cloth silk quilts were on the beds of the British nobility as early as the 1300's. One literary work from that period describes a "rich quylt....with crimson sendel [silken stuff] stitched with thredes of golde."[5] Records also show that Henry VIII gave his fifth wife, Katherine Howard, 23 quilts as a wedding gift,[6] and that in 1609 James I gave his daughter, Elizabeth, three quilts as marriage gifts.

If quilted bedcoverings were found in the households of the wealthy, it might be assumed that the noblewomen of the time were creating these quilts. Creating fine needlework was an important activity among aristocratic women in this period, but there is another possible source for these quilts. From the mid-1500's or earlier professional quilters were at work making quilted petticoats, jackets, hats, and perhaps even fabrics to line carriages. They may have marked fabrics for others to quilt as well as making bed quilts to sell.[7]

By the 1600's whole-cloth quilts had been on the beds of the British aristocracy for centuries. But at the time the settlement of the American colonies began, there is no indication that the ordinary people in Britain had any quilts at all. Dorothy Osler reports that the sparse inventories from less affluent households show few textiles and no quilts. The ordinary people slept on a sack of straw and were lucky to have one sheet, blanket, or coverlet as additional bedding. Thus, the very earliest settlers in America are unlikely to have brought the quiltmaking tradition with them.[8]

The Craze for Printed and Painted Fabrics From India

At the time the American colonies were being founded, the whole-cloth quilts of the British elite were made of wool, linen, silk, or satin. Cotton does not appear to have been common. The surviving quilted clothing of the period shows that lovely and intricate quilting designs were available to embellish bed quilts. Stuffing, cording, embroidery, and even small amounts of appliqué are recorded as decorative features on quilts, but no evidence of pieced designs is found in the 1600's.

It may be hard for the modern quilter, whose work is based on an abundant supply of printed cotton, to envision a time in which all fabric was either a single color or was woven of simple stripes or checks. Techniques for printing designs on cloth were not in common use, and embroidery and appliqué were the usual methods for adding color to otherwise monochromatic fabrics.

Then all of this changed. In 1635, shortly after the first British colonies were established in North America, colorful printed or painted cottons were first imported into Britain from India. These exotic, colorfast fabrics eventually proved so popular that, by 1702, they were banned as a threat to the existing British textile industries. The Indian chintzes were also prohibited in France for the same reason, but the ban was not very successful in either country.

PLATE 23. TREE OF LIFE, 1777, 100" x 106". Made in the Palampore style, this quilt is a masterpiece of appliqué. The central motif was cut from a single printed textile and stitched to the background fabric. Additional branches were expertly added to give the design needed width. Free-form leaves were appliquéd in the corners above the tree. The extremely fine quilting includes crosshatching and tiny clamshells the size of the end of a finger. The quilt is said to have been made by one of the daughters of John Hart of Hopewell, Mercer County. Hart was one of the signers of the Declaration of Independence. This quilt is housed in the Drake House Museum in Plainfield, Union County, and owned by the Historical Society of Plainfield.

The appealing Indian fabrics were the height of fashion in both countries, and the scarcity caused by the bans made them even more desirable. Prominent people ignored the ban, including Mme. Pompadour, the legendary mistress of Louis XV, who dressed in Indian calicoes, used them to decorate her chateau, and gave them as gifts. The public demand for these prohibited fabrics created many of the same problems the prohibition of alcohol did in the 1920's in America, including smuggling, clandestine production, inflated prices, corruption of enforcement officials, and even the creation of bands of armed thugs to protect illegal activities.[9]

This would suggest a possible connection between the shortage of the popular Indian chintzes and the evolution of a fad for patchwork among the British upper classes. The earliest surviving British patchwork quilt, the Levens Hall Quilt, dates from 1708, just six years after the importation of Indian chintz was forbidden. The quilt, attributed to the daughters of an affluent family in the Lake District, appears to be a skillful effort to stretch a collection of Indian fabrics. The first written reference to patchwork occurs only a few years later in 1726; in *Gulliver's Travels* Jonathan Swift describes a suit of clothing made by the Lilliputians as looking like "the patchwork made by the ladies of England."[10] No other patchwork quilts survive from the early part of the 1700's, but by the time of the American Revolution in the 1770's, examples of patchwork quilts are found on both sides of the Atlantic.

As patchwork came into fashion sometime in the eighteenth century, quilting on bedding went out of style among the affluent and moved down the social ladder into the homes of the less wealthy. The Levens Hall Quilt of 1708 utilizes both patchwork and quilting on the same bedcover, but by the

1790's patchwork bedcovers were deliberately being left unquilted on the beds of the upper classes.[11] Also by this time, quilting had appeared as a social activity among poorer and more rural women, including the wives of Welsh miners and the Methodist women in the northern counties of England.[12]

Thus, at the time the American colonies were being settled, the skill of making patchwork apparently was evolving among the British upper classes and the skill of quilting was moving down the social scale. Although the Levens Hall Quilt uses both patchwork and quilting, by the end of the century patchwork bedcovers were deliberately being finished as unquilted counterpanes.

Quilts Come to America

Up to the time of the Revolution, the record of quilts in America is similar to that of the British Isles. The estate records from Virginia and Massachusetts document the presence of quilts in prosperous households before the Revolution. Sally Garoutte studied early records from the Plymouth colony, Providence, Rhode Island, New Hampshire, and the Hartford, Connecticut, area and found only 10 quilts mentioned out of 868 references to bedding. When the value of bedding items was listed, quilts averaged a much higher value than other bedding items: 52 shillings for quilts as compared to 10 to 15 shillings for rugs, blankets, and coverlets.[13] The quilts described in estate inventories before the 1770's seem to be whole-cloth quilts. Virginia records show an East Indian quilt in 1655, a crimson satin in 1702, and a blue-and-white Holland (linen) in 1746.[14] Similar quilts are found in the Massachusetts records. An Indian silk quilt is listed in the 1729 estate of Governor William Burnet, and several quilts appear in the 1743 estate of wealthy Boston merchant Peter Faneuil,

including two green silks, a yellow mohair, a blue silk, a chintz, a "workt" (embroidered) fustian and harrateens (worsteds) in green, blue, and red.[15] Both the Virginia and Massachusetts records contain references to merchants selling quilts, some of which are described as made in England.

In America, as in Britain, several cotton patchwork quilts have survived from the last quarter of the 1700's. After about 1760 the British textile industry had learned how to produce quantities of attractive printed cottons at prices that made them more accessible to the general public. The increase in surviving patchwork seems to coincide with this greater availability of English printed cottons. Most of the surviving quilts from both sides of the Atlantic are in medallion format. However, the Project documented two cotton quilts from this period that are in block format. One is an Uneven Nine Patch, later called Puss in the Corner (Plate 17, right), and the other is a simple star block set with squares like an Irish Chain (Plate 17, left).

The early history of quilts in America is summed up in the quilts owned by that quintessentially American couple, George and Martha Washington. In 1757, George Washington received a chintz quilt valued at over £1 that he had ordered from London.[16] By the time Martha Washington died in 1802, she owned one quilted bedcover and nine counterpanes, two of which have survived.[17] Both of Martha Washington's surviving pieces are in classic medallion format. Although records do not specifically show that Mrs. Washington pieced these quilts herself, the idea that America's first First Lady might have pieced quilts may have helped establish the erroneous idea that making patchwork was a common activity before the American Revolution. It certainly does establish the place of quilts in the homes of the affluent of the period. ■

Floral Printed Cottons & Whole-Cloth Quilts

New developments in textile printing and dyeing processes resulted in new varieties of whole-cloth quilts.

About the time that British settlers began arriving in New Jersey, some of their countrymen at home were trying to master the fabric printing methods that had made the colorful textiles of India so popular in Europe. By the 1740's British textile printers had gained some skill with the Indian techniques of using mordants to apply designs to fabrics before the cloth was placed in the dyebath.[18] Mordants are not dyes themselves, but rather are chemicals, usually metal oxides, that "fix" colors and increase the fabric's ability to retain dyes. The British learned to use a number of mordants with a dyebath of Indian madder (a reddish root). Each produced a different color, including rose, brown, purple, and black, in addition to madder's more usual red. In many parts of India the various mordants were applied by hand, but the English adopted the practice of applying mordants with carved blocks of wood that measured from hand-size up to 15 or 18 inches square.[19] When a series of mordants was applied with coordinating wood blocks, a single pass through the madder dyebath would produce a fabric printed with several of the madder-based colors. If blues were also desired in a particular fabric, they

would then be applied by hand, a technique called penciling.[20]

Although reds and related colors could be produced using mordant printing methods, indigo, the dye most commonly used for blue in the 1700's (and until as late as 1900),[21] was not affected by mordants. Therefore, patterns in blue fabrics were created by sealing off areas with a material that would not allow the dye to penetrate the cloth. The sealing material, such as wax, might be applied freehand or through openings in a stencil. Indonesian batiks are familiar contemporary examples of this technique. Mid-to-late eighteenth century examples of fabrics printed by this process are the blue resist fabrics in quilts found in American collections of historic textiles (see Plate 24 top). Since blue resist textiles have not been found in European collections or elsewhere in the world, the question has been raised as to whether this fabric was printed only in the New World, either in the American colonies or in one of the islands of the West Indies, both locations where indigo was grown and exported successfully.[22]

In Ireland, in 1752, Francis Nixon devised another process of applying color to fabric: by engraving a design into a sheet of copper, forcing the dye into the carved lines, wiping the sur-

face of the plate clean, and pressing fabric against the metal plate so that the dye in the lines was transferred to the fabric.[23] The copperplate process was more efficient than the wood block printing method because it allowed the printing of 36 inches of fabric at one pressing. The use of metal rather than wood permitted finer lines and more elegant designs, sometimes called *toile de Jouy*, for the location of the French manufacturer most famous for using this technique beginning in 1783. But the copperplate process allowed the use of only a single color because additional colors could not be aligned with the first one printed. Therefore, from the mid-1700's to sometime in the first half of the 1800's, both multicolored wood block prints and single-color copperplate prints were manufactured. A subtle example of copperplate printed fabric is the tan-and-white fabric in the center of Plate 24 (middle). The fabric is similar in appearance to the early copperplate fabrics produced by Nixon.[24]

Near the beginning of the 1800's, several new developments added different looks to the textiles being printed. First, a process called discharging was perfected: wherever a bleaching chemical was applied, color was removed or "discharged" from the dyed fabric. Although this method was particularly suitable for creating patterns in mordant-resistant indigo blue, it was also sometimes used to create white spaces in which to reprint flowers and other decorative items.[25] A second advance at this time was the increasing availability of a new, more permanent dye for yellows and browns. This dye was called quercitron and was derived from the bark of the American oak tree.[26] Although it was initially patented in 1784 by Dr. Edward Bancroft, an American chemist, it did not gain popularity among British textile producers until the patent expired 15 years later. This new dye was suitable for mordant-dyeing techniques and produced yellow, buff, olive, and brown. It probably was responsible for the "drab" background colors that are so often seen even in the relatively fresh glazed chintz floral prints of the first half of the 1800's (see Plate 25).

Perhaps the most significant development in the textile printing processes of the first half of the 1800's was the perfecting of the roller printing method around 1815.[27] This process took the copperplate principle, but engraved the design into a metal cylinder rather than a flat plate, which allowed long yardages of fabric to pass against the revolving and continuously re-inked cylinder. Fabric widths from 36 inches up to 52 inches could be printed with design repeats of about 13 inches.[28] Because of the mechanical nature of this process, several cylinders could be positioned to apply different colors to the fabric in sequence. In skillful hands, this process allowed colors to be aligned perfectly in register with each other. Since the roller print process allowed the efficient printing of multiple colors, by the 1850's it had largely replaced the wood block and copperplate processes. The third whole-cloth quilt in Plate 24 (bottom) seems to have been produced by the roller printing process since it uses both red and blue in a design with a 13-inch repeat. ■

PLATE 24 (Top, Detail). BLUE RESIST WHOLE-CLOTH QUILT, c.1760, 92" x 94". Probably made by Elizabeth Waln, Walnford, Monmouth County, New Jersey. Blue resist fabric is unique to the American colonies. The pattern of this blue resist fabric is also seen in Florence Montgomery's Printed Textiles, figure 204. Although the quilt is now so worn that it is in pieces, some fragments retain the lovely intense blue of the original print. The quilt has thick wool batting and is bound with striped fabric also of a blue resist print. The quilting is diagonal lines crossing at 2-inch intervals. The probable maker's husband, Richard, owned a mill complex in the Walnford area, conducted an extensive textile import business through Philadelphia, and was a prominent Quaker of his time.

(Middle, Detail) TAN AND WHITE WHOLE-CLOTH QUILT, 1760-1796, 100" x 104½". Probably made by Elizabeth Waln or her daughter-in-law, Sarah Waln, Walnford, Monmouth County, New Jersey. This quilt was owned by the same family as the Blue Resist. The fabric of the top uses a design repeating in 34-inch intervals and is similar to those produced by Francis Nixon, an originator of copperplate textile printing, before the American Revolution. However, the back of the quilt bears the cross-stitched initials of Sarah Waln, who married into the family in 1796. Possibly Elizabeth made the quilt when the fabric was new and later presented it to her son's bride. An alternative explanation is that the quilt was made around the time of Sarah's marriage using fabric saved from an earlier era. The similarity of the batting and quilting lines between this quilt and the Blue Resist would favor Elizabeth as the maker. This quilt is in excellent condition for its age: examination of the seams does not suggest that it was once a brighter color.

(Bottom, Detail) RED AND BLUE FLORAL WHOLE-CLOTH QUILT, c.1820, 68" x 77¼". Made in Monmouth County, New Jersey. This quilt was found in an historic Monmouth County building and may be associated either with the Dutch Longstreet family or with others interwoven with families of English origin. Although this quilt was not associated with the Waln family, it is another example of whole-cloth quilts in Monmouth County. It has very thick batting, although of cotton rather than wool. Like the Waln quilts, it is quilted in intersecting diagonal lines, but these are placed 6½ inches apart, rather than 2 inches apart as in the Waln quilts. The quilt is backed and bound with a brick-red fabric printed with rows of dime-sized flowers. Four-inch strips of the backing fabric are also used as borders on two sides of the quilt. The floral print repeats in 13-inch intervals, and the blue of the leaves appears to have been added mechanically rather than by hand. All three quilts owned by the Monmouth County Park System.

Trenton Tape: A New Jersey Phenomenon

**A distinctive binding produced in the first half of the 1800's
has helped establish the New Jersey origin of some quilts.**

Trenton tape is the local quilt historians' name for a tan-and-usually-green commercially woven tape with a distinctive longitudinal stripe that is sometimes seen as the binding on New Jersey quilts made between the 1830's and the time of the Civil War. The fibers have been described as cotton or as cotton woven on a linen warp. The tape is significant because it can sometimes help confirm that a quilt may be of New Jersey origin.

Several local historical societies have identified this tape on the quilts that they own, but they have not been able to suggest the manufacturer's name or dates of operation.[29] However, an advertisement placed in a Trenton paper describes the Bloomsburg district as being a place "where extensive cotton factories are now established," confirming the Trenton area's capability to produce such a tape as early as 1815. In addition, records from 1814 show that Robert Waln and Gideon Wells were considering including a tape manufacturing operation in their Eagle Factory, which was to be built to produce cotton fabric. The Waln and Wells company was in operation from 1815 to 1845, which included the time when many of the Trenton tape-bound quilts were made.[30] However, there is no specific evidence to confirm that the Eagle Factory, rather than some other Trenton company, was the source of this distinctive binding material.

The New Jersey Project recorded Trenton tape on quilts made as far south as Swedesboro in Salem County (Plate 35) and as far north as Plainfield in Union County (Plate 40). Since Trenton is on the Delaware River, which divides New Jersey from Pennsylvania, some Pennsylvania quilts with Trenton tape may eventually be identified. However, the range in which the tape was used in New Jersey suggests that the area of use in Pennsylvania will also be rather small.

Trenton tape has been recorded on a variety of types of quilts including whole-cloth quilts, samplers (Plate 35), pieced quilts with repeat blocks (Plate 29), blocks arranged in strips (Plate 58), one patch quilts, and even a *broderie perse* medallion. Quilts with Trenton tape bindings are in the collections of several New Jersey museums and historical societies, as well as other museums nationally:

- A *broderie perse* medallion with Trenton tape binding and presumed date of 1830 to 1840 is in the collection of the Newark Museum. The quilt is shown in the museum's publication *American Quilts in the Newark Museum Collection*.[31] Since *broderie perse* medallions are not otherwise recorded in New Jersey, the presence of Trenton tape on this quilt confirms a New Jersey attribution which might otherwise have been questionable.
- Several whole-cloth quilts with Trenton tape are known, and some are shown in Plate 25. These may be among the earliest recorded examples of Trenton tape as binding, but their use of a single fabric and their lack of inscribed dates makes them hard to firmly date.
- A New Jersey sampler quilt with

Trenton tape binding is owned by the Art Institute of Chicago and was featured on the cover of the calendar the museum produced for 1990. This quilt has the dark printed lattice strips and diagonal set that suggest a Quaker origin. It bears an inscribed date of 1842 and an inscribed location, "Mt. Holly."[32] The town mentioned is about 20 miles southeast of Trenton and seems to have been a major center of quilt-making in the 1840's as well as a center of Quaker activity.

• A post-Civil War One Patch quilt made of right triangles was brought to the Project for documentation. It bears no inscribed date or place name. Its fabrics were produced both before and after the Civil War. Possibly the tape used as the binding was produced at the time of the earlier fabrics and was saved along with them to be incorporated into the quilt later.

As quilt historians, museum curators, and others become more familiar with Trenton tape, its geographic range and dates of use should become better understood. In any case, it may prove useful in helping quilt lovers appreciate the New Jersey origins of some quilts that have previously been attributed to other states. ∎

PLATE 25. TRENTON TAPE BINDINGS. *The variety of shading found in Trenton tape bindings can be seen on these whole-cloth quilts. These tan-and-green commercially woven tapes were sometimes used as bindings on quilts made in central and southwestern New Jersey from the early 1800's to a few years after the Civil War. Local historical societies believe the tape was manufactured in Trenton, although the name of the manufacturer and its dates of operation are still in question. The chintz whole-cloth quilt in the upper right-hand corner retains its original glaze. It was acquired from the estate of the Woodward family which had lived along the border between Monmouth and Burlington Counties since the late 1600's. Their property was located about 8 miles from Bordentown, which is near Trenton. All quilts owned by Phyllis Mount.*

The Dutch: An Early New Jersey Presence

**Dutch immigrants maintained their separate identity
from first settlement through seven or eight generations.**

The first Europeans to set foot on New Jersey soil were probably Henry Hudson's crew, who explored the mid-Atlantic coast in the summer of 1609. They sailed under the Dutch flag and claimed the territory for The Netherlands, although Hudson himself was English and his men were of several other nationalities. The Dutch were already trading successfully in many other parts of the world and saw the Delaware and Hudson River Valleys as promising areas for fur trade. They built trading settlements from the present state of Delaware to Albany, New York. By 1626 they had established New Amsterdam on Manhattan Island as their principal settlement in the New World. Although the main intention of the Dutch was to trade with the native people, they made several attempts to set up farming communities in New Jersey, just across the Hudson River from Manhattan. But these Dutch farming settlements were not successful at first because they were repeatedly attacked by the native tribes.[33]

During the years that the Dutch controlled the mid-Atlantic coast, the British also claimed it, but for fifty years they did little to challenge the Dutch in the area. Initially, only the Swedes, who claimed the Delaware Valley from 1638 to 1655, competed with the Dutch by maintaining a few small settlements in New Jersey on the east bank of the lower Delaware.[34] By 1664, the British had established several successful colonies both north and south of the Dutch-held territory and decided to evict the Dutch from the land that separated their northern and southern colonies. When the British took over Manhattan without a fight, many of the Dutch fled to New Jersey as well as to the areas of New York surrounding Manhattan.[35]

As a British colony, New Jersey drew a diverse group of settlers, especially in its eastern counties. Unlike other British colonies in America, New Jersey did not have an established religion so it attracted a variety of dissenting British Protestant groups, such as Presbyterians and Baptists, as well as several northern European nationalities, including Germans and French. By the mid-1700's New Jersey had one of the most diverse populations in the American colonies. People of English origin represented less than half the New Jersey population, although other Britons – Scots, Irish, and Welsh – made up another sixth of the people in the colony. The Dutch comprised an additional sixth of the New Jersey pop-ulation, making them the largest non-British nationality. The Dutch, like the Germans, Swedes, and French, often lived in separate communities so that up to the time of the American Revolution, languages other than English predominated in many areas of New Jersey.[36]

In many ways the Dutch and the Quakers played similar roles in opposite corners of the state. The Dutch were among the original settlers in the northeastern part of the state as well as the central Raritan Valley, and provided a cultural link with the New York Dutch in the Hudson River Valley and on Long Island. Similarly, the Quakers were the founding group in the southwest part of New Jersey and were in regular contact with Quakers in other states through their annual meetings in Philadelphia.[37] Both the Dutch and the Quakers prospered in their own regions and came to represent a substantial part of the population in their areas. Just before the American Revolution, the Dutch had 30 churches in the state while the Quakers had 40 congregations. Only the Presbyterians with 50 churches and the Baptists with 30 were as well represented.[38]

Perhaps the greatest similarity between the Dutch and the Quakers was their determination to maintain their separate identities by keeping their own styles of speech, dress, religion, and other cultural features. Both groups were able to maintain their distinct cultures well into the 1800's. In 1833 when writer Washington Irving took a trip down the Hudson River from Kingston, New York, with stops at the Dutch communities of Tappan and Harrington, New Jersey, he found communities of farmers who were "still culturally Dutch despite the fact that their families had been in America for 7 or 8 generations....They lived in neat Dutch stone houses, their wagons were Dutch, their speech was Dutch...the women wore Dutch sunbonnets" and the men "wore calicoe pantaloons."[39] At the same time, the Dutch in some other areas had begun to become more integrated into the general society. Florence Peto quotes diaries of young Dutch women on Long Island who wrote in English in the first quarter of the 1800's. However, most of the social contact these women described was with people with Dutch surnames such as Bergen, Voorhees, and Schenck, suggesting that they still maintained their separateness as a social group despite their fluency in English.[40] In central New Jersey's Raritan Valley in 1837 and 1838, Margaret Ten Eyck, a single woman of Dutch descent who earned her living by sewing and quilting, also kept a diary in English, recording that she worked both for households with English surnames such as Cox and for households with Dutch surnames such as Elmondorf and Van Pelt (see her diary excerpt on page 46).

The contributions of the Dutch to the American quilting tradition have not been explored as fully as those of other cultural groups such as the Quakers and the Pennsylvania Germans. At the time the Dutch first settled New Jersey in the late 1600's, their bedding practices were more like the Germans' than the British. In the 1600's

and early 1700's, both the Dutch and Germans often used beds built into wall cabinets. In the British Isles, only the Scots used built-in beds with any frequency.[41] Most of the settlers from Britain were accustomed to using freestanding bedsteads, with as extensive fabric curtains as circumstances permitted. Only a few quilts are listed among the possessions of British settlers before 1700, and no actual quilts survive from before about the 1770's. One early written reference to quilts among the possessions of the British is from New York in 1672, just eight years after the British took the area from the Dutch; in the inventory of the items owned by British sea captain John Kidd are listed quilts as well as featherbeds, linen sheets, 10 blankets, and four bedsteads.[42] The date that the Dutch in the colonies adopted quilts has yet to be established, but the translation of Dutch inventories into English should be of assistance to those who wish to search for early Dutch references to quilts.

Although quilts were occasionally listed in inventories of British colonists' possessions in the years before the American Revolution, the oldest surviving actual quilts of British heritage date from about the time of the Revolution in the 1770's. One of the earliest surviving quilts of known Dutch origin, now owned by the Shelburne Museum, was made in about the same period, the late 1700's. The quilt was made by the great-great-grandmother of the donor, who was the last surviving member of an old Dutch family. The quilt was given to the museum with the notation that it was to be a reminder of the contributions "of the Dutch who settled that part of our country."[43] This Dutch quilt, like many of the early quilts recorded by the Project, is made in blocks alternating with squares of plain fabric and set on the diagonal. However, unlike most New Jersey examples, the Shelburne quilt is surrounded by a large border of floral

chintz and uses the Reel pattern, a design not recorded in New Jersey except as part of the Oak Leaf and Reel pattern. The Eight Pointed Star in Plate 26 is similar in overall format to the Shelburne's Dutch quilt, except that the Eight Pointed Star pattern has been substituted for the Reel design.

Florence Peto has suggested that the Reel pattern began with the Dutch in the Kinderhook section of the Hudson River Valley, but she does not provide further information on the probable date of its origin.[44] Mrs. Peto does, however, record early references to familar patterns mentioned in the diaries of young women of Dutch origin who lived on Long Island or Staten Island. Among the Dutch-made quilts she shows or describes are a Wild Goose Chase made in 1803, a Star of Bethlehem made in 1825, a Chips and Whetstones also made in 1825, and an appliquéd Oak Leaf begun before 1830.[45] The diaries she quotes clearly document the fact that, by the first quarter of the 1800's, young women of Dutch descent commonly made at least one quilt in anticipation of marriage, sometimes before they had accepted a particular suitor.

By the middle of the nineteenth century, the Dutch in New Jersey were finally becoming more integrated into the general society. This integration can be seen in the surnames inscribed on a quilt made in Newark, New Jersey, in 1853 for a Methodist missionary to the Choctaw Indians (Plate 55). The British names listed include Bell, Taylor, and McVey, and they are accompanied by the Dutch names of Bergen, Boorum, and Schenck, indicating that Americans of British and Dutch descent belonged to a single church congregation. The gradual disappearance of the Dutch as a separate cultural group has helped obscure the particular contributions Dutch women may have made to the American quilting tradition. ■

PLATE 26. EIGHT POINTED STAR, 1830-1840, 85" x 86". Made in New Jersey. The extravagant use of border material, as well as the consistent use of the same material in the alternate squares, seems to indicate a quiltmaker with means to purchase sufficient yardage for her quilting needs. Even the stars are made of only six different materials. The sole use of scraps is in the Sixteen Patch blocks found on the corners of the quilt. The back is coarsely woven cotton. The quilt is a strong example of an early quilt in good condition. Owned by John L. Lutz.

Chapter Three

The Golden Age

Walnford Dec 23rd 1861

Dear Elisa

I have laid aside my work to acknowledge your kind letter....last evening I read a sermon and psalm to the children. To day I have been making pies and crust for tarts &c. &c., which has tired me out – to morrow I expect to cook Doughnuts. And spend Christmas in Trenton, wind and weather favourable...it has stormed to day in a variety of ways: rain, hail and snow, and now it is blowing furiously – the goose's loone, however, indicates a mild winter – I dined on one in Phil, week from last, where I stayed three nights at Aunt S. Waln's....

...I left little Jim's mother here, who went back to the city the day after I got home. She was here nearly 3 weeks – she made herself quite useful. We quilted and saved other garments for the soldiers and now they want more quilting, which I perhaps might be induced to do, if I had your assistance, as you are fond of it – Mother thinks I have done my share. We [c]are for the sick and wounded. I have some knitting to do yet. Em Comly gave me some yarn for them. My cousin Isaac Wistar (now Col. Wistar), who was wounded at the time Baker was killed, they think will never be able to use his right arm. A ball passed through his arm at the elbow, others in his legs.... Yet, still he is likely to recover....

...Martin Emly, who worked for us, died with the Dyptheria in Imlaystown, where the disease has prevailed extensively for so small a place....It is reported Lib is engaged to George Wiles, yet she contradicts it. Nicholas & Unity are invited to Annie Kirby's wedding, Newyear's eve. Your friend Caleb Newbold is engaged to Cecelia Abbott, George's daughter. All very pleasing, I believe....

...give our love to all inquiring friends and believe me as ever   Sallie

–Letter from Sarah Waln, Jr. to Eliza Smith
Collection of the Historical Society of Princeton

PLATE 27 (Folded). SUNFLOWER, c.1850, 65" x 88." This striking quilt is in excellent condition. The unusually wide and well-designed border gives a three dimensional look to a classic red and green quilt. The heavy quilting is done in three colors: red, green, and white. Included in the quilting designs are clustered and single laurel leaves, other leaf designs, and clamshells. The quilt is shown on the fence of the Mount Salem Methodist Church north of Pittstown, Hunterdon County. Built in 1864, the church is now home to the Alexandria Township Historical Society. Quilt owned by the Vineland Historical Society, Cumberland County.

1840 to 1870

Samplers, Signatures & Classic Calicoes

From 1840 to 1870, uniquely American quilt styles developed in the mid-Atlantic region.

In the early 1840's, New Jersey and perhaps adjacent areas of Pennsylvania made a unique contribution to the development of the American quiltmaking tradition. Both signature quilts and sampler quilts are believed to have originated in the early 1840's either in the Delaware Valley[1] or in a wider area stretching from New York City to Baltimore.[2] By either interpretation, New Jersey formed a major part of the area in which these styles apparently evolved. Many major museum collections contain 1840's sampler quilts made wholly or partially in New Jersey.

The appearance of signature quilts and sampler quilts was accompanied by the increasing popularity of the block-style quilt and the evolution of a repertoire of pieced and appliqué designs that had not previously been seen.[3] The extent to which New Jersey made lasting contributions to the range of American block designs is not yet clear. However, New Jersey does seem to have been among the leaders in the shift from medallion to block-style quilts. The New Jersey Project recorded both cotton and wool block-style quilts made before 1800, the same time period in which the original Southern states seem to have been concentrating on medallion quilts. In the 1840's, the block-style quilt gained national popularity over medallion and strip formats and became synonymous with American quilt design for nearly a century, until medallion quilts were revived in the floral appliqués of the 1920's to 1940's.

The reasons that the block style came to dominate American quilts is a subject for further historical research. However, a few possible contributing factors may be proposed. First, the division of the quilt top into blocks not only made the piecing process more portable, but also provided many separate units that could be constructed, and perhaps signed, by several people in different places. One example of a quilt made of blocks worked in widely spaced locations is owned by the Smithsonian Institution. It is a signature quilt assembled in Indiana with some blocks created by the maker's relatives in Gloucester County, New Jersey. Quilts in medallion format did not offer the same opportunity to have parts of the quilt constructed by a variety of widely separated people. Second, the designs in the printed cotton fabrics of the 1840's were moving from the large printed florals that had been popular for the past one hundred years to smaller scale prints in more strongly geometric arrangements. It is hard to know whether interest in block-style quilts created a demand for the smaller scale prints or whether the smaller scale prints created the interest in block-style quilts; the two did seem to attain popularity at about the same time.

The block-style quilts that New Jerseyans made between about 1840 and 1870 may be seen as two types: the darker quilts set on the diagonal (Plate 35), and quilts with more white space set on the square (Plate 40). The darker-and-diagonal-set quilts are seen from 1840 (or perhaps even earlier) to about 1855. The whiter-and-square-set quilts are occasionally found as early as 1842, but they become more common in the late 1840's and predomi-

PLATE 28. DIAGONAL CROSS, c.1870, 88" x 88". Probably made by Adah L. Drake Blackwell (1835-1926), Hopewell Township, Mercer County, New Jersey. In perfect original condition, this quilt shows bright colors in a somewhat unusual combination. The yellow sashing dominates the design with the squares carefully color balanced. The strong central focus was a common design element for New Jersey quilters of this time. The quilting is done with tan thread in simple parallel lines. Owned by Jane Grove, great-granddaughter of the maker.

nate in New Jersey quilts in the 1850's and 1860's. The Project recorded the darker-and-diagonal-set quilts only in the southwestern area of the state from Hunterdon County south along the Delaware Valley to Salem County. This area of the state had a large Quaker population, and the darker-and-borderless diagonal-set quilts may be a product of Quaker taste, even when these quilts contain forms or dates that suggest their makers were not Quakers (Plate 34). On the other hand, an early whiter-and-square-set quilt shown in *Remember Me*[4] was made for a circuit-riding Methodist minister in Monmouth, Burlington, and Ocean Counties, establishing an early Methodist association with the whiter style of quilts. By the 1850's, the focus of New Jersey quiltmaking seems to have shifted out of the Quaker southwest counties of the state, and the whiter-and-square-set style of quilts, sometimes even with simple appliquéd borders, dominated the New Jersey quiltmaking scene. ∎

PLATE 29. *VARIABLE STAR ALTERNATING WITH DIAMOND IN A SQUARE, c.1840, 106" x 106". This quilt retains its original bright colors. One print has a chain design and another is a small-scale pillar print. The border triangles are glazed flowered chintz. The quilting is done in the crosshatch style. The binding is Trenton tape. Housed in the Drake House Museum, Plainfield, Union County, and owned by the Historical Society of Plainfield.*

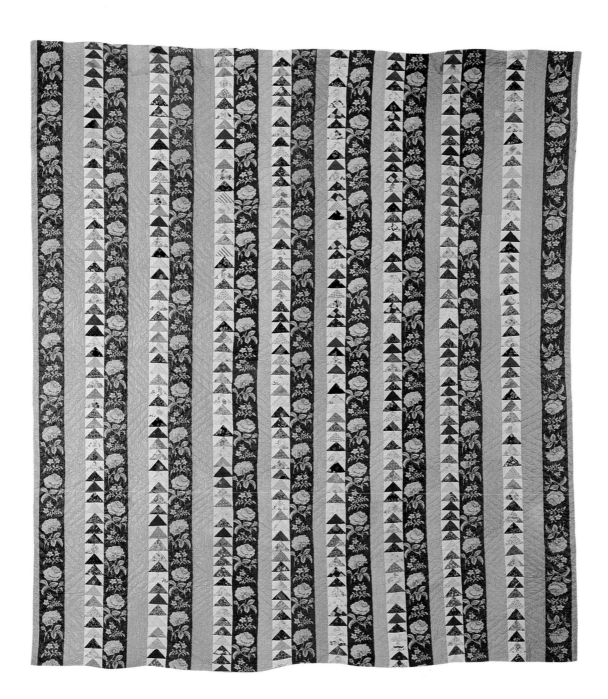

PLATE 30. FLYING GEESE, 1830-1840, 87½" x 95". Made in New Jersey. This is a crisp-looking quilt in near perfect condition, never having been used or washed. The polished chintz looks shiny and new. An early example of "cheater cloth" can be seen in the flowered and tan stripes which are a single piece of fabric. It is quilted in straight lines. The quilt has come down in the family of William (b. 1868) and Debbie Magdalena (b. 1867) Woodruff, who lived in New Providence, Union County, New Jersey. William was the first superintendent of schools in Berkeley Heights, Union County, New Jersey, where there is a school named for him. Owned by The Morris Museum, Morris County.

PLATE 31. LONE STAR WITH FEATHERED EDGE, c.1845, 102" x 104". *This quilt is a marvel of construction, made of tiny diamonds. It features* broderie perse *and appliquéd triangles around each star point as well as around the edge of the quilt. Like many early New Jersey quilts, this one is bound with twill tape. Quilting includes straight lines, outline, and stencil designs. Even though the origin of this quilt is unknown, it is very similar to one in the collection of the Burlington County Historical Society attributed to Anna Chambers Deacon of Burlington County, and published in* Lady's Circle Patchwork Quilts *(Summer 1983). Owned by Arline Hines (Mrs. Earle D. Hines).*

PLATE 32. SQUARE IN A SQUARE, 1843, 96" x 100". Made in Lambertville, Hunterdon County, New Jersey. New Jersey quiltmakers were enthusiastic participants in the friendship quilt fad which became popular in the 1840's. This is a particularly fine local example with many visible stamps and signatures from the prominent Lambert and Coryell families. (The town of Lambertville was formerly called Coryell's Ferry.) Martin Coryell was the engineer for the construction of the Delaware and Raritan Canal. He later moved to Williamsport, Pennsylvania, and this quilt may have been made as a parting gift for one of the family members. A graphic piece, it is well designed and makes good use of a variety of shaded floral and striped fabrics in the individual blocks as well as in the border triangles. Owned by the Hunterdon County Historical Society.

PLATE 33 (Folded). DIAGONAL CROSS, c.1845, 92" x 94". Probably made in Hackettstown, Warren County, New Jersey. The Diagonal Cross (or Album Patch) block is often seen in 1840's scrap quilts. This example is unusual both for the strip with square corners that surrounds each block, and for the limited number of fabrics used. The vibrant blue green stripe of the pieced blocks is complemented by the large flowers in the sashing. The small floral fabric that forms the border apparently was printed as a companion to the sashing fabric for both have the same tiny black dots in the background (picotage). Stencil quilting designs are used on the sashing and border, but they are obscured by the printed fabrics. The maker of this elegant quilt is unknown, but the quilt was found in a house with an extensive array of furniture from the 1840's, suggesting it was part of a prosperous pre-Civil War family's possessions. Privately owned.

FIG. 12. Mary Brown Batten

PLATE 34. DOUBLE X, 1845, 106" x 108". Made by Mary Brown Batten (b. 1814), Swedesboro, Gloucester County, New Jersey. Good contrast of fabrics in the blocks and the unusual paisley print sashing give this quilt its distinctive look. The polished floral chintz stripe material used on the back is exactly the same as the backing of the sampler quilt in Plates 35 and 36, another signature quilt made in Swedesboro in the same time period. The two quilts also share some other fabrics, particularly the acid yellow and one red print. Stamps and signatures of both men and women with dates ranging from 1842 to 1845 mark it as an early example of the signature quilt that was starting to become popular at this time. At least one signature is dated in the Quaker style: "5th 7th 1845." The owner also has a sampler made by Mary Brown in 1828 when she was 14 years of age and a purse made by her in 1830. Owned by Eleanor Shoemaker Spencer, great-great-granddaughter of the maker.

PLATE 35 (Top). PIECED SAMPLER, 1842-1843, 102½" x 106". Made in Swedesboro, Gloucester County, New Jersey. This is a friendship quilt with each block having a signature and date (some dates written in the Quaker style), some stamped and others signed in ink. It is a wonderful collection of mostly pieced blocks in a variety of patterns and colors that continue on the back of the quilt with still more blocks and signatures. Again we see the familiar New Jersey sampler with blocks set on the diagonal and use of strip sashing. The sashing here makes good use of an unusual striped fabric. Note, as well, the appearance of the Oak Leaf and Reel block, a favorite New Jersey design. The fabric on the back of this quilt is exactly like that of the Double X quilt in Plate 34, also made in Swedesboro in the same time period. The two quilts also share some other fabrics. The edge is bound with Trenton tape, and the quilting is done with tan thread. Many of the signatures carry the name of Robbins, which was the owner's maiden name, although the quilt came down through a different branch of the Robbins family. Owned by Marjorie R. Brooks.

PLATE 36 (Right). Reverse of PIECED SAMPLER, Plate 35.

PLATE 37 (Left, Detail). CHIMNEY SWEEP, 1840-1850, 91" x 98". Made by Anne Baker. This quilt in original condition gives us a fascinating study of early fabric, including glazed cotton and many stripes and plaids. The eight-inch-square blocks are set on the diagonal and surrounded by sashing made of floral stripes. Owned by the Hopewell Museum, Mercer County.

PLATE 38 (Right, Detail). RAMBLER VARIATION, 1856, 91" x 106". Made by Rachel Anne Evans Braddock (1833-1904), Medford or Marlton, Burlington County, New Jersey. An exciting display of beautifully pieced blocks, this quilt features a variety of the soft blue-red prints of the time period. The blocks, stamped and signed with signatures, are complemented by exquisite quilting in outline and stencil designs. The quiltmaker's sister, Lydia Evans, made the classic Oak Leaf and Reel quilt in Plate 4. Both sisters' quilts display excellent workmanship, and both are marked with the date 1856, the year that Rachel married Jesse Braddock. Owned by the maker's granddaughter and namesake, Lillian Rachel Braddock Gerber, who still has the frame on which it was quilted.

FIG. 13. Rachel Anne Evans Braddock and her first child, Mary, born in 1858

PLATE 39. DOUBLE IRISH CHAIN WITH SAWTOOTH STAR, 1840-1850, 82½" x 93". Made by Mrs. Frank Miles, Watchung, Somerset County, New Jersey. This quilt of many pieces is an interesting version of a pattern which is more commonly made in two colors. It is a marvelous display of early fabrics including many floral stripes, and is beautifully framed with a swag and bow border. Owned by Ruth Miles Barrett, granddaughter of the maker, and Barbara Barrett Diem and Betsy Ripley, great-granddaughters.

PLATE 40. APPLIQUÉ SAMPLER, 1857, 86" x 103". An outstanding example of the New Jersey signature quilt, this piece shows a connection to the well-known Baltimore Album quilts with both New Jersey place names, such as Martinsville and Elizabeth City, and also Baltimore and Baltimore County place names. The quilt seems to be the work of several different hands, with one heavily stuffed block in the center. The quilting is done in crosshatching, clamshell, and hearts. This quilt is housed in the Drake House Museum in Plainfield, Union County, and owned by the Historical Society of Plainfield.

PLATE 41. SUNBURST, c.1850, 84¾" x 86". A classic signature quilt of its time period, this piece has the distinction of imaginative sashing and borders. Appliquéd oak leaves surround each block to form the sashing, while peonies parade across the outer edge. Finally, a Sawtooth border encloses all. Although faded, many of the signatures written in ink are still visible. Some New Jersey towns named are Spring Mills, Flemington, West Amwell, Higginsville, Asbury, and Youngs Mills. Two entwined hearts in the quilting design may indicate that this was made for a marriage. The use of leaves, the tendency to fill up all available space, and the simple outline quilting are characteristic of New Jersey quilts of this time period. The quilt is housed in Fleming Castle, which was built in 1756 and is the oldest house in Flemington, Hunterdon County. The house and quilt are owned by the Colonel Lowery Chapter, D. A. R.

PLATE 42. PEONY VARIATION, c.1840, 87¼" x 94". Made in Mount Royal, Gloucester County, New Jersey. Flowers – all red except for a gold one near the center – march across this quilt. The current owner was told that the one gold flower was a deliberate imperfection to guard against the Evil Eye, an example of the superstitious belief that God would not look favorably on a human's attempt at perfection, and that the deity must be appeased by making an intentional "mistake." Whatever the reason for its origin, the inconsistency here adds interest and excitement. The elaborate border, rare in a New Jersey quilt, may be indicative of the family's German heritage. The border has a primitive look that contrasts with the expertly pieced flowers. A bird, the moon, oddly shaped leaves, and vines that do not connect add individualistic charm to this unusual piece. The quilt came from the Fell family who were distant relatives of the owner, Mrs. Jeanette L. Soukup.

PLATE 43. SAMPLER OF STARS, c.1860, 90" x 95½". *This impressive galaxy of stars is beautifully planned and pieced around a central star of more complex design. A thoughtful eye to color coordination is shown in the consistent use of yellow surrounding the center of each star and the blue or green of the star points. The eight pointed stars of the sashing are separated by the same green fabric as the first border. Tying the whole piece together is the background material, a print of brown squares on pin dots. The pieced border on three sides has an appliquéd heart in each lower corner. Owned by the Camden County Historical Society.*

PLATE 44. APPLIQUÉ SAMPLER, c.1860, 72" x 74½". Made by Ada Birdsall, Bergen County, New Jersey.
Blocks of original interpretations of floral appliqué designs give this quilt its charm. Each block is either signed
in embroidery or ink or stamped with names. A name common to this quilt as well as one other documented
quilt is that of Zabriskie, a noted Bergen County family. One block signed by Martha Zabriskie shows the use
of slits as a decorative technique, an appliqué method seen in some other New Jersey quilts. Several of the
designs feature reverse appliqué and stuffed work. This quilt shows some other characteristics of New Jersey
quilts of this time period: the use of leaf motifs, the Oak Leaf and Reel block, and minimal quilting. Well preserved with very little fading except for the borders, this quilt is a good example of the brightness and hue of
original colors. Owned by Joan E. Cleveland, whose husband's grandmother was the maker.

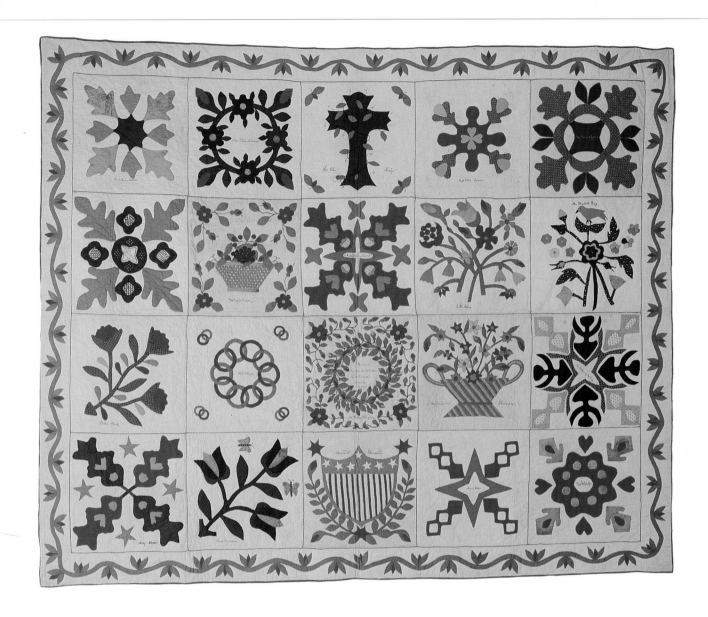

PLATE 45. APPLIQUÉ SAMPLER, 1867, 76½" x 95". Made by ladies of the Old First Church (formerly the Middletown Baptist Church), Middletown, Monmouth County, New Jersey. Signed blocks of original design have been made into a presentation quilt: a New Jersey version of the Baltimore Album quilt. Each block is a masterpiece of design and workmanship featuring appliqué, reverse appliqué, and piping around each block. Many of the colors, including the electric blue, are startlingly bright, particularly in contrast to the faded green in some of the corner blocks. Early machine top stitching is used on the binding. An inscription in the center reads, "Presented to Reverend Mr. and Mrs. D. B. Stout by the ladies of Leedsville Dec. 1867." Rev. David B. Stout was pastor of the Middletown Baptist Church from 1837 to 1875. In April of 1988, at the 300th anniversary of the establishment of the church, Mrs. Harry E. Johnson, the great-great-granddaughter of Rev. Stout, presented the quilt to the Old First Church, the current owner.

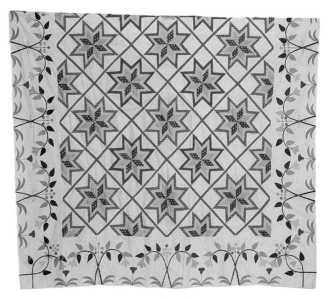

PLATE 46 (Top). APPLIQUÉ SAMPLER, c.1850, quilted 1951, 95½" x 98". The delicate appliquéd stems and bows would make this a distinctive quilt, no matter what its origin. While not made in New Jersey, it provides an interesting example of the possibilities found in the experimentation with appliqué design that took place in the mid-nineteenth century. A fine collection of beautifully stitched and appliquéd floral blocks is surrounded by a wide border of swags and bows. The presence of hearts in many of the blocks may indicate that it was made for a marriage. The owner purchased the quilt in Fredericksburg, Virginia, in 1950 and it was then quilted by her grandmother in Middlesex County, New Jersey. Owned by Glorianna H. Gibbon.

PLATE 47 (Bottom, Folded). EIGHT POINTED STAR VARIATION, c.1850, unquilted, 86" x 93½". Mady by Sarah Moore Kinne (1843-1878), probably Ferndale, Sullivan County, New York. This cheerful quilt is a delight to the eye. The substantial Eight Pointed Stars surrounded by thin strips of yellow and red fabric give way to a delicate narrow red sashing and a masterfully appliquéd border. Flowers, stems, and leaves are appliquéd with bows and details embroidered. Some of the green leaves have faded with time. While most of the fabric is cotton, some of the leaves are of silk. Although Sullivan County is not too far from New Jersey's northwest corner, such an elaborate border would be rare on a New Jersey quilt. Owned by Anita Ringen, great-granddaughter of the maker.

Uncommon Appliqués

Mid-nineteenth century experimentation in appliqué technique produced a variety of unusual and rarely seen designs.

"The broad range of appliqué patterns in the sampler album [quilts] of the mid-nineteenth century indicates that the makers were exploring the design possibilities of a new technique. Certain patterns caught on and spread around the country: others disappeared after a few years or one single use."[5]

The "uncommon appliqué quilts" recorded by the New Jersey Project seem to be a part of this experimentation process. The Project also sometimes called these quilts "the undatable appliqués" since their exclusive use of solid fabrics makes them more difficult to date. However, an increasing familiarity with the pre-Civil War New Jersey quilts led the Project to eventually assign them to the period between 1840 and 1870 based on the fabrics and characteristics they share with other quilts of that period, as well as that indefinable quality of their overall "feel" or "hand."

The original appliqué in Plate 48 is different from other New Jersey quilts in its four-block format and in its extensive use of slits in the appliqué motifs. Only one or two other quilts among the 2,100 documented in New Jersey were made of four large blocks. The extensive use of slits as a decorative motif was also rare in New Jersey quilts, and all of the examples seen were from the northwestern part of the state. The yellow-orange solid fabric used as an accent color also appears in a New Jersey sampler with dates of 1853 and 1857 (Plate 40).

The pattern of the original appliqué in Plate 49 suggests experimentation with "snowflake-type" paper cutting as a source of design. As many remember from childhood, this technique, which was a common nineteenth-century folk art among Middle Europeans including the Swiss, Germans, and Poles, involves folding a single piece of paper (or perhaps the fabric itself) and cutting it into four or more symmetrical "arms" to form a design. A more common variation of this technique is usually called fleur-de-lis. The book *Forget Me Not* shows both the fleur-de-lis and a design similar to the original appliqué.[6] It calls both of them fleur-de-lis, but they are clearly two different variations of the decorative paper-cutting tradition. The examples in *Forget Me Not* are attributed to eastern Pennsylvania and are dated at about 1846 and 1866, respectively. The New Jersey example has an appliquéd border of a simple design that seems to have been created by folding a long strip of fabric and cutting it like paper dolls. A second example of this type of fold-and-cut appliquéd border can be seen in the Circle Design quilt (Plate 52). These fold-and-cut appliqué borders seem to suggest that quiltmakers were seeking greater elaboration in their quilts without having access to a complex design tradition to draw upon for inspiration. The use of yellow-orange in the original appliqué (Plate 49) as the single color is an unusual feature. Most of the single-color quilts of the period feature red or green: yellows are normally used only as an occasional accent. However, this distinctive "cheddar" color can also be seen in smaller amounts in other New Jersey quilts of the period including the sampler in Plate 40.

PLATE 48. ORIGINAL APPLIQUÉ, c.1850, 81½" x 83". Probably made in New Jersey. This is one of the few quilts made in the four-block format that the Project documented. It is an example of the technique of folding and cutting paper to make a pattern. An unusual cutwork border in two colors with two rows of scallops echoes the designs in the center blocks. A rare feature is the extensive use of slits in the appliqué designs. Both the fold-and-cut technique and the use of slits may indicate that the quilt is related to Pennsylvania quilts where these methods are more common. The colors are still vibrant and the teal green is a color found in other New Jersey quilts of the period. The quilting was done at a time later than the original piece. Owned by the Roseberry Estate.

The original appliqué in Plate 50 also suggests experimentation with folded paper or folded fabric as the source of the design. Of particular interest on this quilt are the "fish hook" units appliquéd as the border motif. Although this type of border is unusual, it is not without precedent. A pieced signature quilt with sections of the fleur-de-lis design appliquéd around the border can be seen in *Forget Me Not*.[7] That example, like the fleur-de-lis quilt, is attributed to eastern Pennsylvania. A more elaborate version of the "fish hook" appliquéd border can be seen on a New York quilt dated about 1875, shown in *New Discoveries in American Quilts*,[8] perhaps indicating that quiltmakers continued to experiment with the possibilities of paper or fabric cuttings as a source of new designs even after the Civil War. However, the New Jersey example includes the dark teal fabric also seen in the sampler in Plate 40 which suggests that it probably dates from before the Civil War. ∎

PLATE 49. ORIGINAL APPLIQUÉ, c.1850, 88" x 90". Made in New Jersey. The pattern for this quilt was probably made from folded and cut paper, and the border pattern of connected ovals was done in the same manner. It is beautifully appliquéd and quilted. An unusual and distinctive touch is the wide use of the yellow-orange color, more commonly reserved for an accent color. A quilt of similar design done in pink can be seen in the collection of the Township of Lebanon Museum at New Hampton, Hunterdon County. The quilt is housed in Fleming Castle, which was built in 1756 and is the oldest house in Flemington, Hunterdon County. The house and quilt are owned by the Colonel Lowery Chapter, D. A. R.

PLATE 50. ORIGINAL APPLIQUÉ, c. 1850, 67" x 67½". Made in the Swartswood area of Sussex County, New Jersey. One senses a mystery and symbolism in this unique and original piece. The appliqué designs appear to be made from folded and cut paper patterns. Note the unusual "fish hook" appliqué design in the border. A similar design can be seen in New Discoveries in American Quilts by Robert Bishop. Quilting motifs include stars, half moons, hearts, and circles. The teal color is found in other New Jersey quilts of this time period. The quilt was passed down from the grandmother and mother of the owner, Mary Engemann.

The Quilts of Ruth Diament Brown

While rural New Jersey life was demanding, women found time to quilt, and the results of their labors have been treasured.

R uth Diament Brown was born in Cumberland County, New Jersey, on August 29, 1821, the daughter of Benjamin and Phebe (Black) Diament. She seems to have made her three elegant quilts when she was in her twenties, probably in anticipation of her marriage. The fabrics in her quilts have a consistency that suggests they were all made within a few years' time.

In 1847 at the age of twenty-six, Ruth married Francis Elmer Brown. They lived on a farm in Hopewell Township in Cumberland County. The farm they owned adjoins the one her great-granddaughter, Eleanor Sheppard, the owner of the quilts, lives on

today. Ruth and Francis had three children: Isaac, Caroline, and Edward. The family does not have any quilts Ruth made in her later years. However, Albert, Caroline's son and Eleanor's father, remembered his Grandmother Ruth as a skillful craftswoman, able to knit items for her family even in the dark in this rural area that remained without electricity until 1934. Three generations of Ruth's descendants have treasured her quilts and passed them down in nearly perfect condition except for some damage characteristic of 1840's prints.

Family history doesn't recall the details of Ruth's life; she was busy helping on the farm and raising three

children. We can imagine her performing the age-old tasks of cleaning, washing, cooking, and sewing. Perhaps she made soap and candles, and preserved fruits and vegetables grown on the farm. She knitted, darned, and sewed new clothes and mended old ones. She tended to the demanding needs of her children. Although the rigors of raising a family in a rural setting no doubt required a life of hard work, Ruth's portrait taken in her later years suggests the same sense of elegance and style that is revealed in her quilts. ∎

From information provided by Eleanor W. Sheppard, great-granddaughter of Ruth Diament Brown.

FIG. 14. Ruth Diament Brown

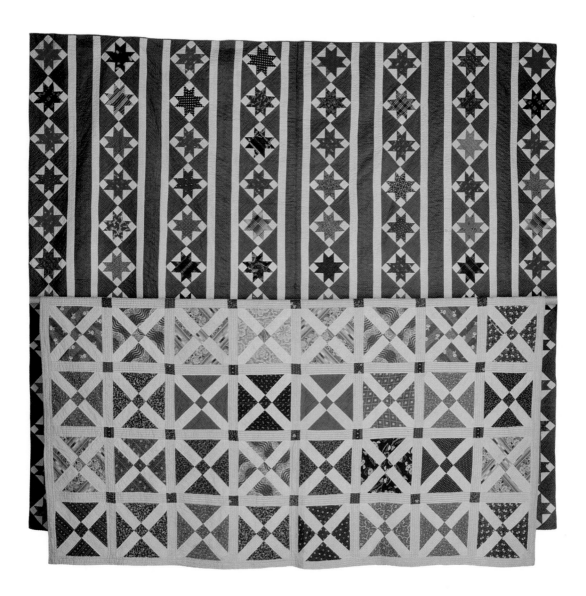

PLATE 51 (Top, Folded). SAWTOOTH STAR, c.1840, 93" x 105". Made by Ruth Diament Brown (1821-1904), Hopewell Township, Cumberland County, New Jersey. A myriad of well-preserved fabrics appears in the stars: one blue paisley fabric is the same as that used in the maker's Cross Variation. The crisp rust, brown, and blue stars sparkle in the fresh green strip setting which is often found in New Jersey quilts.

(Bottom, Folded). CROSS VARIATION, c.1840, 87" x 97". Made by Ruth Diament Brown. Four blue blocks and four green squares provide the central focus that so often appears in New Jersey quilts. There is a wonderful selection of vibrant fabrics in this precisely executed work. The small squares of rust and brown at the intersections of the pale yellow-striped lattice add intricacy to the overall impact of this quilt. The outline quilting is also typical of New Jersey quilts. Both quilts owned by Eleanor W. Sheppard, great-granddaughter of the maker.

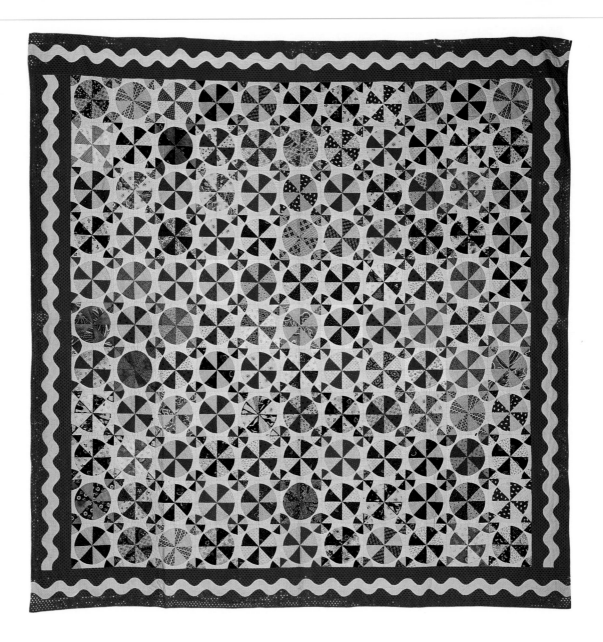

PLATE 52. CIRCLE DESIGN, c.1840, 93" x 94". Made by Ruth Diament Brown, Hopewell Township, Cumberland County, New Jersey. There is a lovely selection of early fabrics in this quilt, including a predominantly blue glazed chintz. Each block has been carefully pieced in light and dark fabrics, using the same fabrics in each corner as are in the larger circle. When the blocks are pieced together, smaller secondary circles are formed where the block corners meet. The dark red border highlights the rust reds of the circles. The wavy white border is reverse appliqué done in exquisitely tiny stitches. Owned by Eleanor W. Sheppard, great-granddaughter of the maker.

Signature Quilts for Friends & Family

New Jersey quilters were leaders in the use of elegant script and exquisite illustrations as embellishments.

Some of America's earliest signature quilts, as well as sampler quilts, were made in New Jersey. Two quilt historians, Jessica Nicoll and Barbara Brackman, have searched published photographs and museum collections and have concluded that both of these trends originated either in the Delaware Valley, which provides the border between New Jersey and Pennsylvania,[9] or in a somewhat larger area from Morristown, New Jersey, to the Chesapeake Bay.[10] Brackman located at least one quilt with an inscribed date as early as 1839. The New Jersey Project recorded several quilts with dates of 1841 or 1842. (Plate 35). By either quilt historian's interpretation, New Jersey is within the area where these two styles apparently arose.

If the period from about 1840 to 1844 can be considered the "formative years" for these two related styles, the quilts made during these five years should be useful in showing the ways in which the styles developed. The limited number of early samplers recorded by the Project corroborates

Brackman's observation that early samplers do not use familiar appliqué designs, except for the Oak Leaf and Reel. Instead, they include pieced blocks, chintz appliqué (*broderie perse*), a few blocks with applied needlepoint, and many unfamiliar appliqué designs. Brackman describes the appliqué designs of the early samplers as looking as if "the makers were experimenting with the design possibilities of a new technique."[11] In one early sampler recorded by the Project, the maker had even constructed her appliqué pattern out of the scraps from an adjacent appliqué block. The sampler-style quilt quickly spread beyond New Jersey, and some quiltmakers outside the area apparently looked to quilting stencils as inspiration for appliqué patterns. But this option may not have been available to many New Jersey quiltmakers since stencil-style quilting was not common in early New Jersey quilts.

The color range of early sampler quilts, like their appliqué patterns, often has a certain tentative or experimental quality. The striking red-and-

green-on-white color scheme so characteristic of sampler quilts after about 1844 is not common before that date. The early samplers are often either darker or paler than later examples. They frequently use printed lattice strips and a diagonal set. They omit elaborate borders, simply finishing the diagonal rows with large triangles of printed fabric. Most of the early samplers found in publications, as well as those recorded by the Project, are from the Quaker area of the state, and several are of known Quaker origin. Dated quilts made by Quakers can be identified by the placement of the day before the month and the use of a number for the month, for example "7th 4th 1842" (Plate 59). Since many characteristics of early samplers are also typical of other Quaker quilts of the time, early non-Quaker samplers (if any can be identified) should provide interesting insight into the sampler's evolution.

By about 1845, the classic red-and-green sampler using familiar appliqué designs began to appear over a wide area along the Eastern seaboard and into the states of the Middle West. By

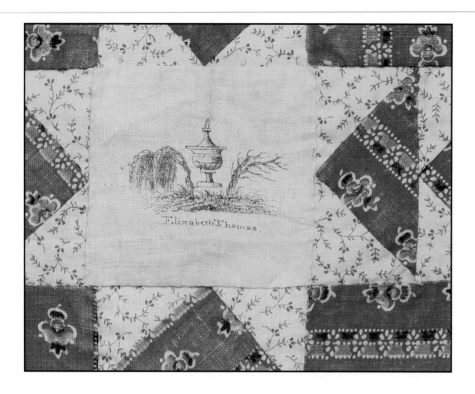

PLATE 53. *Detail of WILD GOOSE CHASE VARIATION, pieced 1843-1847 (Plate 55, Bottom, Left).*

this time, associations with other religious groups also became more common. For example, from November, 1846, to November, 1848, in Mount Holly, Burlington County, New Jersey – a town which may have been a great center of quiltmaking in the 1840's – a chintz appliqué quilt with 110 blocks now owned by the Burlington County Historical Society was made for Marvin Eastwood, the Reverend of the First Baptist Church. The years from 1848 to 1852 are considered the height of album quilts made in Baltimore, and the Methodist associations of these quilts are well-documented. Although sampler quilts are much rarer after the Civil War, one late New Jersey example was made by Baptists in Monmouth County in 1867 (Plate 45). Still later, around the end of the 1800's, a wool sampler was made for a minister in Alloway or Clinton, Salem County (Plate 87).

Single-pattern signature quilts are much more common than sampler quilts, even though both first appear in about the same time and place. Since

many of the early examples of single-pattern signature quilts in publication or recorded by the Project are of Quaker origin, it is tempting to speculate that this style originated with the Quakers. However, one early Methodist example dated 1842 can be seen in Linda Lipsett's book, *Remember Me.*[12] This quilt was made by Methodist women from several churches in three adjoining New Jersey counties: Monmouth, Ocean, and Burlington. The recipient was David Graves, the itinerant minister who served these widely separated congregations. In Burlington County, Quaker women were already actively making signature quilts, suggesting perhaps that the women of a Burlington congregation may have been the organizers of the minister's quilt. This Methodist quilt, though quite early, uses the red-and-green-on-white color scheme that later was to become popular for sampler quilts. The pattern is referred to as Full Blown Tulip and is similar to the later Dresden Plate design. It is described as being both pieced and appliquéd,

although the design could be executed in piecing alone, unlike the Dresden Plate. Other pieced designs found in New Jersey single-pattern signature quilts include Chimney Sweep (Plate 57), Lend and Borrow, Feathered Star (also Plate 57), Double X (Plate 34), Square in a Square (Plate 32), Nine Patch (Plate 17), a Wild Goose Chase Variation (Plate 55), and an unnamed block using concentric squares. Surprisingly, the New Jersey chintz appliqué signature quilts that are often seen in print were absent from the quilts brought to the Project's Documentation Days.

Many pre-Civil War signature quilts commemorated life's milestones including marriages, important birthdays, deaths, and departures. For some of the quilts recorded, the recipient is known, but the occasion for which the quilt was made is no longer remembered by the family. In other cases, it would seem that a quiltmaker collected the signatures for her own quilt, perhaps a logical step if she carried both her autograph album and her needlework with her when she went visiting. The early signature quilts recorded in New Jersey often have signatures in ink, sometimes accompanied by exquisite little illustrations. By the 1850's, some quilts mixed ink signatures with tiny cross-stitch initials and dates reminiscent of the initials occasionally found on the backs of quilts made before about 1840.

PLATE 54. *Detail of APPLIQUÉ SAMPLER, 1853 (Plate 55, Top).*

PLATE 55 (Top, Folded). APPLIQUÉ SAMPLER, 1853, 85" x 85". *Probably made by a missionary society of Newark, Essex County, New Jersey as a gift for missionary Elias L. Boring. The twenty-five blocks of this quilt have a variety of appliquéd designs, including some* broderie perse *using large paisley motifs. Each block contains one signature and, where the first name is given, it is always a woman's. Several blocks contain the date "1853." Some blocks are signed in ink, and some in cross-stitch. One very fine cross-stitched example says, "Newark, N. J. – June, 1853. Sarah Corwithe – Num. Chap. VI 24-26., Choctawe, IND. TER." (Plate 54). Although the quilt was previously attributed to the Presbyterian Missionary Society of Newark, research into Methodist archives shows that several members of the Boring family were Methodist missionaries to the Choctaws. The Elias Boring named has not yet been located, but he is believed to be a second or third generation member of this Methodist missionary family. Owned by The Morris Museum, Morris County.*

(Bottom, Left, Folded). WILD GOOSE CHASE VARIATION, *pieced 1843-1847, quilted 1876, 92" x 92". Made in Mullica Hill, Gloucester County, New Jersey. This lovely example of a single design signature quilt is signed with many stamps and signatures of both men and women. A pen and ink sketch in the center has the following inscription: "For Miss Sarah M. Thomas 1843 – on her birthday. Designed by F. T. Dunlops 1876." This inscription with the two different dates and the machine stitching on the quilt's edge suggest it was quilted in 1876, having been pieced much earlier. The well-preserved colors are remarkable, indicating how bright the colors of the period really were. The owner of the quilt, Beryl Skinner, is the great-granddaughter of the initial recipient and can trace many family names among the quilt's signatures.*

(Bottom, Right, Folded). TULIP, *1852, 94½" x 95". Made in the Rosemont area of Sergeantsville, Hunterdon County, New Jersey. Red tulips, contained by the green sashing, seem to burst forth in an explosion of color and pattern. Each block is signed in ink, with names of both men and women. One block is inscribed, "Elizabeth Rose, May 20, 1852." This is a well-preserved quilt, showing the beauty and variety of the blue-red colors of the time period. The owner of the quilt is Skip Johnson. His grandmother (1895-1973) reported that her mother had worked on the quilt. However, her maiden name is unknown, and her married name does not appear.*

Single-pattern signature quilts were occasionally made in New Jersey after the Civil War, and one 1885 wedding quilt recorded was very similar in design to an example made in the 1840's. In one case, the idea of a signature wedding quilt was translated into a classic 1880's fancy fabric quilt (Plate 86) with elaborately worked initials and flowers replacing the ink signatures and drawings of the 1840's wedding quilts. By the 1890's quilts with a large collection of embroidered signatures became popular. While most of these were fund-raisers for churches or fraternal groups, occasionally they would contain inscriptions like "Grandpa" or "1893 Charlie 6 years" (Plate 90), confirming that the quilt was made for a family member rather than as a group fund-raiser. ■

PLATE 56. Detail of FEATHERED STAR, 1850 (Plate 57, Top).

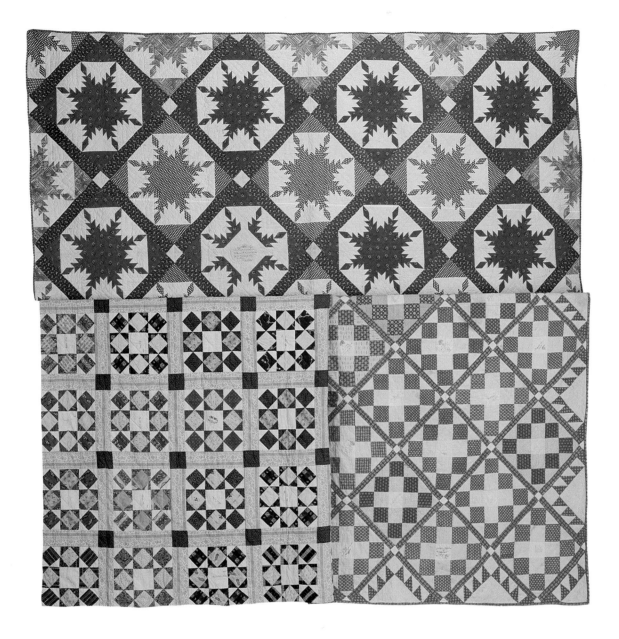

PLATE 57 (Top, Folded). FEATHERED STAR, 1850, 73½" x 97". Made by Mary Mount, Monmouth County, New Jersey. This intricately pieced quilt in a somewhat unusual color combination has an inked inscription that reads, "1850 This quilt presented to William B. Mount at the age of 14 years, by his mother, Mary Mount." It is thought that William later went to California. Owned by Phyllis S. Mount.

(Bottom, Left, Folded). SQUARE IN A SQUARE, 1844, 84¾" x 86¼". Made four miles north of Absecon, Atlantic County, New Jersey. This friendship quilt with many handwritten signatures and dates is a good example of a single pattern signature quilt. It was made by the family and friends of Peter Boice II (b. 1805) and Sarah Ann Chamberlain Boice as a gift celebrating their twentieth wedding anniversary in 1844. The farm of Peter Boice II is now the grounds of the Sea View Country Club, Atlantic County. Owned by Estella B. T. McCormick, great-granddaughter of the original recipients.

(Bottom, Right, Folded). CHIMNEY SWEEP, 1854, 100" x 103". Made in southern New Jersey. This is a mourning quilt, made in memory of loved ones. It is inscribed with many handwritten names and towns. Some of the names are preceded by the phrase "in memory of" and have ink drawings of weeping willow trees. Note the use of the early azure blue color. Owned by the Camden County Historical Society.

The Quakers

From the times of the earliest settlement, quilts in southwest New Jersey were influenced by Quaker style preferences.

In the last half of the 1600's, members of The Society of Friends, commonly called Quakers, began to come to the New World to escape religious persecution in Britain. Even before the British claimed New Jersey from the Dutch, a few Quakers settled in Rhode Island, Massachusetts, and Maryland. However, Massachusetts did not welcome dissenting religions, and four Quakers were hanged in Boston in 1656, the same year that they had arrived in the colony. By 1663, some Quakers had found a more tolerant atmosphere in Shrewsbury in East Jersey.[13]

When the entire western half of New Jersey became available for purchase in 1674, four wealthy Quakers, including William Penn, acquired it for £1000 and began planning to establish a Quaker colony. Between 1675 and 1682, nearly 1,500 Quakers came to Salem, Gloucester, and Burlington Counties along the Delaware River in the southwest part of the state. They joined the few settlers already there because of the earlier colonizing effort of the Swedes. After 1682, the influx of Quakers to New Jersey slowed as Pennsylvania became the center of Quaker settlement. Meanwhile, other English Protestants, particularly Anglicans (Episcopalians), began settling in the Quaker areas, diluting the Quakers' dominance over the region.[14]

The founders of the West Jersey Quaker colony believed that when they purchased the land, they also acquired the right to govern it. They drew up a plan of government, called The Concessions and Agreements, that took the revolutionary step of giving the power of government to an elected assembly. This early document also guaranteed religious freedom and trial by jury. Eventually, the British declined to recognize West Jersey's right to govern itself. But many of the religious and civil liberties guaranteed by the Concessions continued to be honored and to serve as a model for later American documents insuring personal liberties.[15]

In the 1700's, the Quakers in New Jersey enlarged their farms, established trade, and built the ornamentally patterned brick houses that record the Quaker presence in several of the original colonies. As the Quakers' own position became more secure, they took the lead in trying to improve the condition of less fortunate groups in the colony. In 1758, a Quaker organization called "The New Jersey Association to Help the Indians" convinced the New Jersey legislature to set aside 3,000 acres for the use of the few native people remaining in the colony. The Quakers also took an official stand against slavery in 1758 and began lobbying the legislature to forbid the continuing importation of slaves. In addition, the

Quakers encouraged slave owners to make plans to free their slaves. Although New Jersey did not start the process of abolishing slavery until 1804, the Quakers in New Jersey had begun their role as the conscience of the colonies, and later the nation, well before the Revolution.[16]

The Quakers also took the lead in promoting education and in advocating policy making roles for women. Within their religious structure, they established separate meetings in which women could discuss and influence church policies, free from the inhibiting presence of their fathers, brothers, and husbands. Women were accepted as religious writers and preachers, sometimes traveling to distant congregations to present their religious thoughts.[17]

Although Quaker doctrine advocated simplicity in material possessions, many Quakers acquired enough wealth to allow them to use the most expensive of materials, including brick for their houses and silk imported from China for their clothing. They compensated for using luxurious fabrics by making their clothing in simple styles and using drab colors, such as olive green and brown. Writers of the 1700's and 1800's who were not Quaker often commented on the apparent contradiction between the Quakers' ideal of plainness and their use of expensive materials. However, in the early 1800's, cotton was the fashionable choice for fabric so the use of silk, despite its expense, did in a sense represent a rejection of fashion.[18]

The drab silks of Quaker clothing also appeared in their quilts. In fact, the presence of drab silk in a quilt is one clue that it was made by Quakers.[19] Another major clue to the Quaker origin of a dated quilt is its designation of the month by number: "7th" rather than "July." Although many Quakers adopted cotton printed fabrics for quilts by the 1840's, some Quakers continued to wear silks in Quaker-style dresses up to the 1930's.[20] The Project recorded one small brown Quaker silk quilt with crosshatch quilting said by the owner to have been made in the early twentieth century.

Although the new red and green printed fabrics of the 1840's proved irresistible to many Quaker quiltmakers, their quilts continued to show a certain restraint of color that is characteristic of New Jersey quilts in general. Unlike the Amish, whose religion also advocated plainness in material possessions, the Quakers did not usually use elaborate stencil-type quilting designs, limiting themselves to straight line or outline quilting patterns. Quaker cotton quilts of the 1840's and 1850's are often characterized by printed lattice strips, an absence of borders, the frequent use of a diagonal setting, a distinctive center block, and a profusion of signatures and other inscriptions. Many of these features of Quaker quilts are also typical of southwestern New Jersey quilts in general, perhaps suggesting that non-Quaker quiltmakers in that part of New Jersey may have been influenced by Quaker style preferences.

The 1840's and 1850's, the time when the finest of the Quaker quilts were being made, also seem to have been a time when the Quaker religion was losing its hold on some of its members. Interviews with southern New Jersey quilt owners sometimes revealed that the makers of 1840's and 1850's quilts had been raised in the Quaker faith even though the families were not now Quaker and did not particularly think of the quiltmakers as Quakers. Two examples of quilts made by

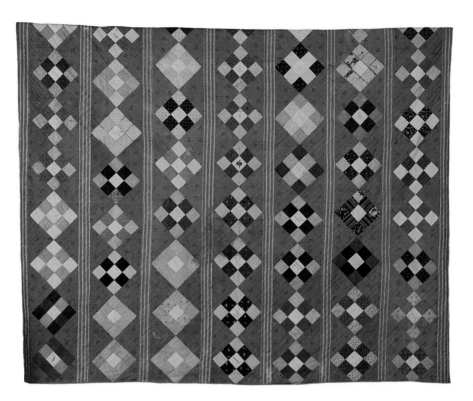

PLATE 58 (Folded). NINE PATCH, 1840-1845, 111" x 126". Made in Moorestown, Burlington County, New Jersey. Although inscribed to "Anna Warrington Jr.," this is known as the Roberts family quilt. The Roberts were a prominent family in Moorestown, and it was made by their Quaker friends. The many hand written names include those of Stokes, Lippincott, and Warrington along with dates of 1840 to 1845. Family names are grouped on the strips and include records of children's deaths. Verses from the Bible also appear. Some of the blocks are signed by men and some of the fabric is from men's vests. The quilt is bound with Trenton tape. Owned by the Historical Society of Moorestown, Burlington County.

women who were raised Quaker and left the religion as young adults can be seen in the Oak Leaf and Reel quilt in Plate 4, made by Lydia Evans, and the Rambler quilt in Plate 38, made by Lydia's sister, Rachel. Family history says that in the years before Rachel's marriage, the two sisters would go to dances and leave their Quaker upbringing with their Quaker hats and other outer garments so that they could enjoy

the dancing the Quakers prohibited. The permanent change in the sisters' religious affiliation can be seen in the fact that they are buried in a Baptist cemetery. Other quilt owners in the area occasionally reported finding a Quaker-style hat or some other item among their families' possessions, suggesting a Quaker affiliation now almost forgotten. ■

PLATE 59. Detail of PIECED SAMPLER, 1842-1843 (Plate 35), which shows Quaker-style date.

PLATE 60. NINE PATCH AND DIAGONAL CROSS, 1841, silk, 93" x 108". Made in Philadelphia, Pennsylvania. This fascinating quilt is signed and dated, mostly with the family name of Stratton. Place names include Philadelphia and Mount Holly, New Jersey. It is unusual to find an inscribed silk quilt from this era. The inscriptions seem to be in the form of advice. One says "Time is the way of life, he said, oh tell the young, the gay, the fair to weave it well...." Another reads, "Go to the ant thou sluggard, consider her ways and be wise." The quilt is bound with tape. Repairs near the edges are of modern silk. The quilt was purchased by Mrs. Elsie Pye and is now owned by Dolores L. Ewan, a friend of the Pye family.

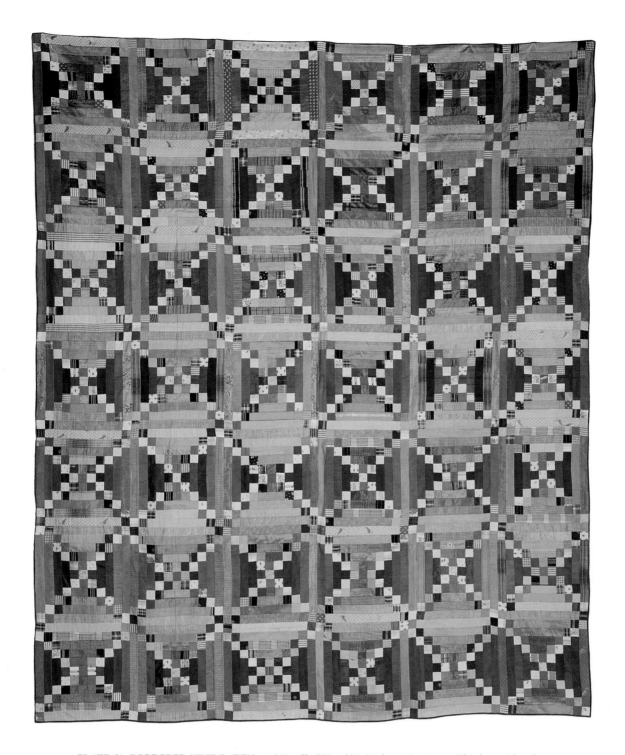

PLATE 61. BORDERED NINE PATCH, c.1840, silk, 75" x 88". Made in New Jersey. This beautiful quilt is made of silk scraps set in an unusual design. This is a family quilt passed down through the owner's mother's family. The owner's grandmother, Josephine Curtis Packer, may have been a Quaker. Excerpts from her diary can be found on page 106. Owned by Josephine H. Fink.

Imitation Patchwork

Faux patchwork or "cheater" cloth was printed as early as 1850 and reflected the patchwork styles of the time.

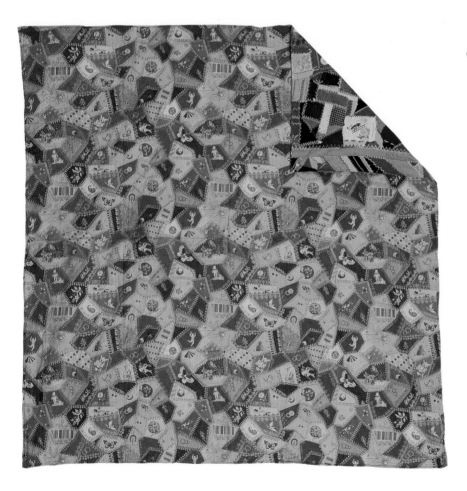

PLATE 62. Whole-cloth reverse of CRAZY QUILT, 1885 (Plate 81).

Several terms are used to describe imitation patchwork: simulated, printed, or faux patchwork, pre-printed patterns, and cheater cloth. The earliest examples go back to the 1850's. In fact, Florence Peto in a 1942 article for *Antiques* wrote that "the printing of cotton cloth to simulate patchwork appeared at least as early as 1849, for a wide border of realistic baby's building blocks or cube work finishes a quilt so dated in my collection."[21] This "cheater" cloth has always appeared as a reflection of the patchwork styles popular at the time, and continues to do so today.

The early printed designs of mid-nineteenth century are patterns – often imitations of woven damasks – that offered inexpensive substitutes for the silk "furnishing" fabrics which we now call decorator fabrics. Many of the designs were printed on chintz, a glazed fabric that is noted for floral and bird designs in bright colors, and often resembled needlework.[22] Yard-wide squares were printed for the centers of patchwork quilts and used as substitutes for the appliquéd squares which traditionally were made of motifs cut from fabrics with large floral patterns. Some chintzes imitated the popular tumbling blocks design which gave the illusion of stepped blocks;

PLATE 63. WHOLE-CLOTH QUILT, c.1850, 47" x 61". The front and back of this quilt are both made from the same glazed cotton printed patchwork fabric. The design is composed of a large diamond shape with a floral bouquet in an urn which is surrounded by smaller diamonds that have birds alternating with four different printed patchwork patterns. The quilting is done along the diamond lines on one side. A hole reveals the remains of another quilt inside, used as filler. Quilt owned by the Hopewell Museum, Mercer County.

others used birds or floral motifs within a geometric shape, such as a diamond or square, to give the appearance of separate patches. One piece was roller printed with scenes from Gilbert & Sullivan's *H.M.S. Pinafore*, presented in 1878,[23] another, from *The Mikado* which made its debut in London in 1886.[24] The printed "pieces" on both fabrics resemble other patterns of the time and include stripes, geometrics, florals, and calicoes. The Cocheco Print Works of Dover, New Hampshire, has been identified with the manufacture of "The Mikado" print. Interestingly enough, David S. Brown, who was born near Dover, established the Washington Manufacturing Company in Gloucester City, Gloucester County, New Jersey, in 1844. At the turn of the century the designs continued to imitate popular patchwork styles of the time and included Log Cabins, Crazy Quilts, and charm quilts. In the 1930's, the Sears catalog offered cottons printed in the patterns that were the current rage: Dresden Plate, Double Wedding Ring, and Grandmother's Flower Garden.[25]

The New Jersey Project documented four whole-cloth quilts made from printed patchwork, one of which is featured in Plate 63. A second example, Tumbling Blocks Medallion, c.

1850, was found to be in pristine condition, having never been washed. The third quilt documented by the Project is made of fabric identical to one found in a quilt in the collection of the Smithsonian Institution and pictured in *Clues in the Calico*.[26] In our example, this simple geometric design was printed in a rather dark, rust and brown monochromatic color scheme.

A twentieth century example exhibits a Cathedral Window design in red, green, and yellow and dates to 1933. In addition, several documented quilts displayed printed patchwork on the back (Plate 62). Other quilts contained only small pieces of printed crazy quilt or six pointed star designs which added to the variety of fabrics used. ∎

New Arrivals Enrich New Jersey

European skill and vision contribute to an American tradition.

PLATE 64 (Folded). MEDALLION, 1860, unquilted, 76" x 80½". Made by Margaret Howat, Netherwood Farms, Galston, Scotland. Leaves cut from fascinating striped, floral striped, and plaid fabrics decorate this quilt that was made in Scotland, using tracings of leaves from the family farm. The quilt, which is very finely stitched, bears the appliquéd initials. "M.H." and the date, "1860." The fringe on the edge is handmade. The maker never came to the United States, but sent the quilt to her daughter, Janet Howat Wilson who came here in the 1840's. The Wilsons lived in Scotch Plains where Janet's husband, John, worked for John Taylor Johnson, the president of the Central Railroad of New Jersey. Later the Wilsons moved to Washingtonville (now Watchung), where John Wilson built Wilson Pond for harvesting ice. Owned by Margaret H. Demler, great-granddaughter of the recipient.

At the time of the first United States census in 1790, less than half the New Jersey population was of English ancestry. The Dutch made up 16 percent of the population, Germans 9 percent, Scots 8 percent, and African Americans nearly 8 percent. Other groups represented included the Scots-Irish, French, Finns, Swedes, Welsh, Walloons (Belgians), and small groups of other nationalities. Of the original thirteen states, only Pennsylvania had a more diverse population.[27]

Over the next century, from 1790 to 1890, 80 percent of the Europeans to arrive in New Jersey came from the British Isles or Germany. By 1900 half of the state's population had either been born in Europe or had parents who had been born there. The mechanical skills of these immigrants were particularly welcomed by manufacturers in the northeast section of the state, where the largest percentage of immigrants settled. One example of the technical contribution of German-speaking immigrants was the scissors and cutlery industry founded in Newark by Rochus Heinisch of Austria and Jacob Wiss of Switzerland in the 1840's and 1850's.[28] Similarly, Clark Thread Company's large scale installation established in Newark in the 1860's was an American expansion of the thread company's original Scottish

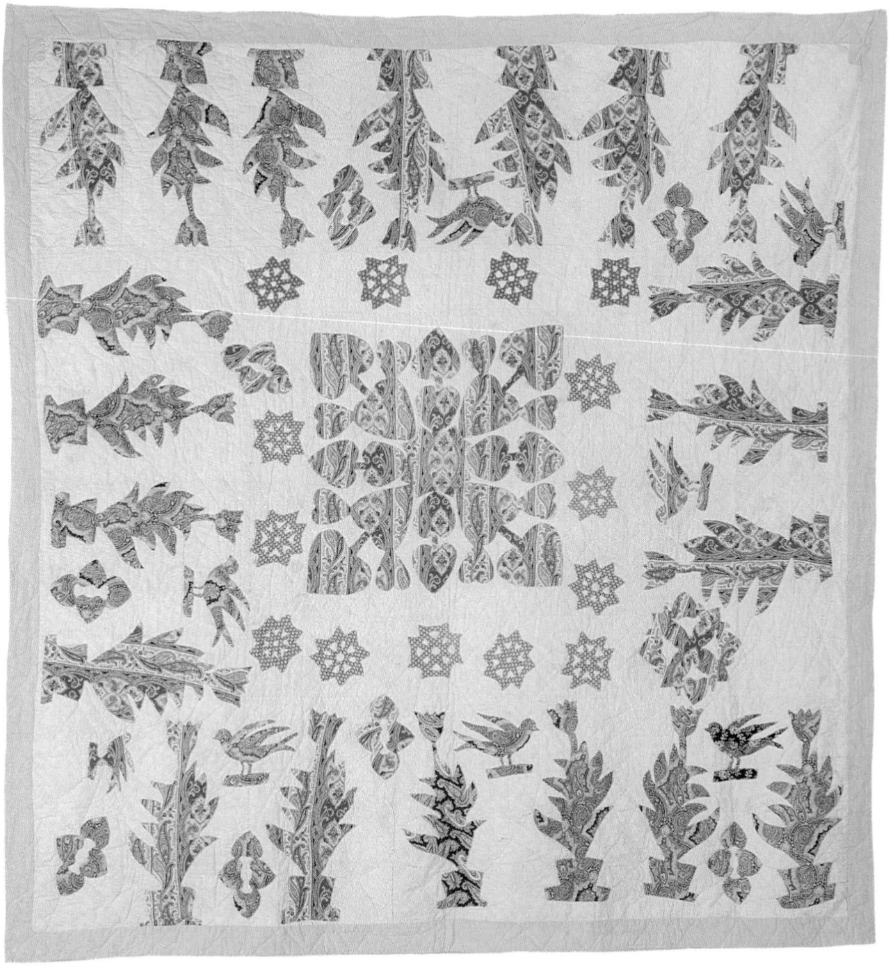

PLATE 65. ORIGINAL APPLIQUÉ, c.1870, 81" x 83½". Made by August and Barbara Schlank Happ. This quilt was made by an immigrant couple on board a ship on their way to America from Germany. August helped with the cutting, while Barbara did the sewing. The quilt top was passed down through the family and presented to the present owner at her bridal shower in Walpack, New Jersey, in 1949, having been recently quilted by the ladies of the Methodist Church of Walpack. Owned by Ellen R. Moffett, great-granddaughter of the makers.

operations. In the years after the Civil War, great numbers of skilled silk workers from England, Germany, Switzerland, and France arrived in Paterson to work in the silk mills, later to be replaced by Italians and Central European Jews.[29]

Although the vast majority of quilts recorded by the Project were made by women whose families had resided in the state for more than one generation, two exceptions are particularly interesting. The appliquéd leaf counterpane in Plate 64 with the large date "1860" was made in Scotland by a mother for her daughter who had come to America in the 1840's. The patterns for the appliqués were actual leaves from the family land the daughter had left many years before. (This documented use of appliquéd leaves as souvenirs of a particular location suggests an explanation for the naturalistic leaves occasionally found on quilts made in New Jersey in the same period.) The other quilt illustrating mid-nineteenth century migration to America (Plate 65) has a top that is said to have been made by a couple en route to America from Germany in 1873. The family tradition indicates that both wife and husband worked on the top while on the ship. Both of these quilt tops have a certain similarity of style, using large scale fabrics and rather free-form appliquéd shapes representing parallel European interpretations of American quiltmaking styles.

From 1890 the flow of immigrants from the British Isles and Germany declined sharply and immigration from eastern and south Europe increased, bringing Armenians, Byelorussians, Croatians, Czechs, Estonians, Greeks, Hungarians, Italians, Jews, Latvians, Lithuanians, Poles, Serbs, Slavs, Slovaks, Ukrainians, and others into the state. The Immigration Act of 1924 slowed immigration into New Jersey as well as the rest of the country. Yet in 1970 about 30 percent of the New Jersey population had either been born abroad or had parents who had been. Over half of this group was of Italian, German, or Polish origin. Recent immigration has shifted to Latin America, the Middle East, and Asia, and, in 1976, the New Jersey Bicentennial Ethnic Council was able to identify at least fifty ethnic groups within the state.

Many of the women of these ethnic groups brought an extensive tradition of handwork from their homelands. A few became avid participants in the quiltmaking fashion of the 1930's and 1940's. Among these was Elizabeth Moravek, whose quilts may be seen in Plates 134 and 135 and who sought to learn quiltmaking skills from her neighbors when her Czech mother could not provide them. ■

Chapter Four

Expanding Horizons

1875

February 25th– *Very rainy cutting rags*

26th– *P. Green of [?] here to dinner. Meds here a little while this after*

27th– *Sunny this afternoon*

March

4th– *Very busy washing and sweeping. J. G. [?] and wife H. [?] and wife here to tea*

6th– *Quilting this afternoon. 20 here to tea supprise party at Mr. Strictlands to night – he was presented with silver tea set – cost 35$*

8th– *Went out to Clarksboro yesterday morn. Minister's last day. went to Tomlins to dinner, then to sunday school home with Maggie H. and staid all night came home this morn. Med and Lizzie have gone to Mantua. I am keeping children*

9th– *Ironed this morn. meeting down at the Friends*

1879

February 9– *Lizzie staid all night. the baby little better. I went to Church this eve.*

12th– *Quilting at Ridgways. Lizzie & Debbie went,*

13th– *Went over to Georges, to Church this eve. and then to Joes to sew.*

17t – *Very stormy*

18th– *Went down to Rulons sale. down to see Tom Th[?] at Swedesboro this eve*

March   1st– *Took my chair out to Paulsboro to have shortened.*

4th– *Dyed rags.*

6th– *J V Clark married. Going up to Joes,*

8th– *[?] wedding at E. W. Packers*

10th– *Very warm for this time of year.*

11th– *Meds gone to B. Owens sale*

17th– *Quilting my quilt*

19th– *Washed.*

20th– *Went to the Literary Entertainment at Mullica hill. Very dark and rainy coming home ran into the fence & broke shaft*

– From the diaries of Josephine C. Packer, born November 7, 1852, Woodbury, Gloucester County, New Jersey.

PLATE 66 (Folded). LOG CABIN, Streak of Lightning Variation, c.1880, 61" x 74". Credit for this beautifully made quilt goes to an unknown quiltmaker. The fabrics are typical of the period, with warm reds and browns predominating. The edges have been re-bound. The quilt is part of the textile collection of the Clinton Historical Museum in Clinton, Hunterdon County, New Jersey. It is pictured here in front of a reconstructed log cabin on the grounds of the museum village.

1870 to 1925

Cottons, Wools & Fancy Fabrics

During the late nineteenth and early twentieth centuries a variety of fabrics found their way into New Jersey quilts.

If New Jersey quilts made between 1870 and 1925 have an underlying theme, it is the use of silk, satins, velvets, brocades, and wools in addition to the familiar cottons. Of course, wool quilts had been made in the state in the late 1700's, and a few silk quilts were made between 1800 and 1860, usually by women with a special access to silks: Quaker women in the southern part of the state who traditionally wore silk clothing[1] and women in the northern part of the state whose families manufactured silk items such as umbrellas.[2] With these exceptions, New Jersey quilts were almost exclusively of cotton until after the Civil War. Many of the more elegant pre-Civil War cotton quilts were examples of their makers' best handwork and were preserved because they were considered too special to be subjected to everyday use.

Sometime in the mid-1800's, silks and other fancies replaced cotton as the fabrics considered suitable for quiltmakers' best efforts. These fancy fabric items were often intended for display in parlors while cotton quilts were made for daily use as bedding. An early example of the trend toward silk items made for display is the small Tumbling Blocks piece shown in Plate 155. It measures less than two feet square and bears an ink inscribed panel indicating that it was made in 1860 by a woman in her eighties for her daughter. It may be considered a forerunner of the darker silk "parlor quilts" that would be made in New Jersey and in many other states in the second half of the 1800's. From the 1870's through the 1890's, New Jersey women used silk, satin, velvet, and brocade for the Victorian darkness and richness that cotton could not match. Popular designs worked in fancy fabrics included Log Cabin, Tumbling Blocks, and patterns based on hexagons. One interesting unbacked example was assembled on a foundation of squares and Eight Pointed Stars, with Log Cabin blocks worked on the squares and crazy quilt units assembled on the diamonds that make up the points of the stars. The effect of this quilt, which can be seen in Plate 83, is dazzling – or perhaps even dizzying.

In the 1880's, crazy quilts became as popular in New Jersey as they did in many parts of the country. However, New Jerseyans did not limit their crazy quilts to fancy fabrics, often working this design in cotton or wool. In fact, cotton crazy quilts retained a certain popularity in the state into the 1930's.

In addition, fancy embroidery was not reserved for crazy quilts: some of the most lavishly embroidered quilts recorded in New Jersey were made in simple silk squares or diamonds. Examples of these silk quilts can be seen in Plates 5, 85, and 86.

As the nineteenth century ended, wools came to replace silks, satins, and velvets as the popular alternative to cotton for New Jersey made quilts. New Jersey's late nineteenth century use of fancy fabrics had been part of a national fashion. Its early twentieth century use of wool may be part of a more regional trend, perhaps more prevalent in the northern states than in the South. The establishment of successful woolen manufacturers in Passaic helped move New Jersey woolen manufacture from thirteenth place nationally in 1900 to fifth place in 1912.[3] The turn-of-the-century New Jersey wool quilts do not have the sheen of the earlier silks and satins, but, at their best, they have a strong graphic presence and a richness of color even when their fabrics are considerably deteriorated. Most of the early twentieth century wool quilts use simple pattern pieces, including strips, triangles, and squares. However, one interesting exception is the full-size sampler quilt

(Plate 87) made for a minister using a variety of pieced blocks, reminiscent of the cotton presentation quilts common 50 years earlier. According to their inscriptions, several of the wool crazy quilts made in this period are also presentation pieces, although their use of simple stem stitch embroidery suggests a utilitarian, rather than "special" quilt. One of these wool crazy quilts clearly made as a gift has an embroidered hand with the message, "1893 Charlie 6 years" (Plate 90).

One characteristic of the New Jersey cotton quilts carried over from the pre-Civil War years is the limited use of open white space in pieced quilts. Although white is seen as the background of individual blocks, it does not appear as lattice strips or plain squares to separate the blocks; no open space is left to permit elaborate quilting designs. However, one elaboration of organization sometimes seen is the Streak of Lightning set, which allowed New Jersey quiltmakers to fill background space without leaving open areas of white. However, large areas of white do begin to appear in New Jersey quilts in about 1895 when red embroidery quilts displaying signatures, pictures from purchased transfers, and, occasionally, appliquéd stars

PLATE 67. SAWTOOTH STAR, c.1890, 65½ x 65¾. Probably made in north-western New Jersey. Small stars twinkle in a bold zigzag setting in this quilt still in its original condition. Note the three stars on bright yellow backgrounds that give an added sparkle to the other mostly neutral colors. A small embroidered initial "L" is all that is known of the maker. Privately owned.

became popular as fund-raisers, family gifts, or personal mementos. In the 1920's the red of turn-of-the-century embroidery quilts was replaced by a blue that can be seen in the quilt with the charming children's embroideries in Plate 159.

From 1870 to 1925, New Jersey quiltmakers were a part of the mainstream in their creation of crazy quilts, Log Cabin quilts, and embroidered signature quilts. However, they maintained their own characteristics in their rejection of complex piecing, open areas of white space, elaborate borders, and stencil-style quilting designs. By the 1930's New Jersey's differences from the national mainstream had come to an end as New Jerseyans adopted the patterns distributed and popularized nationally to create floral appliqués, Dresden Plates, and Grandmother's Flower Gardens indistinguishable from those made anywhere else in the country. ■

PLATE 68. BLAZING STAR VARIATION, c.1895, 67" x 84". Made by Elizabeth Stillwell Mason (1869-1948), Holmdel, Monmouth County, New Jersey. This is a pleasing utility quilt made from scraps. The alternate colored corner triangles provide an interesting secondary design, set off by the border fabric. Elizabeth (Lizzie) Stillwell grew up in Allendale, Illinois. In September of 1893 she was introduced (by mail) to Charles Wesley Mason (Wes), a farmer from Monmouth County, New Jersey. A two-year correspondence followed, and at Christmas of 1895, Wes was able to make the trip to Illinois to meet Lizzie in person. They were married on December 31, 1895, and shortly thereafter departed for New Jersey. Lizzie's new home was a farm in Holmdel which Wes had purchased in 1893. Lizzie was descended from the Stillwells of Monmouth County, and, in fact, returned to her great-grand-father's home county when she married Wes. There Lizzie and Wes lived and raised their three children. The owner of the quilt, Wayne Mason, is their grandson and is restoring the farmhouse built by his grandparents.

FIG. 15. The Masons (clockwise from top): Elizabeth Stillwell, Charles Wesley, Ray W., Atlanta S., and (center) Furman T.

PLATE 69. PEONY VARIATION, c.1880, 86½" x 88¾". Made by Kesia Stiles English (1817-1894), Willow Grove, Salem County, New Jersey. The classic red and green color scheme is emphasized here with the use of double sashing and a pieced border on all sides. This quilt is representative of many Peony variations found in the New Jersey quilt search; however, this one is particularly pleasing with its small, diamond-shaped appliquéd leaves echoing the shape of the larger pieced leaves. Owned by Diana Scotton, great-great-grand-daughter of the maker.

FIG. 16. Kesia Stiles English

PLATE 70. LIVE OAK TREE, 1880-1890, 67" x 83". *Probably made by Mrs. Hickman, mother of Ethel Hickman Giberson, who was a friend of the current owner, in Scullville, Atlantic County, New Jersey. A forest of oak trees sparkles with the occasional gold leaf and the one block with gold background. This is one of the more unusual tree patterns and is more difficult to piece than some because diamond-shaped patterns are used instead of triangles. The border and quilting are recent. Owned by Anne Nickles.*

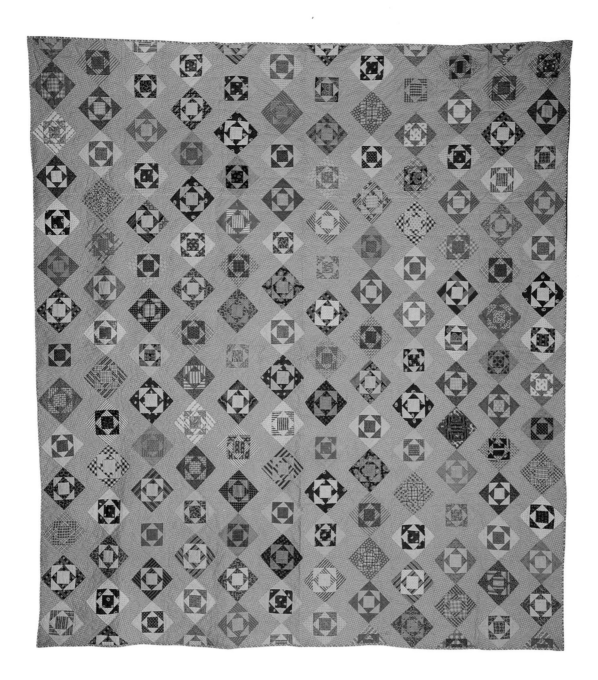

PLATE 71. TWELVE TRIANGLES, c.1870, 81" x 82". Made by Emma Mae Hoagland Losey and her mother-in-law, Lavina Sked Losey, Unionville, Hunterdon County, New Jersey. This is a fresh looking quilt in a characteristic mid-century design made special by the zigzag setting. Many New Jersey quiltmakers seemed to favor this set, especially for simple patterns made from scraps. A close look reveals the use of a great variety of fabrics, many of which have been reproduced in modern times. The quilt is backed with a brown and white plaid. Owned by Grace B. Cronce.

PLATE 72. BASKET, c.1870, 74" x 75½". Made in Hunterdon County, New Jersey. This is a beautifully designed and executed quilt with the baskets in the center set on the diagonal while the baskets in the two side rows face the center. A special touch is the one contrasting triangle in the center of each basket. Note the straight handle instead of the more commonly used curved handle. In excellent condition, this quilt has bright unfaded colors. Privately owned.

PLATE 73. DOUBLE HEARTS WITH BASKETS, c.1900, 75" x 75". Made by Elizabeth Bateman Gates Allen (1887-1973), Newport, Cumberland County, New Jersey. This is a cheery quilt showing originality of design in its diagonal row of baskets as well as in the corner basket blocks. Each basket contains a sturdy looking bud and two leaves. It is quilted in straight lines and the edges are finished by bringing the backing to the front. Elizabeth was born in Newport and lived her adult life there as well, with her husband, Harry, and daughter, Emma. She was known for her love of home and family and enjoyed sewing, crocheting, and quilting in her spare time. Owned by Dr. Emma G. Allen, daughter of the maker.

FIG. 17. Elizabeth Bateman Gates Allen

PLATE 74. ROBBING PETER TO PAY PAUL, c.1890, 73½" x 84½". Made by Mercy Anna Clarkson Garretson (1834-1908), Middlebush, Somerset County, New Jersey. Robbing Peter to Pay Paul is said to be a very old Quaker name, given to many different patterns that are all designed on the same principle of alternate light and dark blocks in which the pieces left after cutting one block can be used to make the next. This particular quilt is a fine example of a classic nineteenth-century design, enhanced by a pieced border. The cotton fabrics are those manufactured by the Ely & Walker company, which were popular and used by quilters for over one hundred years from 1878 to the early 1980's. Another quilt by this maker can be found in Plate 94. The quilting was done in 1983 by the current owner, Ann G. Bering, granddaughter of the maker.

PLATE 75. CRAZY QUILT, c.1890, 68" x 69". Made by Ephraim B. Watson (d.1898), Hurffville, Gloucester County, New Jersey. The maker of this crazy quilt lived with his wife, Anna Jane Murphy Watson, on a farm with their seven children. Mr. Watson, a farmer, took up quiltmaking when tuberculosis kept him from regular employment. He made a quilt for each of his seven children. Each quilt carried its recipient's initials. The boys' quilts were appliquéd with farm implements: rakes, hoes, and plows. The girls' quilts had appliquéd household objects: utensils, lamps, and pitchers. This quilt, initialed "T. C. W.," was made for his youngest daughter, Theressa Camp Watson (1885-1967), and is the only one known to remain. When Theressa was thirteen, Mr. Watson passed away. The quilt is sewn in strips and is quilted in the Baptist Fan pattern. Owned by Emma L. Evers, granddaughter of Ephraim and daughter of Theressa.

FIG. 18. Watson Homestead with Anna Jane Murphy Watson, widow of Ephraim B. Watson, and three of their seven children

PLATE 76. LOG CABIN, *Barn Raising Variation, c.1880. 78" x 80". Made by Althea Orr Diament (1865-1957), Cedarville, Cumberland County, New Jersey. This quilt is representative of the many Log Cabin quilts documented by the Project. This quilt was taken to school by the maker's son, Lewis Ramsey Diament, when he left home to attend Rutgers University. His name tag (in her writing) is still attached. Owned by Ellis and Dorothy Diament. Ellis is the grandson of the maker.*

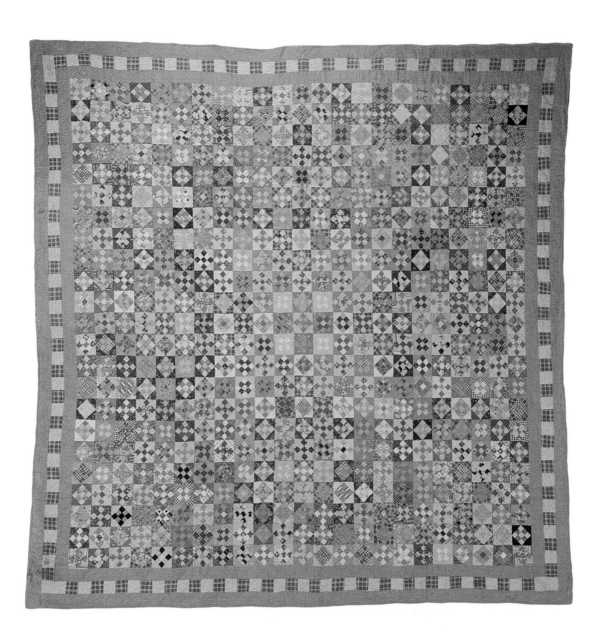

PLATE 77. NINE PATCH IN A SQUARE, c.1880, 77½" x 80". Made in Mullica Hill, Gloucester County, New Jersey. Small scraps of material from a forty year time span were used to make this quilt. Tiny ⅝" squares are sewn into a Nine Patch, which is set on point and surrounded by four triangles to make a 3" block. The use of yellow background fabric to form a large "X" from one corner of the quilt to the other echoes a New Jersey tradition of changing background color to subtly highlight the center area of the quilt. Two pink border strips enclose a pieced border made of alternate brown plaid 1½" squares. Owned by Carolyn Rueda.

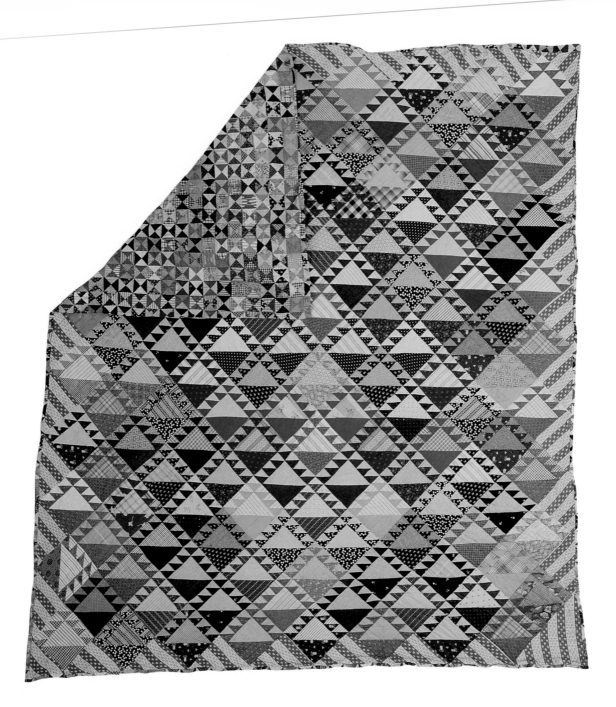

PLATE 78. SAWTOOTH/BROKEN DISHES, 1870-1890, 85½" x 96". *Made by Rachel C. Wilkins, Lumberton, Burlington County, New Jersey. This quilt is reversible, with a different pieced pattern on each side. A true scrap quilt, it makes use of tiny pieces of material covering a wide time span. A turned down corner of the Sawtooth pattern reveals the Broken Dishes pattern on the reverse side. The maker lived on a farm neighboring that of the owner's family. Owned by Ruth Evans Kutteroff, great-niece of the maker.*

PLATE 79. CHURN DASH, c.1880, 66½" x 87". A simple block in a simple setting, this quilt is made special by the secondary designs formed by the alternate pink and white prints in the corner squares of each block. The pink Eight Pointed Stars which appear add dimension and interest. Owned by Joan S. Danskin.

PLATE 80. CRAZY QUILT, 1885, 64" x 64¼". Made in Morristown, Morris County, New Jersey. This is an exquisite silk, brocade, and velvet quilt that displays a variety of embroidered figures and objects including a spider, a pig, a ladder, and an assortment of Japanese fans. Other embellishment techniques include chenille worked into sprays of daisies and goldenrod, hand-painted floral bouquets and appliquéd pansies and butterflies. It is believed this piece was made as an engagement or wedding gift for Katrina Becker whose initials "K. B." appear near the center along with the date "1885." An embroidered horseshoe sends "Good Luck" wishes. Owned by Louise Zuber.

PLATE 81. CRAZY QUILT, 1885, silk, 62" x 62". Made by a member of the Pedrick family, Glassboro, Gloucester County, New Jersey. An enchanting personal and historical document, this quilt pictures the maker's town, home, and family members, all embroidered in lavish detail. The house depicted in the center of the quilt was Dr. Pedrick's house, nicknamed The Pines or The Mansion. While this house is now gone, a smaller neighboring home shown on the quilt still stands. It is known as the Whitney House and is located on West Avenue (Route 322). Embroidered under the figure of a woman is the inscription, "Born June 16, 1826." This is thought to be the maker, probably the grandmother of the recipient, since another inscription reads, "Mother's hand work presented to Charley 1885." The original recipient is believed to have lived in the house at the time the quilt was presented to him. One fascinating detail includes a copy of a campaign panel embroidered with what appears to be the figure of Grover Cleveland, a New Jersey native son, and the date of his first Presidential inauguration, March 4, 1885. The figure Liberty stands behind him, holding a panel inscribed, "Peace, Prosperity, Progress." Other details include a rocking chair and a man sitting in an upholstered chair. The back of the quilt, made of printed patchwork in a crazy quilt design, is shown in Plate 62. Owned by Vic and Karen Martinson.

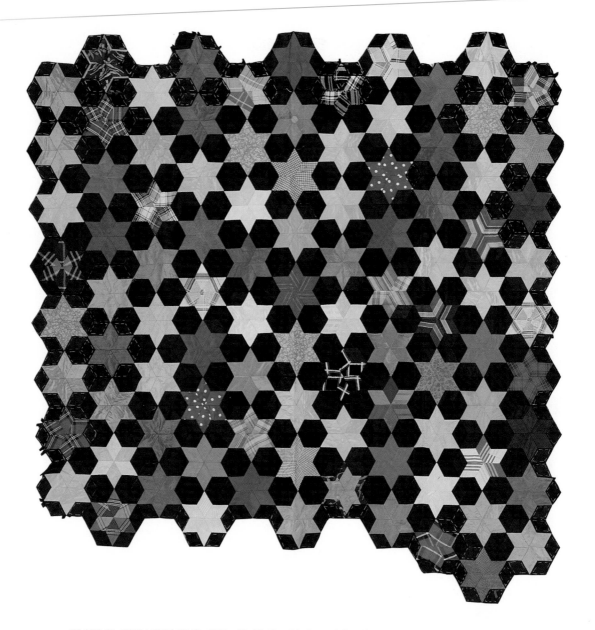

PLATE 82. HEXAGON STAR, 1888, silk, 50¼" x 54½". Made by Albatine Gaskill Stalford (1863-1948), Bridgeton, Cumberland County, New Jersey. A bright collection of silk and satin stars, this unfinished piece was constructed using the paper piecing method. Because it is incomplete, the back reveals fascinating glimpses of pieces of catalogs, advertising, and letters, including one with a postmark of "Bridgeton, N. J., Aug. 24, 1888." Owned by Winifred J. McLees, granddaughter of the maker.

FIG. 19. Albatine Gaskill Stalford and granddaughter, Winnie McLees

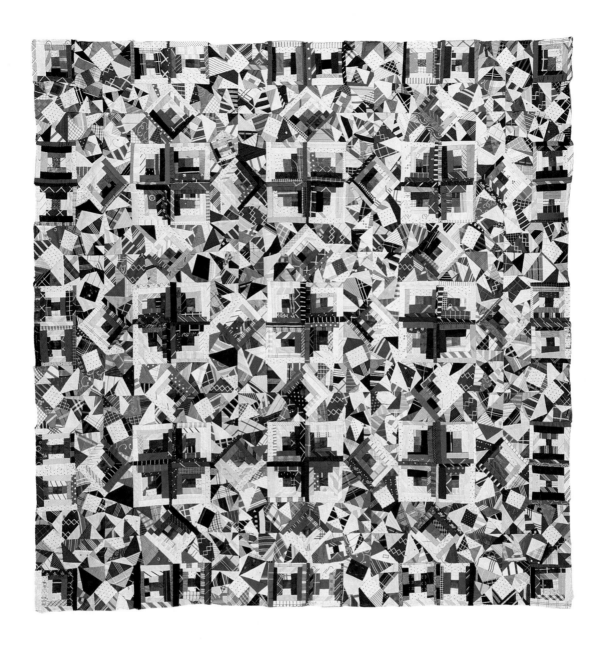

PLATE 83. CRAZY QUILT, c.1890, 73" x 73½". Made by Mary Cole (Mrs. Vanderenver Cole), Sergeantsville, Hunterdon County, New Jersey. The Log Cabin design appears prominently on the face of this quilt, but it is not until the quilt is turned over, that the distinctive star and block pattern of the foundation pieces can be seen. This pattern is almost lost on the front of the quilt. It is not only the unique construction of this quilt that draws our interest, but also the contrast of the fabrics used on the front and the back. The jeweled array of silk, corduroy, brocade, and velvet on the front is sewed to foundation pieces from a much earlier era, that include early cottons, indigo, and polished chintz. Owned by Elaine Jakubco.

PLATE 84. Reverse of the CRAZY QUILT in Plate 83, showing the foundation pieces used to create the top.

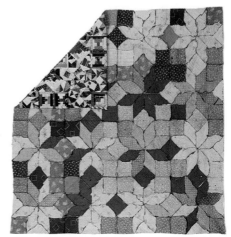

PLATE 85. FLORAL QUILT, c.1880, silk, 53" x 67½". Made by Hannah Elizabeth Huylar, Monmouth County, New Jersey. Finely embroidered realistic floral designs decorate this outstanding piece of needlework. A border of daisies is finished with a ribbon edge. The quilt is tied with the thread hidden on the top. A faded signature appears on the back of this artistic masterpiece. Owned by Margaret M. Cleveland (Mrs. Hugh M.), great-grandniece of the maker.

PLATE 86. FRIENDSHIP QUILT, 1884, silk, 72¼" x 81¼". "Fancy work" at its best, this is a well-documented friendship quilt made for the engagement and marriage of Lydia Davis Jones. She was from Germantown, Pennsylvania, and married Charles Collins Haines of Maple Shade, New Jersey, on February 26, 1885. Black satin pieces were given to friends and relatives who were asked to embroider them with their initials and anything else they wished. The ladies did their own initials and those of their men as well. There are 72 squares, and at about 85 years of age, Lydia Haines remembered the names of all but two of the people. Owned by Marion C. Willits, granddaughter of the original owner, who has a detailed record of all the contributors.

FIG. 20 (Left). Charles Collins Haines

FIG. 21 (Right). Lydia Davis Jones

PLATE 87. SAMPLER, 1896, wool and cotton, 87" x 90". Possibly made in Alloway, Salem County, New Jersey. A wool sampler quilt is rare indeed. This one is a bold mixture of color and design, signed with many signatures and initials. Although much of its history is lost, we know that it was made for a pastor and is embroidered with the initials "A. Mac K" and the date "1896." Owned by Gerry Downer.

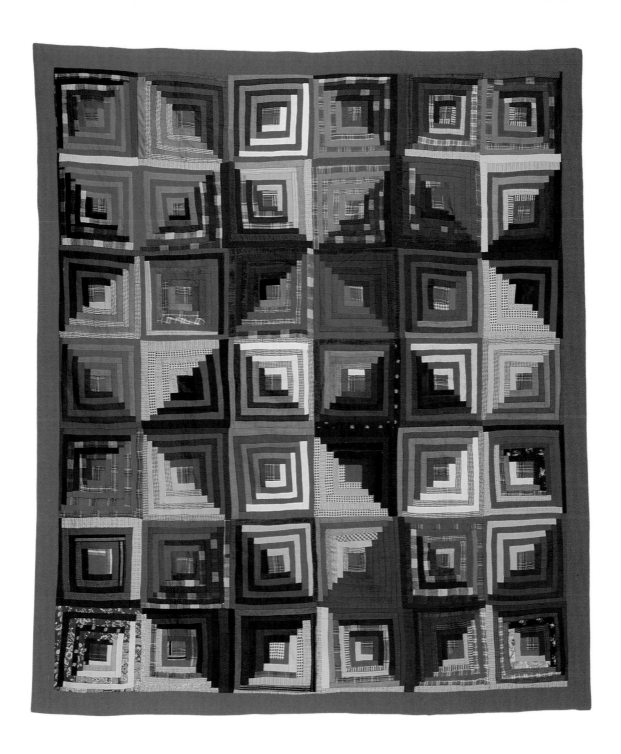

PLATE 88. LOG CABIN, *Light and Dark Variation, c.1900, wool, 74½" x 85". Made by Mary Barber (1870-1965), Scotts Mountain, Old Port Warren, Warren County, New Jersey. Wool Log Cabin quilts were frequently documented by the Project. This is a typical example of the dramatic result of the pattern's use of light and dark contrasting fabrics. The maker, who lived to be 95, was a descendant of John Barber, one of the earliest settlers of Lopatcong Township. At the time of the Lopatcong Township Centennial Celebration in June 1963, Mary was honored as the oldest resident as well as the oldest native resident. Owned by Virginia B. Smith, friend of the maker.*

FIG. 22. Mary Barber

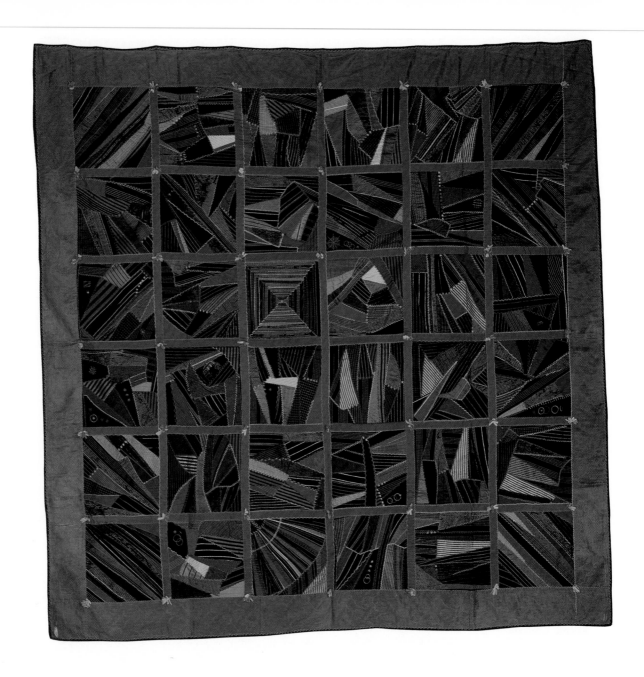

PLATE 89. CRAZY QUILT, before 1900, silk, 84" x 85". Made by Blanche Stokes Hillman Stratton (1878-1955), Delaware Township (now Cherry Hill Township), Camden County, New Jersey. This is a lovely contained crazy quilt, surprisingly made of pieces of men's suit linings. The maker's cousin obtained the materials at work, but it is not known whether the fabrics were samples or manufacturer's scraps. Various embroidery stitches decorate the quilt, and it is held together with ribbon ties. This quilt was made just prior to the maker's marriage in 1900. Blanche and her farmer husband, Levi, purchased a farm adjacent to her birthplace, and there they reared eight children. Owned by Retha E. Batten, granddaughter of the maker.

FIG. 23. Blanche Hillman Stratton

PLATE 90. CRAZY QUILT, 1893, wool, 68" x 83". Made by Martha Hulsizer Worman Hamlen (Mrs. George Hamlen), Stewartsville, Warren County, New Jersey. Here is a delightful quilt lovingly and thoughtfully made by a mother for her child. One block contains the outline of a small hand and the inscription, "1893 Charlie 6 years." It is embroidered with many common household objects of the period. Initials on the quilt are those of the recipient, Charles C. Hamlen, his mother, and his father. Owned by Martha L. Sikra, daughter of the recipient and granddaughter of the maker.

FIG. 24. Martha Hulsizer Worman Hamlen

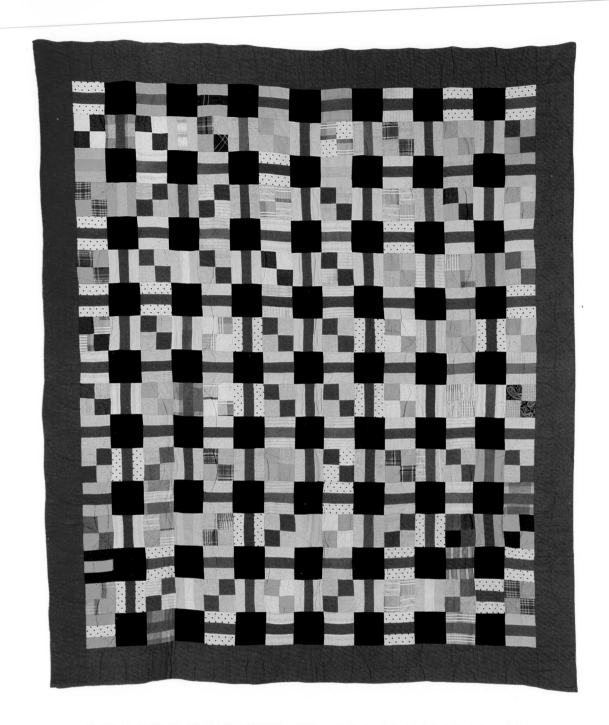

PLATE 91. LONDON ROADS VARIATION, c.1895, wool, 71½" x 81". Made by Minnie Jones (1868-1931), Manahawkin, Ocean County, New Jersey. Wool quilts tend to show sharp clear contrast, and this graphic piece is no exception. The navy squares give a three-dimensional quality to a somewhat unusual design. The quilting is done with black thread in the laurel leaf or pumpkin seed pattern. Owned by Karen M. Truhan, great-granddaughter of the maker.

PLATE 92. CRAZY QUILT, 1924, wool, 70½" x 76". Made by Eva Nichols (1859-1937), Burlington County, New Jersey. This attractive quilt shows the evolution of the crazy quilt from its fancy decorative silk beginnings to this plain utilitarian and startlingly modern collection of wools. The pastel wool colors foretell the colors of the cottons of the coming decades. Eva Nichols, who was born in London, made this quilt for her grandson when she was sixty-five. The fabrics were from a mill in Burlington County. Owned by Lucy C. Johnson, whose husband was the grandson of the maker.

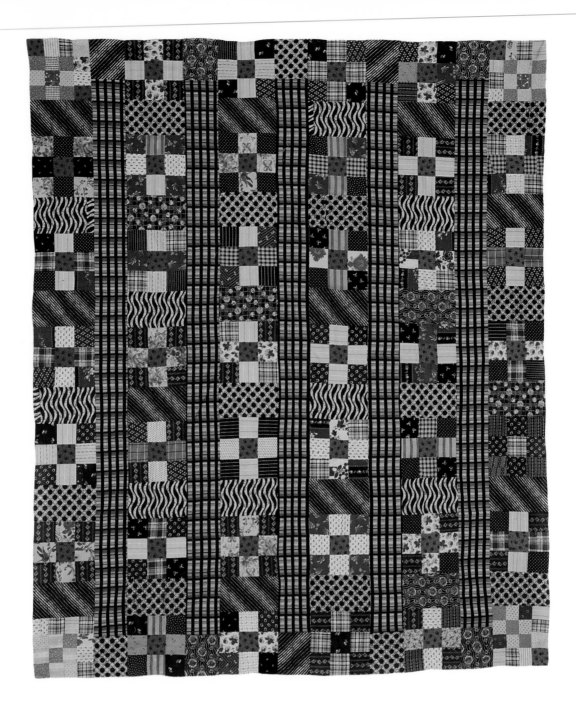

PLATE 93. NINE PATCH, c.1930, unquilted, 67" x 79". Made by Ruth Fenwick and relatives, Clifton, Passaic County, New Jersey. Fabrics from a forty-year time span were used to make this quilt. The dominant squiggly looking dark prints are most unusual and very unlike the pastels coming into vogue. Note the Sixteen Patch blocks in each corner. Owned by Cheryl Gormley, niece of the maker.

PLATE 94. NINE PATCH VARIATION WITH CENTER STAR, c.1880, 74" x 76". Made by Mercy Anna Clarkson Garretson (1834-1908), Middlebush, Somerset County, New Jersey. Even though this quilt was probably made for utilitarian reasons, several of the design elements lift it above the ordinary. One is the star in the center. Not only does it give the quilt a focus, but it is also cleverly pieced to take advantage of striped and plaid fabrics, a technique much in vogue among today's quiltmakers. Another interesting effect is the secondary Four Patch design formed at the corners of the blocks when they are set together side by side. This is a quilt of strong light and dark contrasts, as is the quilt in Plate 74 which was made by the same person and, like this one, quilted in recent times. Owned by Ann G. Bering, granddaughter of the maker.

PLATE 95. RISING STARS, c.1915, unquilted, 79" x 88¼". Made in Tuckerton, Ocean County, New Jersey. Many small pieces of striped fabric were used to make this patriotic looking quilt top. Interesting to note are the light colored blocks that form an X through the center of the quilt. Owned by Virginia Scheetz.

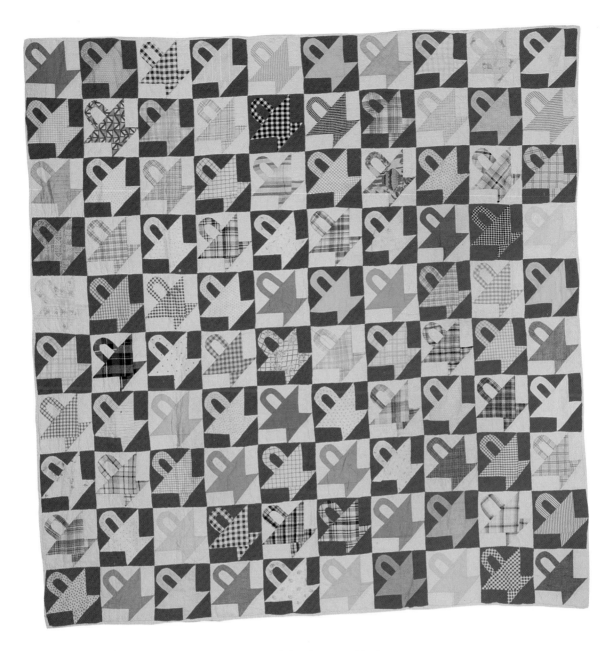

PLATE 96. BASKET, c.1930, 78½" x 78½". Made by Clarence Lashley (1884-1945) and Anna Mary Lashley (1882-1944), Mays Landing, Atlantic County, New Jersey. This was one of several quilts made by husband and wife; Clarence pieced the blocks, Anna put them together, and a local church group quilted the top. The basket fabrics are mostly cotton but include seersucker, flannel, and wool. Delicate florals and vigorous plaids and checks have been placed on a bold red and white checkerboard background. This is a strong scrap quilt that uses a great variety of fabrics: the makers' daughters and granddaughter can recognize scraps from dresses they wore as children. Other quilts made by Clarence can be seen in Plates 143 and 144. Owned by Emma L. Cline, daughter of the makers.

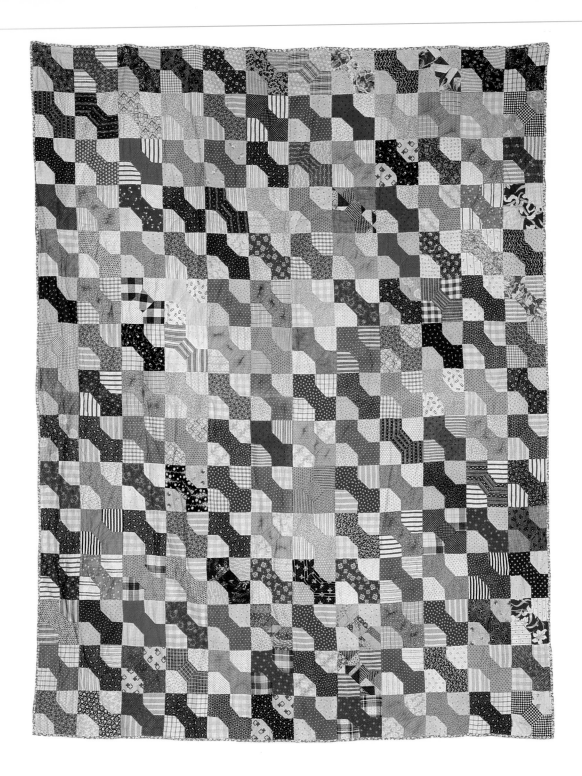

PLATE 97. BOWTIE, c.1920, 66¼" x 83¼". A large collection of scraps went into the making of this tidy looking quilt. It is an example of the transition period of the 1920's, with some pieces from the turn of the century (mainly the dark blues, maroons, and blacks) being used along with the lighter colors and grayed blues that were coming into vogue. Pieces of printed patchwork in two different color combinations appear. Owned by Judith K. Grow.

Paterson: The Silk City

Many of the silks found in fancy quilts of the period were probably produced in Paterson's thriving mills.

The waterfall of the Passaic River at Paterson in Passaic County has a perpendicular drop of nearly 80 feet through a narrow gorge and, except for Niagara Falls, is the largest waterfall east of the Mississippi River. Alexander Hamilton was so impressed with the potential water power of the falls that he encouraged its selection as the site for the creation of the Society for Establishing Useful Manufactures (SUM), incorporated in 1791, and the beginnings of America's industrial economy.[4] Indeed, Paterson has been called "the cradle of American industry" and it was here that the cotton-duck sail was developed, a significant portion of the nation's locomotives were produced, the Colt revolver was manufactured, the first submarine was invented, and Wright's airplane engines were made.[5] Paterson also became the world's leading silk manufacturing center.

It was under the supervision of John Colt, son of one of the owners of the only cloth factory in the new nation,[6] that the first Paterson mill was built in 1793. It had machinery for spinning, weaving, bleaching, and printing.[7] Known as the Bull Mill because it was initially driven by ox power, it switched to water power in 1794 and was the new nation's second successful attempt at spinning cotton by machinery, the first being in 1790 in Rhode Island. While the Bull Mill failed in 1795, the industry in Paterson attracted workers of various skill levels. As the SUM would not use slave labor in the mills and farmers didn't want their children moving off the farm into factories, European workers with skills lacked by Americans were recruited from New York City and Europe.[8] In 1822 Colt gave another boost to the cotton industry in Paterson when he made the first cotton duck that didn't require a special finishing to protect it from mildew. The material was particularly well-suited for sails, and the demand was such that by 1824 he had developed a method for manufacturing the fabric on a power loom. By the 1830's all the sails used by the U.S. Navy were manufactured in Paterson. By 1840, only Lowell, Massachusetts, exceeded Paterson in the amount and quality of its cotton production.[9] After a boom during the Civil War, cotton gradually declined as Paterson's main product, partially because of increased competition from the South. Yet it remained an active industry through the end of the nineteenth century.[10] When silk became the rage, it was the manufacture of cotton that provided a base for the development of the silk industry: the skills and equipment used in cotton production were easily transferable to silk.

Silk production in Virginia had been encouraged by James I as early as 1608. Experiments in England hadn't been successful and it was hoped that the colonies would provide a better environment for raising silkworms and the production of raw silk. While some raw silk was produced in the colonial period, it wasn't enough to be successful. In the 1830's the American government encouraged the growth of mulberry trees to feed silk worms. Unfortunately the climate wasn't favorable for the silkworms, but some of the mulberry trees did survive, and signs that say "Mulberry Street" are reminders of this brief mulberry madness.[11] After this, manufacturers of silk goods had to import raw goods from the Orient and the Mediterranean. As interest in silk manufacturing increased, more silk industry professionals were recruited from Europe.[12]

Christopher Colt brought the first silk making machinery to Paterson around 1838. When his first attempt at silk manufacturing was unsuccessful, Colt's facilities were bought in 1840 by George Murray, "a traveler whose own silk business had been destroyed by fire." Murray employed John Ryle, a young Englishman who had worked in a Northhampton, Massachusetts, fabric mill and who had established a silk importing business in New York City, to run the business. A partnership was formed in 1843, although Murray retired in 1846. The business continued to grow until by 1850 Ryle employed more than 500 workers and more than 1,000 pounds of silk were produced weekly. Ryle has been recognized for being the first person to produce sewing silk in the United States, the first to wind silk on a spool, and as the maker of the first silk American flag, which flew over the Crystal Palace at the New York World's Fair in 1852.[13]

When the English silk industry suffered a severe decline in 1860, silk industry workers, managers, and former business owners emigrated to Paterson, which benefitted from their skills and experience. Other silk makers such as John Benson, John Birchenough, Thomas Dale, Benjamin Tilt, and Catholina Lambert added to Paterson's fame and "The Silk City" continued to grow, until by 1881 there were 15,000 workers employed by 121 firms involved in silk production. Two-thirds of all raw silk imported into America went to Paterson where it was turned into flags, neckties, dress goods, tassels, ribbons, and trims for uniforms, for household decorations, for carriages, and for use by undertakers. No doubt much of the silk found in the fancy quilts of the period was produced in Paterson.

In 1902, a fire destroyed the entire commercial hub of Paterson and, less than four weeks later, the Passaic River flooded. Despite these disasters, the town rebuilt and by 1910 experienced renewed growth and prosperity, with several hundred silk plants that employed 25,000 workers.[14]

While labor unrest existed as early

PLATE 98. RAINBOW QUILT, 1906-1912, silk, 60" x 79". Made by Alice Mosier Bennett (1890-1960), Passaic, Passaic County, New Jersey. Sparkling silks from the famed Paterson silk mills are displayed in this striking scrap quilt. The combination of solid black and string-pieced triangles forms the basic block. By arranging the blocks in groups of four with the string halves together, they give the appearance of string-pieced and single fabric blocks set on point. The velvet border and backing were added in 1979. At the time this quilt was made, Paterson was still known as "The Silk City" and had over 300 silk mills. Owned by the Meadowlands Museum, Bergen County.

as 1879, it was after the damaging strike of 1913 organized by the Industrial Workers of the World that Paterson's silk production began to slip. In contrast to wealthy "silk barons" such as Catholina Lambert were the mill workers, who worked long hours in miserable conditions for little pay. As industry competition intensified, the workers were pushed to work harder – often asked to double the number of looms each weaver operated – for even less pay.[15] For twenty-two weeks – with 24,000 silk and dye workers on strike amidst violence and food shortages – labor and management struggled. Ultimately, the IWW's unity was broken and the strike collapsed, but a mortal blow had been dealt to the dominance of Paterson's silk industry.[16]

Despite an upsurge during World War I when the number of Paterson silk companies nearly doubled so that by 1923 at least 30,000 workers were involved in some phase of silk production or dyeing,[17] the crash of 1929 hit Paterson particularly hard. Its mills were reluctant to convert to rayon, the "artificial silk" which, along with other synthetics, many manufacturers foresaw as the replacement for silk. By 1934, New Jersey had 200 rayon looms out of 47,000 nationwide, and none were located in Paterson.[18]

During World War II Japanese silk supplies were cut off, which forced an increase in the use of the synthetics that Paterson was reluctant to manufacture. By the 1950's, Paterson, though no longer recognized as "The Silk City," still had over a hundred plants engaged in various phases of silk and rayon production and was known as the American center of textile dyeing and printing.[19] ∎

PLATE 99 (Detail). CRAZY QUILT, c.1890, silk, 74" x 78." Made in New Jersey. A quilt with a strong New Jersey heritage, this fascinating work features pieces of many different labeled hat linings. Thornton's and Lurch's both of Newark, New Jersey, are named, as well as a hatter from Poughkeepsie, New York. Several of the labels are from Paris and London firms, including one that says "Hatter to the Queen." Some of the embroidered initials suggest that the quilt may have been made by the relatives of one of the hatters. Initials include two different capital letter "T"'s which may indicate a possible connection to the Thornton firm. Another set of initials is "m.h.a.t." and the name "Maggie" and the number 11 are embroidered on the quilt. Privately owned.

The Split Nine Patch Design

Use of this design seems to have been a modest New Jersey trend.

One of the first local quilt-making styles identified by quilt historians was the Baltimore appliqué quilt made in the late 1840's and early 1850's. While no other local trend will probably ever have the impact of the Baltimore appliqués, some state projects have identified more subtle local styles in their states. In Tennessee, one region continued to make exquisite all-white quilts until about 1900 even though the rest of the country had lost interest in that style by about 1840.[20] In Pennsylvania in the last half of the 1800's, quiltmakers around Berks County in the southeastern part of the state developed a preference for backgrounds in strong colors such as orange or blue, while quilters in the middle of the state retained their preference for the white backgrounds of the previous decades.[21] More examples of local quiltmaking preferences will undoubtedly be reported as additional state projects present their findings.

In New Jersey, certain styles of quilts were documented at almost every Quilt Day. Some of these, such as

crazy quilts, Dresden Plates, and Sunbonnet Sues, were New Jersey versions of nationally popular quilt styles. However, one design frequently seen at northern New Jersey Quilt Days is not often seen in publications from other state projects. The Split Nine Patch block, sometimes called Hayes Corner, is like the Log Cabin block in that it is divided diagonally into two areas, one dark and one light, with a center square of a consistent color, usually red. The dark and light diagonal

areas allow the block to be arranged in any of the Log Cabin settings, such as Barn Raising, Straight Furrow, and many others. Because the Split Nine Patch block is made mostly of squares instead of strips, it requires only 11 pieces per block rather than the 17 to 33 pieces of the typical Log Cabin block. There is even a variation of the Split Nine Patch combining some of the squares so that the number of pieces per block is reduced to 5. An even further simplification can be seen

FIG. 25. Split Nine Patch

Split Nine Patch, 11 pieces

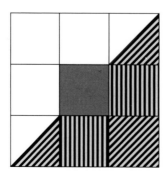

Split Nine Patch, 5 pieces

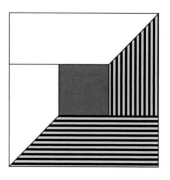

in a few quilts using Split Squares of one dark and one light triangle to achieve the Barn Raising or Streak of Lightning effect.

Although quilts in the Split Nine Patch design have not been published frequently, a few can be seen in print, usually with a Pennsylvania attribution. An Amish example in Barn Raising set, probably of Pennsylvania origin, is shown in an advertisement in *The Clarion* magazine, published by the Museum of American Folk Art.[22] Nancy Roan has reported that two valleys in central Pennsylvania – the Perkiomen Valley and Center Valley – each adopted a complex arrangement of the design as its own speciality. She notes that the intricacy of the set used in each valley required a quiltmaker to have a completed quilt on hand in order to copy the layout correctly.[23] A Perkiomen Valley style Split Nine Patch is attributed to New Jersey in Jonathan Holstein's book, *The Pieced Quilt: An American Design Tradition.*[24]

However, in keeping with New Jersey quiltmakers' usual preference for simplicity of design, the Split Nine Patch quilts seen by the Project include only the more basic settings. The arrangements recorded include Barn Raising, Streak of Lightning, and a variation of Barn Raising in which the blocks are set on point to form a central square rather than a central diamond. In one New Jersey family, two sisters were each given a Split Nine Patch quilt – one in Barn Raising set and one in Streak of Lightning. The only additional set recorded was a Sunshine and Shadow variation seen in an unfinished top. All of these settings could easily be accomplished by a quiltmaker familiar with Log Cabin arrangements.

The Split Nine Patch quilts recorded in New Jersey were usually made between 1900 and 1925, a time period that has not gained much popularity, perhaps because of its rather grayed color schemes. This may account for the design's infrequent publication. Perhaps once other states are alerted to the Split Nine Patch design, it will be reported in areas other than the adjoining states of New Jersey and Pennsylvania. ■

PLATE 100. SPLIT NINE PATCH, c.1920, 76" x 78". Made in either Schooleys Mountain, Morris County or Montclair, Essex County, New Jersey. This quilt is representative of a design that appeared repeatedly in New Jersey. Found mostly in the northwest part of the state, the style is similar to a pattern which is called Perkiomen Valley in Montgomery County, Pennsylvania. The basic block is a Nine Patch with a red center dividing it into dark and light fabrics. All the quilts could be considered utilitarian and the pattern made good use of fabric scraps. This quilt shows an imaginative setting. Note that some of the light fabrics are darker than others, adding interest and motion. Owned by Mr. and Mrs. Langdon Palmer.

PLATE 101. SPLIT SQUARE, c.1880, unquilted, 84" x 86". Done in the Barn Raising variation, this piece is another example found in New Jersey showing the use of dark and light contrast to produce a Log Cabin-like design. It is similar to others of its kind in the use of scrap fabric, particularly red. The use of yellow is more unusual, resulting in a brighter look than others of this type. Some of the fabric dates back to the 1850's. Owned by Sue Huesken.

PLATE 102. SPLIT NINE PATCH, c.1930, 76½" x 78". Possibly made in White House Station, Hunterdon County, New Jersey. An example of the Split Nine Patch design, a configuration of dark and light squares, this quilt is done in a Streak of Lightning set. In this particular variation, the Nine Patch block is divided into light and dark shades in the center by the use of two triangles. This quilt, like most others of this design, makes repeated use of the color red. Older fabrics from the turn of the century were used for the dark areas while the lighter sections are made from 1920's and 1930's pastels. Owned by Carolyn Briggs Stenzel, whose mother was a friend of the maker.

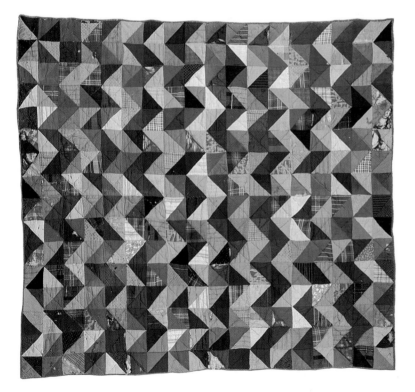

PLATE 103. SPLIT SQUARE, c.1890, silk and wool, 70" x 77". Although this quilt is considerably damaged, it is still a striking example of the New Jersey quiltmaker's fondness for simple patterns making use of light and dark contrast. Done in a Streak of Lightning set, this quilt is made of silk and wool scraps. Owned by the Clinton Historical Museum, Hunterdon County.

The African-American Presence

**African-American quilts documented by the New Jersey Project
feature well-defined blocks, familiar designs, and careful workmanship.**

here has been an African presence in New Jersey nearly as long as there has been a European one. The Dutch imported Africans as slaves in the 1600's when they had settlements on the Eastern seaboard, and in the 1640's they are believed to have unloaded slaves at Jersey City, then known as Harsimus.[25] Early English settlement policies encouraged the importation of Africans as slaves, and by 1680 Colonel Morris Lewis of Shrewsbury, Monmouth County, owned sixty to seventy slaves. In the same decade, two free blacks, who were among those brought to New York by the Dutch, owned land in the Hackensack River Valley. The families of these two free blacks eventually sold their land and retreated into the Ramapo Mountains, becoming one of several black groups to form separate communities in New Jersey.[26]

The historic differences between East and West Jersey are evident in the attitudes in the two areas toward the African-American population. East Jerseyans reflected New York's attitude and actively imported blacks as slaves

to fill their labor needs. Land was so readily available that Europeans interested in farming were able to acquire their own land but laborers for farm work were often in short supply. Therefore, farmers with large holdings, particularly the Dutch, used slaves and indentured workers on their lands.[27] The port of Perth Amboy, Middlesex County, was a center of the New Jersey slave trade, and by the end of the 1600's most of its white families are reported to have owned slaves. Similarly, Jersey City, Hudson County, was an important port for the slave trade, and by 1709 New Jersey had 11,000 African-Americans, 2,300 of whom lived in the vicinity of Jersey City.[28]

By the 1700's the East Jersey population was 10 to 12 percent black. At the same time, African-Americans comprised about 4½ percent of the population in West Jersey. As early as 1693, a Quaker writer encouraged other Quakers to avoid buying slaves on moral grounds. Although some Quakers did own slaves in the 1700's, they generally made a greater effort to keep families together and to free their

slaves when circumstances permitted. In 1758 the Quakers began working actively for the abolition of slavery, and by 1776 slave-owning Quakers were banned from religious meetings.

The everyday life of slaves in New Jersey is rarely described in written records, but some indication of the skills they had acquired can be seen in the advertisements for slaves who had run away or who were being offered for sale. Various slaves are described as "a mason," "a shoemaker," "a ship-carpenter," "a good blacksmith," "skilled in the saw-mill business," or "skilled in the care of horses and the management of a carriage." The advertisements also show that some slaves could read and write, speak fluent Dutch or French as well as English, and "play on the violin." Although the advertisements do not describe specialized textile skills among black women, they do refer to general skills of "housewifery." Some advertisements suggest that a particular runaway slave was likely to have gone to the area where his mother or wife lived, indicating a continuing black effort to

PLATE 104. LADY OF THE LAKE, c.1850, 79" x 93". *Probably made by Mrs. Browning, Florida. This lovely pieced quilt with its vine and leaf appliqué border is assumed to have been made by Mrs. Browning, a black woman, for her son, Perry, who was born in 1888. He brought the quilt with him to Schooleys Mountain, New Jersey, where, starting at age sixteen, he worked for the Blake family for sixty years. The quilt was passed down to the late Josephine Blake McKnight by her aunt, Emma Louise Blake. Owned by Dale McKnight.*

maintain family ties under a system that sought to destroy these relationships. In the 1700's New Jersey slaves were subject to capture and whipping if they were found more than five miles from their owner's house without a pass. Yet, some New Jersey slaves were permitted to compete against New York slaves in dance contests at the Catherine Market in New York.

In the Revolution, several New Jersey slaves were soldiers in the Continental Army, and many others served as wagon drivers, horse grooms, and in other supporting functions. No doubt, other blacks worked in support of the British, as did many of their owners. The white colonists' writings supporting their own freedom from British rule showed many clear contradictions in their continued support of slavery. After the Revolution, the original states north of New Jersey abolished slavery, but East Jersey, with its relatively large black population and need for black labor, maintained an attitude similar to that of the southern states. In 1786 New Jersey finally became the last of the original northern states to ban the importation of newly enslaved Africans. It also loosened some of its laws that had made it difficult for slave owners to free their slaves when they wished to do so.

By 1793, New Jersey was the last of the original northern states permitting slavery, and New Jersey abolitionists sought assistance from Pennsylvania abolitionists in their fight against the owning of slaves in their state. In 1804 New Jersey finally adopted an awkward compromise that gradually abolished slavery by making newborn children of slave women free while leaving their parents in bondage.

Although New Jersey was well-placed to be an escape route for runaway slaves from the southern states of the Atlantic Coast, the diverse attitudes of New Jerseyans towards blacks

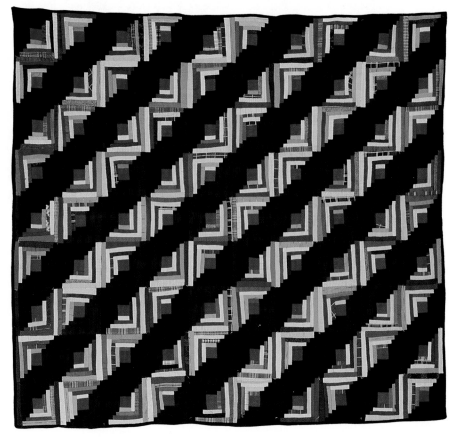

FIG. 26 (Left). Charity Morris

PLATE 105 (Below). LOG CABIN, Straight Furrow Variation, 1910, wool, 72" x 78". Made by Charity Morris, Lafayette, New York. A dramatic interpretation of the Log Cabin design, this quilt is pieced mainly from wool and flannel. Charity Morris, a former slave, was brought to Lafayette from the south by the Freedman's Aid Society. She made the quilt in 1910 for the marriage of Edna Palmer Flint, her employer's daughter. Even though the bride was a New York native, the groom was from New Jersey, and the couple resided there. Owned by Priscilla Flint.

meant that escape through New Jersey entailed considerable risk. The Underground Railroad operated along the Delaware River and along several other routes through the southern counties. It also operated as far north as Jersey City where at least four Underground Railroad routes are said to have converged. There, fleeing slaves were transferred to New York for train or boat transportation farther north along the Hudson River. In 1854, David L. Holden, an ardent abolitionist and amateur astronomer, built a house in Jersey City with an observatory on the roof where he could watch both the sky and the movements of the waters in nearby Harsimus Cove. Holden is said to have housed 25 or more escaping slaves at a time in his basement. Bounty hunters periodically combed the woods behind his home searching for runaways who had not yet reached safety.[29]

A New Jersey law of 1826 provided for the return of fugitive slaves to their owners outside the state. In 1846 the anti-slavery newspaper *New Jersey Freeman* reported the abuse of this law to kidnap New Jersey-born African-Americans. It noted "some of our inhabitants have during the past year been dragged away...into hopeless slavery." At the other end of the spectrum, in 1824 one escaping slave, Daniel (Benjamin) Clark, was fortunate enough to encounter a sympathetic group of whites in Gloucester County who raised the considerable sum of $140 and purchased his freedom from his Delaware owner.

As more African-Americans became free in New Jersey, they formed their own churches in urban centers, started literary societies to promote education, and, in 1849, held a convention in Trenton to seek voting rights. They also organized to oppose the Colonization Societies that influential whites had formed to send free blacks to Africa as Christian missionaries. However, the process of gradual abolition had been so slow that at the beginning of the Civil War several slaves still remained in the state's population of 25,000 African-Americans.

When the Civil War came, New Jersey once again had divided allegiances. In addition to some New Jerseyans' pro-Southern racial attitudes, many New Jersey manufacturers of inexpensive clothing were dependent on Southern buyers.[30] Yet New Jersey fielded its regiments for the Northern cause. While it did not organize an all-black regiment, about 2,900 black New Jerseyans served with regiments from other states.

In 1870, just after the Civil War, the nation's first black to vote under the 15th Amendment voted in Perth Amboy, and in the same year New Jersey's first black juror was seated in West Milford, Passaic County. In 1884 a black minister in Burlington County won a case against school segregation. Yet many New Jersey school districts maintained separate schools well into the twentieth century, and many other forms of discrimination continued unabated as migration from the South increased the black population, particularly in urban areas.

From 1860 to 1940 the African-American population of New Jersey increased tenfold from about 25,000 to about 250,000. The hope of employment opportunities attracted African-Americans from the rural South to the cities of the North where they found established black communities with churches and other social organizations.

The years of World War I opened some jobs for African-Americans in the North as the competing flow of workers from Europe was cut off. Yet, government surveys in the early part of the 1900's had documented a pervasive attitude among both manufacturers and trade unions that deliberately excluded African-Americans from the skilled trades. Thus, when the hard times of the Depression hit, these new immigrants from the South were the most vulnerable to unemployment, inadequate housing, and other urban ills.

Only one of the black-made quilts recorded by the Project was made in a family that had been in the state before the Civil War. However, a few early quilts attributed to New Jersey African-Americans can be seen in print, including a particularly lovely and skillful example with elaborate scalloped edges and an array of appliquéd black figures.[31] The quilts documented by the Project generally reflect the continued northward migration of black families: the makers of all but one of these quilts came from Southern states from Florida to Mississippi (examples are shown in Plates 104, 105, and 123). Whether made before or after leaving the South, whether made for family or friends, all of the quilts recorded used well-defined blocks, familiar designs, and careful workmanship, rather than being of the "improvisational" style with the spontaneous and irregular construction that scholars and museum exhibition curators have sometimes presented as the "African-American style" of quiltmaking. ∎

The Quilts of the Hopper-Goetschius House

Quilts found in this historic building illustrate design trends of the period and the development of cottage industries.

In 1739, when Charles Clinton surveyed what is now the Upper Saddle River area of Bergen County, New Jersey, he wrote, "This year [Abraham Hopper] built a stone house." Most likely this stone structure is now the west wing of the Hopper-Goetschius House, a sandstone Dutch Colonial with a high gambrel roof over the main section and a deep gable on the in-line west wing, additions and changes having been made beginning in the late 1700's through the Victorian era. Located at the crossroads of Lake Street and East Saddle River Road, it is now a museum operated by the Upper Saddle River Historical Society and is listed on the National Register of Historic Places. The Hopper family, having settled in the area in the 1600's, farmed the land which at one time numbered some 278 acres. In addition to the house itself, there were numerous out-buildings necessary for self-sufficiency on a farm.

In 1814 the house was purchased from the Hoppers by the Rev. Stephen Goetschius (1752-1837), a minister to the Dutch Reformed Old Stone Church and a Revolutionary War soldier. It remained in the Goetschius family until the death of its last resident, Lizzie Carlough Goetschius (1888-1983), wife of Rev. Goetschius' great-great-grandson, Stephen J. (1888-1962). In 1985 Clinton and Grace Carlough, Lizzie's nephew and his wife, presented the house to the town to be developed as a museum.

When the Upper Saddle River Historical Society began inventorying the contents of the house, thirty-one quilts were found. Many familiar patterns

---

FIG. 27. The Hopper-Goetschius house in the 1920's

were found among the quilts, including Baskets, Nine Patch, Pine Tree, and Ohio Star. Several may have been made by Maria Eckerson Goetschius (1826-1905), wife of Rev. Goetschius' grandson Stephen (1820-1893). Several were made by Dorcas Courter Carlough (1845-1936), Lizzie's mother. But the majority of the quilts had been made by Kate Fisher Goetschius (1863-1955) – the wife of Rev. Goetschius' great-grandson, George (1889-1936) – Stephen J.'s mother and Lizzie's mother-in-law. Thus, most of the quilts can be attributed to Dorcas and Kate, mothers of the last couple to live in the Hopper-Goetschius house.

Dorcas Courter Carlough was born in Franklin Lakes, Bergen County, New Jersey, in 1845, and after James D. Carlough courted her on horseback from Upper Saddle River, she married him in 1868. James Carlough started the Carlough Apple Orchards, later becoming the largest apple producer in New Jersey. He was also a skilled stone mason whose walls continue to stand today. In 1894 he was elected the first mayor of Upper Saddle River. Dorcas supervised the gardening and the chickens and on Saturdays would take her produce and eggs to the Paterson Market to sell. Her daughter, Lizzie Carlough Goetschius, remembered her mother also making molded butter to take to the market. The Pine Tree quilt made by Dorcas (Plate 106) was probably brought to the Hopper-Goetschius House around the time that Lizzie Carlough married Stephen J. Goetschius in 1910.

Kate's family, the Fishers, lived in Ramsey, not far from Upper Saddle River. After her marriage to George Goetschius in 1882, Kate went to live at the homestead farm. As some of the quilts date from this time, they were probably made by Kate in preparation for her marriage or during its early years. Here, she raised three sons and worked hard, contributing to the life of a farm. In the summer, cooking and chores such as washing and making soap and butter were done outside in the out kitchen which had a large jambless fireplace around which meat was hung to smoke, and a beehive oven.

PLATE 106. PINE TREE, c.1880, 70½" x 94½". Made by Dorcas Carlough (1845-1936), Upper Saddle River, Bergen County, New Jersey. The Pine Tree's postage-stamp-size triangles contain a large selection of prints held together by the center blue and red triangles. The blocks are set on point and sashed by a popular double pink print. The pine trees have been quilted in a geometric pattern while the background has been quilted in overlapping circles and four-petal "flowers." When the contents of the Hopper-Goetschius House were inventoried, this quilt was found in the closet of Lizzie Carlough Goetschius, the last resident. It was probably brought to the house at the time of Lizzie's marriage to Stephen J. Goetschius in 1910. Owned by the Upper Saddle River Historical Society, Bergen County.

FIG. 28. Lizzie (left) & Kate (right) Goetschius in the garden.

Like Dorcas Carlough, Kate and George took their produce to the Paterson Market. In later years, beginning around 1910, produce from the garden was also sold at a roadside stand. In the winter, Kate cooked on the wood stove in what is now remembered as "Kate's Kitchen." The children grew and the farm flourished. In 1910 Kate's son Stephen J. brought his new wife Lizzie Carlough Goetschius to live on the farm. It was around this time that Kate began to work with her sisters, Rachel Fisher Van Blarcom and Lizzie Fisher Barthof, to make quilts to sell. As the sisters lived nearby, they visited Kate often and the three quilted together on the quilting frame Kate kept set up in the back room of the west wing of the house, right behind the kitchen. In this little room heated by the kitchen's wood stove, the three Fisher sisters would sit and quilt. They made quilts to sell, one of which is the Odd Fellows quilt (Plate 108). They would hang them on a clothesline along the Lake Street side of the house, near their roadside produce stand, where passersby might stop and buy. They were a real "cottage industry." ■

From information provided by Kay Yeomans, trustee, Upper Saddle River Historical Society.

PLATE 107 (Top, Folded). DIAMOND IN A SQUARE, c.1880, 70" x 88".

(Bottom, Folded). DIAMOND IN A SQUARE, c.1880, 68½" x 84". Both made by Kate Fisher Goetschius (1863-1955), Upper Saddle River, Bergen County, New Jersey. Known as companion pieces, these two Diamond in a Square quilts share the same bold color scheme and the same green print. In the top quilt, the diamonds are green on white shirt prints and the alternating blocks are red. In the other (bottom), the diamonds are red on white shirt prints and the alternating blocks are green. Both quilts use the same green Ely & Walker print that appears in the Odd Fellows quilt in Plate 108 made by Kate and her sisters around 1915. The backs of the quilts – two different brown plaids – have been brought forward to bind the quilts so a little bit appears around the edge of each. Kate often used plaids to back her quilts and seems to have preferred homespun. Owned by the Upper Saddle River Historical Society, Bergen County.

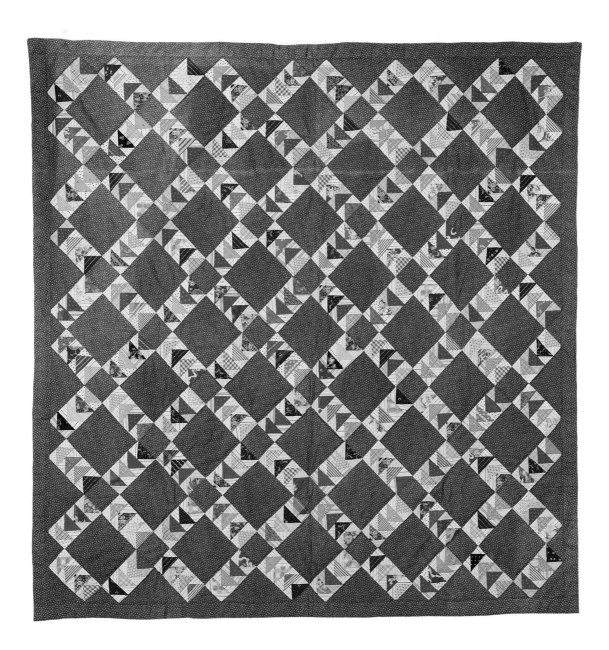

PLATE 108. ODD FELLOWS, c.1915, 79½" x 80". Made by the Fisher sisters, Upper Saddle River, Bergen County, New Jersey. This striking quilt contains a rich sampling of fabrics which remain crisp and new. The colors of the triangles are strong and include a glazed green floral print in addition to a variety of dress fabrics. The green printed background fabric is Ely & Walker, a manufacturer whose style and color of fabric remained popular over a long period of time. First printed in 1878, this type of fabric continued to be printed through the early 1980's. The three Fisher sisters, Kate Goetschius, Rachel Van Blarcom, and Lizzie Barthof, met frequently at Kate's homestead farm, now the Hopper-Goetschius House, where they made quilts like this one to sell at the crossroads of Lake Street and East Saddle River Road. The piecing in this quilt has been done by machine unlike the quilts made solely by Kate which were pieced by hand. The quilting is a very basic outline of the background squares. Owned by the Upper Saddle River Historical Society, Bergen County.

Quilts as Sources of Revenue

Since the 1800's, quilts have been used to raise funds for community organizations and causes.

There are several ways in which quilts have been used to make money over the course of their history. The most obvious has been to make a completed quilt to be sold, auctioned, or, most profitably, raffled if the moral tone of the community permitted. In England, male professional quilters who made whole-cloth bed quilts and quilted clothing had been at work for several centuries before America was even settled.

In the 1700's, as the fashion for quilted whole-cloth bedcovers moved from the aristocracy to the common folk in mining or farming communities, some professionals continued as "quilt designers," marking whole-cloth or strip quilts for special occasions to be quilted by families at home or for church groups to quilt and sell at fairs. In northeast England in the mid-1800's, church quilting clubs flourished just as they did in America in the same period. The north of England was the center of the Methodist movement which had begun in the 1700's. The new Methodist chapels lacked the government funding of the established Church of England, so Methodist women's quilt clubs became an important source of support. However, church fund-raising quilts made in the north of England were sold at bazaars or directly to buyers rather than being raffled because a raffle was considered gambling and

thought to be an inappropriate activity for a church. At the same time, women in the north of England were known to quilt independently for their own support: "Two sisters...in Yorkshire, about 1870 to 1880, used to go to the big houses and farms for several weeks at a time, dressmaking and quilting being paid a few shillings weekly."[32] In south Wales, as in the north of England, the demand for quilts permitted women whose husbands had died or become disabled in the mines to make a meager living for their families by quilting as well as making clothing, taking in laundry, and practicing midwifery. Yet these reports of quiltmaking for profit should not obscure the fact that, in these rural areas of the British Isles, many quilts were made for the personal use of the family creating them. In rural Britain, as in America, quilting around a frame was sometimes a community social event "with tea and cakes" and "music and entertainment for menfolk whilst the women quilted."[33]

No doubt many quilts made to raise money have survived with no clue as to their origin. Fortunately, in America many can be identified because they contain the name of the organization for which they were made or a message in support of a cause. One early example of a fund-raising quilt made in America is an anti-slavery cra-

dle quilt made for a fair held in Boston around the beginning of 1837. The quilt is made of pieced stars and bears an abolitionist message inscribed in ink. In New Jersey no pre-Civil War fund-raising quilts have been firmly identified. Yet questions might be raised about the quilts made for ministers between 1840 and 1870, because the Appliqué Sampler made in 1853 (Plate 55) may have been a fund-raiser for the Methodist Missionary Society. By the time of the Civil War, women of both sides worked actively to make quilts for use as soldiers' bedding as well as to be auctioned to raise funds to help supply the troops.[34]

American fund-raising quilts can sometimes be identified by their use of organization names, moral messages, and an abundance of signatures. In New Jersey in the 1840's many quilts included inked signatures. However, in this period the signatures were limited to one per block and sometimes only a few blocks were signed. The limit to the number of signatures in these quilts and prevalence of personal messages on some of the blocks supports the assumption that these quilts were an extension of the autograph album fad of the time and were made solely as a friendship gesture, without profit motive. Yet, one quiltmaker who worked on a quilt made in 1862 in Pennsylvania was later quoted as

PLATE 109. STAR SIGNATURE, c.1900, 80" x 97". Paterson, Passaic County, New Jersey. One thousand embroidered signatures of Paterson residents decorate this quilt, probably sponsored as a fund-raising effort by the Ark Lodge #110 IOOF. In the center are the names of President and Mrs. William McKinley and Vice President and Mrs. G. A. Hobart. Hobart was a Paterson native, and served as vice president during McKinley's term of office from 1897 to 1901. The quilt was acquired from the estate of Emma Scarr, a Paterson school teacher, whose name is among the signatures. Owned by Oscar Appel, who attended Emma Scarr's fifth grade class in Paterson School Number 5.

describing the quilt as "a friendship quilt; everybody whose name was on it gave a dime"[35] – thus blurring the distinction between quilts made for sentiment and those made for revenue.

In the Victorian era, women were encouraged to be the repositories of taste and virtue, both for their families and for society as a whole. This ideal permitted or even encouraged them to work to raise funds for various causes for public benefit. Since the creation of fancy needlework was also considered a feminine virtue, it was a natural conjunction of these two ideals that they should employ their needlework skills on behalf of churches, temperance organizations, and other causes. Some have suggested that the device of collecting hundreds of signatures for a quilt top at 10 cents per signature became popular as the moral tone of the times came to frown on the profitable raffle quilts, seeing them as a form of gambling. In any case, by the 1890's, fund-raiser quilts with hundreds of signatures, usually embroidered in red stem stitch, came to be a standard women's source of charity funding throughout America.

In New Jersey, quilts clearly known as fund-raisers were not recorded before the 1890's although several Double T quilts were seen which may have been intended to show support for the temperance movement. Among the interesting New Jersey fund-raising quilts is one "acquired by" the Delaware Valley Grange in Sussex County, a national organization for farmers. Since this quilt (Plate 110, bottom left) was apparently not made by the members of the organization or their wives, it may have generated income twice, once for the maker (or makers) and once as Grange members charged those who added their signatures. The fact that the quilt was made outside the group may explain why this quilt has inked signatures rather than the embroidered signatures that were more common in this period. The signature quilt (Plate 109) made for the Paterson chapter of the International Organization of Odd Fellows, a fraternal group comparable to the Masons, uses red appliquéd stars along with its 1,000 embroidered signatures. It has one characteristic of fund-raising quilts of the Civil War, the inclusion of the signatures of famous people, in this case President William McKinley and his vice-president Garrett A. Hobart, who was from Paterson in Passaic County. Their names have been embroidered in the center of the quilt, presumably from their original signatures.

Both the Sussex County Grange quilt and the Paterson Odd Fellows quilt are examples of fund-raisers to support organizations that were primarily social in nature. On the other hand, the embroidered signature quilt (Plate 110, top) made to raise funds for a local library, and the Five Pointed Star quilt (Plate 110, bottom right) made for the Red Cross are examples of women's fund-raising for "good works." The Morristown Red Cross quilt is a somewhat original variation of a fund-raising idea presented in *Modern Priscilla* magazine in December 1917, as the nation entered World War I. Red Cross quilts were made in many communities in response to the *Modern Priscilla* article.[36] Many follow the magazine example and use only red crosses and red signatures with a white background. The Morristown example is different in that it uses primarily blue five pointed stars and blue signatures with a red cross serving as a focal point in the center of the quilt. The Morristown Red Cross Quilt was made in a church context; its inscription reads "Red Cross Auxiliary, Morristown, N.J., 1918, Methodist Episcopal Church."

The embroidered signature quilt continued in New Jersey as an occasional fund-raiser into the 1930's. However, a more common source of church revenue in this period was the quilting and finishing of tops. This activity has been reported among New Jersey church women from the Atlantic Ocean to the Delaware River and from Sussex County in the northwest to Burlington County in the south. Denominations recorded to have generated income by quilting include Methodists, Congregationalists, Baptists, and Presbyterians. Some of these quilting groups disbanded in the 1950's as either the flow of unquilted tops or willing quilters diminished. Yet in some churches, such as the First Congregational Church of Chester in Morris County, quilting for the church has continued uninterrupted for over 100 years. ∎

PLATE 110 (Top, Folded). *EMBROIDERED SIGNATURE, 1895-1896, 76" x 87".* Made in Raritan Township, Hunterdon County, New Jersey. This quilt is a myriad of names and designs embroidered in outline stitch on muslin. On the back a label signed by Katherine S. Merrell tells us that the quilt was made to raise funds to start a library at the Voorhees Corner School in Raritan Township. Ten dollars was raised by the neighborhood folks who each paid five cents to have their name included. Another ten dollars was earned from the sale of the quilt at auction. This twenty dollars was then matched by the state. The label also indicates that the names were embroidered by Mrs. Jesse Merrell, mother of Lou D. Merrell who was a teacher at the school at the time the quilt was made. Owned by the Hunterdon County Historical Society.

(Bottom, Left, Folded). *SCHOOL HOUSE SIGNATURE, 1912-1913, 70" x 86".* Sponsored by the Delaware Valley Grange No. 143, Delaware Valley, Walpack, Sussex County, New Jersey. This is a well documented fund-raising quilt. Each person paid ten cents to have his name written on the edge. The calligraphy, written on the front in black ink, lists the committee responsible and the date made. The inscription states that the Delaware Valley Grange was organized in 1904 and owned its own hall in the village of Layton. The Grange is described as a "vigorous farmers organization devoted to the interests of agriculture and the welfare of the family." Sussex County remains one of the more rural areas of the state. The quilt was won by Mary Alice Hursh who remarried a man named Cook. Thomas Cook's sister, Sarah F. Gumm, bequeathed the quilt to the current owners, William and Gloria Moffett.

(Bottom, Right, Folded). *FIVE POINTED STAR WITH SIGNATURES, 1918, 62" x 79".* Made by Mary A. Mosdale (1857-1931), Morristown, Morris County, New Jersey. This quilt was a fund-raising effort for the Red Cross, each embroidered signature representing a donation of ten cents. Each blue star has at least ten signatures. Blue stars often represented living combatants. The red cross in the center contains the following inscription: "Red Cross Auxiliary, Morristown, N. J., 1918, Methodist Episcopal Church." Owned by The Morris Museum, Morris County.

157

Chapter Five

The Great Revival

My grandmother, Sarah Ann (Leake) Barber...was born in Shropshire, England. She came to America when she was 12 years old....

[She] had 11 children...[and] 36 grandchildren. This quilt [Plate 114] was made when she was 70 or so. She always made dresses for the granddaughters...I loved it when she stayed with us. She could do anything with her hands. [She] designed her own patterns for clothes. She taught me all my handcraft and needlework skills.

She told me about the dressmaking shop she [had] had...to help support her own family. She would go to the homes of wealthy families 2 times each year, spring and fall, to do all their dress-making. They wanted her because she made patterns that no one else had.

Her one dream that she never realized was to learn to fly an aeroplane....She was a feisty little lady. She was young in spirit until she died at 83....Wish you could have known her!

– Letter to The Heritage Quilt Project of New Jersey
from Kay Haulenbeek, granddaughter of the quiltmaker.

PLATE 111 (Below). FLOWERY FIELDS, c.1930 (also seen in Plate 7) a colorful scrap quilt, looks at home in the fall garden of Helen du Toit. Owned by Fred R. Alleman and Winnie Friese.

PLATE 112 (Left). Detail of SUMMER GARDEN, 1943 (Plate 42).

1925 to 1950

Circles & Rings, Flowers & Things

New Jersey quiltmakers participated in the national fads of the era, and also continued to make quilts in traditional geometric designs.

The quilts made between 1925 and 1950 were influenced by at least two co-existing popular styles – Colonial Revival and Art Deco. At the national level, the Colonial Revival movement provided historic restorations, including Colonial Williamsburg in Virginia, Sturbridge Village in Massachusetts, and several New Jersey preservations where George Washington slept, camped, was headquartered, or crossed the Delaware. In the same period, the Art Deco style was expressed in Manhattan skyscrapers, including the Chrysler Building, the Empire State Building, and Rockefeller Center. On a more local scale, the Colonial Revival style lined suburban New Jersey streets with "Dutch Colonial" houses, and the Art Deco style brought "streamlined" stainless steel diners to every rural New Jersey traffic circle. At home, householders could declare their allegiance to one style or the other depending on whether they placed nostalgic wagon wheels or then fashionable flamingos on their front lawns.

At the popular level, the Colonial Revival style did not seem to require strict authenticity, sometimes combining English-style leaded glass windows, American Federal ceiling moldings, and a divided Dutch-style front door with an Art Deco-inspired stainless steel kitchen decorated with "Pennsylvania Dutch" tea towels. So, it is not surprising that many 1930's quiltmakers, who may or may not have thought of themselves as participating in a colonial craft, did not often seek to make literal copies of 100-year-old quilts. They were free to incorporate other popular design elements into their quilts, and these often came from the Art Deco style.

The term Art Deco is derived from a 1925 exhibition of European "modern" decorative and industrial art held in Paris.[1] The style uses both geometric motifs, such as circles and parts of circles, as well as some natural objects, often stylized and sometimes repeated.[2] Quiltmakers of the 1925 to 1950 period could theoretically have chosen from thousands of patterns. Yet several of the most popular quilt designs of the period – Dresden Plate,

Double Wedding Ring, and Fans – are all based on circles, suggesting a public taste attuned to the circular motifs of Art Deco. Even Grandmother's Flower Garden, a genuine 1830's design that 1930's quilters revived, approximated circles by arranging hexagons to form rings of colors. And, having turned hexagons into rings, the quiltmakers of the period extended the same principle to that least circular of geometric shapes, the square, reviving Trip Around the World and Philadelphia Pavements designs of the last half of the 1800's to use squares in rings of colors. In one additional twist to the 1930's taste for circles, quiltmakers turned small pieces of fabric into yo-yos, bottle-cap-size finished circles, which they then arranged into unbacked assemblages of rings, random patterns, or even squares.

While Art Deco clearly influenced quiltmakers' preferences for circular motifs from 1925 to 1950, the connection between the Art Deco style and the quiltmakers' renewed interest in appliqué floral designs is less clear. Much of the credit for the revival of floral quilts goes to Marie Webster, whose original appliqué designs began appearing in *The Ladies' Home Journal* in 1911. Both her designs themselves and the idea of producing patterns for mass marketing were widely copied by other quilt designers in the 1920's and 1930's. By 1929 the Nancy Page quilt pattern series was appearing regularly in the Newark paper, *The Sunday Call*, and the estates of New Jersey quiltmakers show that the newspaper patterns were often saved by quiltmakers and occasionally turned into completed quilts.

The idea of making quilts using repeated stylized images of everyday objects is at least as old as the pieced basket quilts of the 1850's. In the 1880's and 1890's, stylized trees pieced of triangles provided another variation of the theme. In the 1920's and 1930's, pattern designers offered teacups, airplanes, umbrellas, and Oriental lanterns, among other common objects, as designs for quilts. In some cases, the cleverness of the design lay in the fact that the object was to be constructed in piecing, rather than in appliqué. How-

ever, pieced versions of everyday objects either did not reach or did not have much appeal for New Jersey quiltmakers. For example, the pieced airplane quilts that commemorated Lindbergh's 1927 trans-Atlantic solo flight were not seen by the New Jersey Project, although a fabric commemorating this event was printed in great quantity by the Passaic Print Works in Passaic, New Jersey. When New Jersey quiltmakers set about to make fanciful quilts, they were much more likely to choose an appliqué design, such as a juvenile scene or, especially, a Sunbonnet Sue pattern.

The fabrics New Jerseyans used sometimes were printed with whimsical motifs, including balloons, safety pins, lambs, and a miniature Sunbonnet Sue as a pioneer woman tending a campfire near a covered wagon (Plate 126). However, New Jersey quiltmakers of this era had a particular opportunity and inclination to use scraps and other remnants from local factories that made pajamas, aprons, and lingerie. They also made quilts of samples of baseball uniform fabric, drapery fab-

ric from the local "dime store," and so forth. And despite New Jersey's urban image, a quiltmaker from Hoboken used chicken feed sacks from her grandparents' chicken business in her quilts (Plate 147).

Although New Jersey quiltmakers participated in the national fads of the 1925 to 1950 era and made their share of Dresden Plates, Grandmother's Flower Gardens, and Sunbonnet Sues, they also continued to produce pieced quilts in traditional geometric designs, including two-color Ohio Stars, scrap Carpenter's Wheels, and Lone Stars from mail-order kits. And whether they made pieced quilts, appliquéd quilts, or both, they used many sources of designs including newspaper patterns, kits that they ordered by mail, kits from local department stores, and patterns they copied for themselves from older quilts. ∎

PLATE 113. CROSSED PEONY, c.1942, appliqué, 75" x 95½". Made by Elizabeth Allen (1888-1973), New-port, Cumberland County, New Jersey. This cheerful quilt was made as a wedding present for Albert and Anna Gates. The use of solid color fabrics throughout the quilt is somewhat unusual for this time period when print fabric dominated most quilts. Owned by Charlotte Mackie, niece of the maker.

PLATE 114. DRUNKARD'S PATH, c.1920, 70½" x 80". Made by Sarah Ann Leake Barber (1863-1945), Burlington County, New Jersey. The Drunkard's Path pattern gives motion to an interesting assortment of fabric, probably scraps from dresses made for Sarah Ann Barber's granddaughters. Sarah came from Shropshire, England, at the age of 12. A formidable seamstress who could make clothing without patterns, she sewed not only for her own six daughters, but also for wealthy families in the area, including the family of the manager of a mining company. Owned by Kay Haulenbeek, granddaughter of the maker.

FIG. 29. Sarah Ann Leake Barber

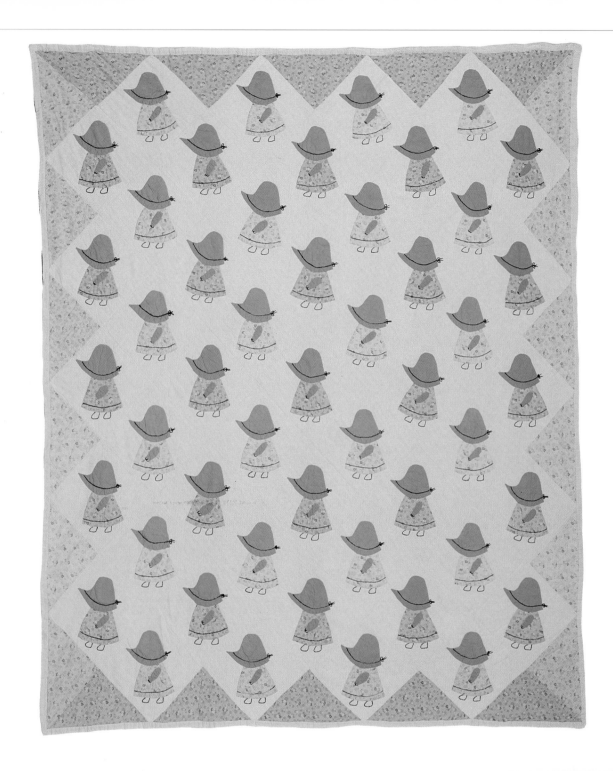

PLATE 115. SUNBONNET SUE, c.1930, appliqué, 73" x 86". Made by Amelia Frantz Sheenan (1900-1960), Paterson, Passaic County, New Jersey. A fresh example of a familiar design, this quilt features black chain stitch embroidery details. The pink and lavender fabrics are two different color combinations of the same material. Matching border triangles surround the figures. Owned by Margaret Zester, whose husband, William, is the nephew of the maker.

FIG. 30. Amelia Frantz Sheenan

PLATE 116. DRESDEN PLATE, c.1940, appliqué, 76" x 95". Made by Mary Allerton, originally from Syracuse, New York. Although it is not known exactly where this quilt was made, it came down through the family of Dorothy Allerton Eden, a long-time resident of Montclair, Essex County, and a great-niece of the quiltmaker. It is an exceptionally well executed version of the Dresden Plate, a popular design of the Depression era. An original touch on this quilt is the addition of the ivy leaves connected with embroidered stems that decorate the corners of the blocks. The border is done in the ice cream cone style with a scalloped edge. Owned by Robert Reynolds, a friend of the Eden family.

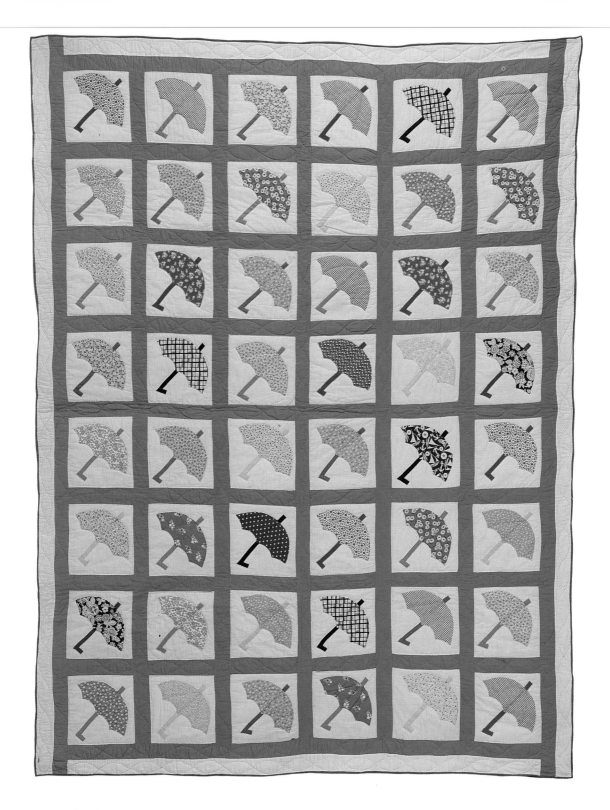

PLATE 117. UMBRELLA QUILT, c.1940, appliqué, 65½" x 84½". Made by Alma Melroy (1918-), Port Colden, Warren County, New Jersey. A popular design of the times, this quilt is one of the few documented examples showing the repeated use of a familiar object. A colorful collection of umbrellas, this quilt was made for the quiltmaker's daughter and present owner, Irene Howell.

PLATE 118. LEADING LADIES QUILT, c.1940, appliqué, 63" x 63". Probably made by Callie Jeffress Fanning Smith, Sulfur Springs, Texas. The blocks of this quilt depict nine movie stars in various roles and settings. The fabrics include silk, rayon, and lace. The figures have hand-painted faces, hair, and hats, with appliquéd clothing and details. Hand-painted nose-gays of roses, violets, green dots, and lace intersect the blocks. Another quilt made in the same style with identical nose-gays is the Eleanor Roosevelt Album Quilt (Twentieth Century Quilts 1900-1950 by Woodard and Greenstein) which is attributed to Callie Jeffress Fanning Smith, Sulfur Springs, Texas. The initials "C.F.S." on the Leading Ladies quilt would suggest the same maker for both quilts. Owned by The Morris Museum, Morris County.

PLATE 119. EVENING STAR, c.1935, 79" x 92". Made by Annie Everingham Kise (1861-1951), Hopewell, Mercer County, New Jersey. The evening stars seem to twinkle across the face of this quilt. The maker's use of the rose fabric lends a sparkle to this quilt she made for her daughter's wedding. All the fabric is Ely & Walker, a brand popular with quilters for over one hundred years, from 1878 to the early 1980's. The owner, Roxanne K. Carkhuff, still has the quilting frame her great-grandmother used.

PLATE 120. LOG CABIN, Straight Furrow Variation, c.1930, 79½" x 82." Made by Frederica
Mueller Vorrath (1871-1939), Richfield (Clifton), Passaic County, New Jersey. The gold center square
of each Log Cabin block gives this quilt its warm glow. Although a variety of prints was used, balance
was achieved by using only two prints in each block. The back of the quilt is a gold and white check
brought to the front as binding. The quilt was made for family use by Frederica, who lived on a farm and
probably participated in a German Lutheran quilting bee. Owned by Fred and Eleanor Meyer. Fred is
the maker's grandson.

FIG. 31 (Left). Frederica Mueller
Vorrath

FIG. 32 (Right). The Vorrath Farm

PLATE 121. YO-YO, 1937, 76" x 78". Made by Etta Bower Davis (1910-1964), Leonia, Bergen County, New Jersey. This is a subtle rendition of pastel and muslin yo-yos that have been organized in a Sixteen Patch arrangement with sashing. Etta made this quilt when she was expecting her first child and it wasn't until 1950 that she returned to quiltmaking. Most of her quilts were made from Mountain Mist patterns and Paragon kits. She later designed detailed appliqué pictures embellished with lace, trims, and embroidery that featured family members. All of her work has been passed down to her family. Owned by Barbara Schaffer, daughter of the maker.

FIG. 33. Etta Bower Davis

PLATE 122. CARPENTER'S WHEEL, c.1940, 71" x 81". Classic 1940's fabrics are used in a design that is more frequently seen in earlier quilts. Some of the scraps feature a print that names the day of the week and shows a woman's domestic activities. For example, Monday is illustrated by a woman hanging wash on a line, while Tuesday shows her ironing. This was made as a utility quilt. Owned by Elizabeth Zak.

PLATE 123. MILL WHEEL, c.1945, 66" x 73". Made by Mary Bell Bunting Callaway (b.1901), Cape May Court House, Cape May County, New Jersey. The colors are still bright in this scrap quilt, even though the quilt is worn from years of use. It is quilted in straight lines and curves. This utility quilt and many others were made by Mary for family use. Mary, an African-American, came to New Jersey from Florida in her youth. She was married to Rufus Callaway, Sr. Owned by Janette Callaway, daughter of the maker.

PLATE 124. EMBROIDERED HISTORY QUILT, 1949, 81"x 92½". Made by Katherine M. Schneider Kolm (1877-1959), Vineland, Cumberland County, New Jersey. An encyclopedia of history and trivia, this quilt is embroidered with the names of hundreds of people, places, and events. Lists of personal friends and local events are documented as well as prominent U.S. and foreign personalities. The categories include movie stars, sports figures, colleges, holy days, U. S. generals, bridges, songs, historical events, states, and politicians. Many headlines from newspapers are noted. Two of the more amusing headlines are: "Mother of Cigar Smoking Baby Deplores Habit" and "Martin L. Smith 89 years old an Expert Knitter." The latest event recorded is the inauguration of Harry Truman, Jan. 20, 1949. All names, including that of the maker, are embroidered in feather stitching. Katherine made this exciting work when she was in her seventies. The owner has an old ledger in which the maker recorded everything that appears on the quilt. Owned by Florence Bacon, a family friend.

FIG. 34. Katherine Kolm (Left) & her daughter Alice (Right)

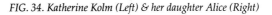

PLATE 125. TRIP AROUND THE WORLD, c.1940, 72" x 75". Made by Charolette La Roe (1864-1967), West Milford, Passaic County, New Jersey. This is yet another example of the soft and comforting look of Depression era quilts. Use of the same print in several different colors, particularly in the center of the quilt, gives a blended look to the whole. The gold and yellow rows add a touch of sunshine. Each square has been carefully cut to show a selected view of the individual print. One unusual print shows safety pins. The binding is applied with a lavender herringbone embroidery stitch. Owned by Bonnie Earl, great-great niece of the maker.

PLATE 126. BLOCK TRIP AROUND THE WORLD. c.1930, 71½" x 91". Made by Mary
DeKryger (1890-1978), Paterson, Passaic County, New Jersey. This somewhat unusual design
takes advantage of the many small pastel prints that were available in the 1930's, as well as the
popular aqua color. The prints were carefully selected to coordinate in each block. A close look at the
fabric reveals a delightful print depicting Sunbonnet Sue as a pioneer woman tending a campfire
near a covered wagon. The overall effect of the quilt is one of soft beauty. Owned by Theresa Wick-
ham, niece of the maker.

Blue & Yellow: New Trends in Color

During the 1940's quiltmakers began to move from the pastels of the 1930's, and incorporated stronger colors in their work.

Even non-quilters can readily identify classic 1930's quilts by their familiar "sherbet" colors, including tangerine, mint green, lavender, and lemon yellow. Popular as these colors were in their own right, they also provided a transition from the colorless grays and milky blues of the first quarter of the twentieth century to the intense and often primary color schemes to be seen from about 1950 to 1980.

The New Jersey Project chose the middle of the twentieth century as its cut-off date partially because this point seemed to coincide with a fairly clear stylistic break between the pastel colors of the second quarter of the twentieth century and the primary colors of the third quarter. Yet changes in quilt fashions often take place over a period of several years, with quilts being made in both the older and newer styles for a certain period of time. The inclusion of the 1940's in the period documented allowed the Project to record the beginnings of the primary colors of the 1950's.

Some nice examples of a quiltmaker working in both the older and newer color ranges can be seen in the works of Amelia (Millie) Clegg, who made eight quilts and tops between 1942 and 1951, most signed and dated so that the sequence in which she made the quilts is known. From these

dates, it is apparent that she worked in both color ranges almost simultaneously. Her medallion quilt appears in Plate 13 and four of her other quilts are shown as a group in Plate 127. Of the quilts as a group, two are dominated by 1930's pastels of peach and mint green while the two others include primary red strawberries and a green that is closer to kelly than to mint. Other quilts that she made in the period are a Rose of Sharon using a charming primary blue check and two sunny yellow Dresden Plates. The collection of her works illustrates a skillful handling of the color schemes of both time periods, and provides an interesting glimpse of the quilts that were to be popular over the next 25 years.

Although Millie Clegg used bright blue and yellow in separate quilts, other quiltmakers of the period sometimes combined these two colors with almost overwhelming effect. The use of blue and yellow together had attained a certain popularity as a decorating color scheme in the 1940's, and the striking blue and yellow quilts of the period are apparently an outgrowth of this decorating trend. For example, in May 1942, *The American Home* magazine featured the bedroom of movie actress Paulette Goddard showing a somewhat grayed blue accented with a quite bright yellow[3]. Similarly, *The Guinness Guide to 20th Century Homes*

illustrates a breakfast nook, a kitchen feature newly popular in the years after World War II, decorated with blue tile, blue wallpaper, and bright yellow curtains.[4]

When New Jersey quiltmakers chose to work in blue and yellow, they sometimes used the bright blue as the background fabric, overshadowing the printed fabrics of the period and occasionally almost overwhelming the pieced design itself. Northern New Jerseyans, in particular, seemed inclined to move away from the white background used in the quilts of the 1930's, shifting to bright solid backgrounds of not only primary blue, but also the bubblegum pink seen in Plate 130. ■

PLATE 127 (Top, Folded). MARTHA WASHINGTON, 1942, appliqué, 68" x 93". Made by Amelia Estelle Clegg (1890-1965), Montclair, Essex County, New Jersey. A beautiful example of appliqué in a design not often seen, this quilt also features an appliquéd vine and floral border. Like other quilts by this maker, it is embroidered with the quilt name, maker's name, place, and date. Owned by Gladys Clegg, sister of the maker.

(Bottom, Left, Folded). STRAWBERRY AND CLOVER, 1947, appliqué, 64" x 69". Made by Amelia Estelle Clegg (1890-1965), Montclair, Essex County, New Jersey. This fresh looking quilt alternates strawberries enclosed in a circle with clover leaves. Characteristic of the style of this maker are the swag and heart border, heavy quilting, and embroidered inscription. Owned by Gladys Clegg, sister of the maker.

(Bottom, Center, Folded). PEONY, 1940-1950, 78" x 97". Made by Amelia Estelle Clegg (1890-1965), Montclair, Essex County, New Jersey. A lovely example of the period, this simple peony design is enhanced by the swag and peony border. The quilting was finished by the owner, Doris Larsen, niece of the maker.

(Bottom, Right, Folded). ROSE OF SHARON, 1949, appliqué, 69" x 90". Made by Amelia Estelle Clegg (1890-1965), Montclair, Essex County, New Jersey. A classic appliqué pattern complemented by a swag and rosebud border, this quilt has the added distinction of heavy quilting. It has the following embroidered inscription: "Amelia Estelle Clegg. Montclair, New Jersey, 1949." Owned by Gladys Clegg, sister of the maker.

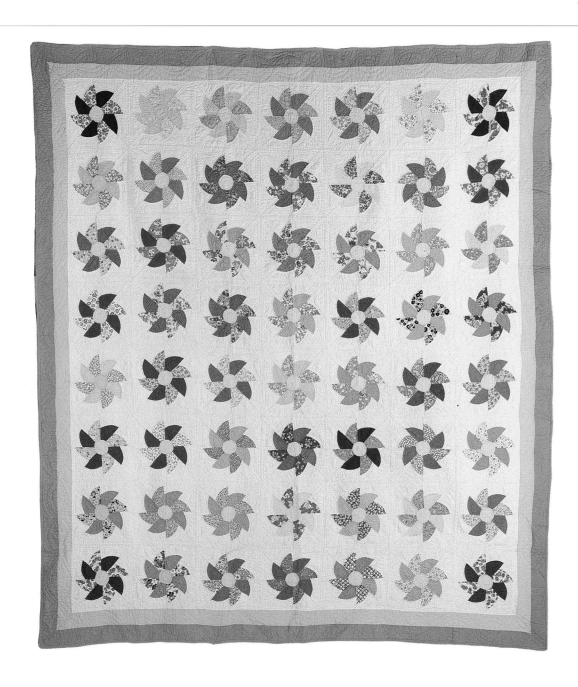

PLATE 128. PINWHEEL, c.1950, 78½″ x 88¼″. *These colorful pinwheels are kept in place by the two border strips. A dynamic motion is at play here with the clever use of prints and solid fabrics. The quilt is one of a matched pair. Unfortunately, the maker is unknown, although she was a friend of a Mr. Washley, for whom they were made. Owned by Minabess Randolph.*

PLATE 129. JEWEL BOX, c.1950, 66½" x 81½". Made by Helen C. Frissell (1893-1984), Dudley, Massachusetts. This is a happy collection of fabrics, representing the end of the time period covered by the Project. The play of yellow against blue makes this simple design sparkle. Owned by Catherine H. Woolley, daughter of the maker.

PLATE 130. JAPANESE LANTERNS, 1930, 59½" x 83½". Made by Virginia Hagerthy (e.d.1960), Woodbury, Gloucester County, New Jersey. This quilt shows the continuing influence of Oriental design on American quiltmakers. It is a colorful array of lanterns on a variety of backgrounds, quilted by the owner in 1982. Owned by Doris L. Reeves.

FIG. 35 (Left). Edith Alvater Bird

PLATE 131 (Top). ALTERNATE SQUARES AND CIRCLES, c.1940, 67" x 76½". *Made by Edith Alvater Bird (1891-1979), Hunterdon County, New Jersey. The pleasing repetitive nature of this design results from a simple Robbing Peter to Pay Paul design. One blue print and one yellow print are the only fabrics used. The quilt top, originally made by the owner's mother, was backed and quilted by Mrs. Avis Pyatt Darago of White House Station, New Jersey. Avis presented it to Grace on her 70th birthday, November 1, 1987. Owned by Grace E. Petersen, daughter of the maker.*

(Bottom). DOUBLE WEDDING RING, 1934, 69" x 83½". *Made by Mrs. Robert Conover, Manasquan, Monmouth County, New Jersey. This quilt is representative of the many quilts of this design documented in New Jersey. This particular quilt was the result of a mother commissioning her neighbor to make a quilt for her daughter's hope chest. Its blue and yellow color scheme follows a decorating trend of the times. Owned by Florence H. Thompson, neighbor of the maker.*

The Quilts of Elizabeth Stanaback Hallas

Elizabeth Stanaback Hallas was born in Sparta, Sussex County, New Jersey, on May 17, 1871. She was the third child and only daughter of Ezekiel Stanaback (1843-1908), principal and school teacher of a one-room schoolhouse in Lafayette, Sussex County, New Jersey, and Sarah Carrie Bird (1843-1914). During her early school years, Elizabeth lived in Lafayette, but when she was about 15 years old, her family moved to Newark, Essex County, New Jersey, where her father continued his teaching career. On November 1, 1893, she married John W. Hallas, a self-employed interior decorator, in Newark. They had four children: Mabel Hallas Soden (1895-1990), Carrie Bird Hallas Cutler (1897-1988), Leonora Hallas (1899-1984), and Fred Hallas (1902-).

Every Saturday the family went by horse and carriage to the farmers' market in Newark located on Raymond Boulevard running from Broad Street to Mulberry Street. There, Elizabeth would buy food and then shop for sewing materials and fabrics in the local shops on Broad Street. Sometimes, though, she would go into New York City to buy fabrics at Wanamaker's. She would buy fabric by the bolt as she made all the clothes for her four children. She preferred Coats and Clark thread for her sewing because the thread was manufactured in Newark and Kearny, Essex County, New Jersey, and the quality was good.

Family history doesn't record how Elizabeth learned her sewing skills. But in addition to sewing clothing for her children and making quilts, she made crocheted tablecloths, needlepoint chair covers, cross-stitch tablecloths, fancy aprons, and embroidered linens. She also caned and made rush seats for chairs. Sometimes her husband, John,

would help her design the quilting pattern after a quilt top was finished. But their big project together was the planting of 1,500 tulip and daffodil bulbs each season and then removing and drying them at the end of the season. Elizabeth has recreated the glory of that garden in her quilts. While she

pieced a few traditional block quilts, she preferred the floral quilts so popular in the 1930's. Although family history doesn't give the source of Elizabeth's patterns, her floral quilts could have come from patterns published in the newspapers of the time and from catalogs published by such

PLATE 132. IRIS, c.1935, appliqué, 72" x 73½". Made by Elizabeth Stanaback Hallas (1871-1966), Newark, Essex County, New Jersey. Similar to patterns from Mountain Mist and the Ladies Art Company, the irises are set in four groups of five and have been meticulously appliquéd. The green in this purple/green color scheme was extremely popular in the 1930's. The plain blocks are quilted in an intricate cable pattern, perhaps designed by the maker's husband. The pieced blocks in each corner add interest to the border. Owned by L. Gordon Soden, grandson of the maker.

companies as Stearns & Foster.

In 1948, Elizabeth and John moved to Bloomfield, Essex County, New Jersey. After her husband died in 1949, she continued to sew but did not quilt anymore. Elizabeth Hallas was actively sewing and cooking until May 1966 when, at the age of 95, she died.

During her lifetime, Elizabeth probably made about 20 quilts for her children, her grandchildren, her friends, and herself. During the 1930's and 1940's, many of her quilts were entered in the New Jersey State Fair in Trenton (Mercer County), the Morris County Fair in Troy Hills (Morris County), and the Rockland County Fair in New York State. Except for one quilt, they all received either a first or second place award. Eleven of these have survived. ■

From information provided by L. Gordon Soden, grandson of Elizabeth S. Hallas.

FIG. 36. Elizabeth Stanaback Hallas

PLATE 133 (Top, Folded). FLORAL SAMPLER, c.1935, appliqué, 73" x 73". Made by Elizabeth Stanaback Hallas (1871-1966), Newark, Essex County, New Jersey. This quilt is a beautifully executed version of a newspaper pattern. The many pastels – particularly the grayed pastel green – are typical of the 1930's. The maker has added embroidery to detail the flowers and used inverted tulips to add interest to the border. The quilting is half-inch crosshatch with cables in the sashing. The edges are scalloped, and great care has been taken to turn them in and then appliqué the thin green binding to the front only, making it look as if the edge were bound in green. Owned by L. Gordon Soden, grandson of the maker.

(Bottom, Folded). TULIP WREATH, c.1935, appliqué, 76" x 83". Made by Elizabeth Stanaback Hallas (1871-1966), Newark, Essex County, New Jersey. Many of Elizabeth's quilts had floral themes, which were very much in keeping with the popular style of the time, but which also spoke of her love of flowers. Elizabeth may have chosen this pattern because it reminded her of the abundant tulips and daffodils in the garden which she and her husband planted and tended every year. The design is very similar to one of the patterns in Nancy Page's Wreath quilt. The quilting is basic crosshatch with ovals and circles in the sashing. Three of the edges are scalloped while the fourth is straight, probably for the head of the bed. Owned by L. Gordon Soden, grandson of the maker.

The Quilts of
Elizabeth Galbavy Moravek

Elizabeth Galbavy Moravek was born in Czechoslovakia on April 16, 1898. When she was six years old, her father – a coal miner in Ohio – had saved enough money to bring the rest of the family to America. In 1916 she married John Moravek, a grocer, and had three children, Elsie and twins John and Milka. A fourth child, Paul, died when he was only 20 months old.

As Elizabeth grew up, she was fascinated by all types of needlework and wanted to know how to do them. As her mother – a midwife – was not knowledgeable in this area, she and her sister, Mary, learned sewing skills from friends and neighbors. She tried all kinds of needlework – knitting, crocheting, embroidery – in addition to quilting, and could make all her clothes, practically without a pattern. After her marriage, Elizabeth's husband made a quilting frame for her and when a quilt top was ready, friends and neighbors would be invited to a quilting bee to finish it. Four to six of Elizabeth's friends would be sitting around the frame, and her daughter, Milka (known as Millie) would be asked to thread the needles because, she explains, "the needles they used were very fine and they said my eyes were so keen."

When the family moved to Manville, Somerset County, New Jersey, in 1927, Elizabeth continued to make quilts, but finished them on her own. She and her husband owned and ran the White Front Market and a gas station in Manville, yet she still found time to make quilts and sew clothes for the family. There were always quilts in use. Millie remembers thinking that homemade clothing and quilts weren't as appealing as those in the stores. So Elizabeth would "trim up" the dresses to look more "store bought." Scraps from clothing found their way into Elizabeth's quilts, but she also liked to shop at W. T. Grant and mail order from the Sears, Roebuck and Company catalog for fabric. In the summer, her sister, Mary, would come to visit from Ohio and they would spend hours discussing and planning new quilts based on patterns which they may have found in books or catalogs. During the

PLATE 134. MEXICAN FEATHER, c.1935, appliqué, 79¾" x 80¾". Made by Elizabeth Galbavy Moravek (1898-1974), Manville, Somerset County, New Jersey. The bold red, green, and gold of this quilt are a far cry from typical 1930's colors. The choice of color may reflect the Czechoslovakian heritage of the quilt-maker. The pattern itself harks back to the previous century, however, it is probably from a Mountain Mist catalog. Small hearts have been appliquéd on the tip of each feather and the quilting is a closely spaced crosshatch. The scalloped edge with applied binding is typical of the period. After this quilt was made, the maker's daughter chose it as a wedding present. Owned by Millie Matyola, daughter of the maker.

winter, they exchanged frequent letters about quilts in progress and plans for others. Apparently they traded quilt patterns and templates, too, which may partially explain why Elizabeth's quilts are not typical of New Jersey ones of the time.

Elizabeth continued quilting into the 1950's. After that, she mostly knitted and crocheted. Her hands were never quiet. She would put the coffee on, and keep knitting until it was brewed. She loved flowers and always grew many different kinds of vegetables which were "put up," so Millie remembers eating "lots of vegetables all year 'round." As Elizabeth got older and continued to rise very early in the morning to tend her garden, her children urged her to stop her "hard work" and rest. But she replied that she would continue because it was "her pleasure."

Elizabeth Moravek died in 1974 at the age of 76. She was a vigorous woman who was proud of her work. It shows in her quilts. ∎

From information provided by Millie Matyola, daughter of Elizabeth Galbavy Moravek.

FIG. 36A. John and Elizabeth Moravek

PLATE 135 (Top). BASKETS WITH FLOWERS, c.1935, 74½" x 75". Made by Elizabeth Galbavy Moravek (1898-1974), Manville, Somerset County, New Jersey. While the colors and stylistic flowers of this quilt are typical of the period, the pattern is a classic. The setting of the basket blocks alternating with plain blocks and the stencil-style quilting are not typical of New Jersey quilts and might result from the quiltmaker's exchange of patterns with her sister in Ohio. Owned by Millie Matyola, daughter of the maker.

(Bottom, Folded). TRIPLE IRISH CHAIN, c.1935, 83" x 83", made by Elizabeth Galbavy Moravek (1898-1974), Manville, Somerset County, New Jersey. This is a crisp example of a favorite pattern. The green is fresh and clean and the scalloped border softens the geometry of the pattern. The white areas have been heavily quilted in a stencil style. Owned by Millie Matyola, daughter of the maker.

A Newspaper Column for Quilters

"Overheard at our Needlework Meetings" and its central character, Nancy Page, provided quilters with patterns and a sense of belonging to a group.

From 1925 to 1940 newspapers across the country published a weekly column written by Florence LaGanke Harris that reported the minutes of the fictional quilt meetings of Nancy Page and the members of the Nancy Page Club. The column appeared under various headings such as "Nancy Page Talks to Women" and "Novel Ideas for Homes" in the *Oregonian*,[5] the "Nancy Page Quilt Club" in the *Philadelphia Record*,[6] and "Overheard At Our Needlework Meetings" in the Newark, New Jersey, paper, *The Sunday Call*, in 1929. LaGanke's column gave a conversational account of these make-believe quilt meetings. During the members' discussions of quiltmaking, Nancy Page, the Club's leader, gave them advice and provided them with ideas, techniques, and the patterns for her original quilt designs. In the summer, the column featured patterns for such novelty items as aprons, porch pillows, towels, and summer table covers because they were more popular for summer work. But in the colder months, patterns were provided for what are now regarded as classic 1930's quilts.

New Jersey readers could send to Nancy Page in care of *The Sunday Call* for any pattern's "direction leaflet," which was free with a self-addressed, stamped envelope. (However, there was a ten-cent charge for ordering missed blocks.) The direction sheet for quilts gave all the dimensions and directions for making a particular quilt along with a diagram showing the design layout. It included general instructions for appliqué and piecing in addition to suggesting color schemes and recommending what materials to use and the amounts needed. For a 90" x 108" quilt, ten to twelve yards of basic white 36" wide fabric were needed for the top and back. Fabrics such as Nainsook – a light weight, soft fabric, slightly heavier than batiste; white gingham – a light to medium weight, closely woven fabric made in solid colors as well as in stripes, checks and plaids; and chambray – a smooth, closely woven fabric with a soft luster, were all suitable.[7] Old fashioned calicoes, referred to as English prints, were preferred for appliqué flowers. "Fast color" bias tape was recommended for the binding.

In one column's chatty account, reference was made to a young observer by the name of Joan, who had been watching "Aunty Nancy" make a beautiful Grandmother's Flower Garden quilt, and wanted to know when she could have a quilt all her own. Nancy responded, "as soon as you know your alphabet child, I will make a quilt especially for you." This was Nancy's introduction to the Alphabet quilt series that ran from October 6, 1929 through March 23, 1930 in *The Sunday Call*.

As LaGanke said in her column, "Nancy Page had done many clever things in her life, but one outstanding achievement was the planning of beautiful quilts."[8] Surely, this was a self-congratulatory compliment, as LaGanke herself, not the fictional Nancy Page, was the designer. When a member of the Club suggested using the idea of Jack's beanstalk for a quilt, Nancy Page designed the Magic Vine quilt.

Starting on September 28, 1930, *The Sunday Call* ran LaGanke's Magic Vine quilt series for 25 consecutive Sundays, ending on March 15, 1931. Nancy Page explained the name "Magic Vine" by telling the Club members about a "vine that never could have grown, for on it there are flowers of spring, summer and late fall. It is a vine that grows in never, neverland where orchids and dandelions are as friendly as the lion and the lamb. It is in truth, a magic vine."[9] Judging from the interest women were showing in her new quilt, Nancy knew "that before long these vines would flourish in many a bedroom from Maine to California."[10]

As reported in the newspaper column, members of the Club got together weekly to sew on their Magic Vine quilts and LaGanke continued to report "overhearing" Club members. Subsequent columns presented the various reasons quilts were being made. One member had been asked to make one for a sorority house at the nearby university to "add the finishing touch to the guest room."[11] Another said the Ladies Aid at her church was going to make one for the next bazaar. As the members progressed in their quiltmaking, Nancy would remind them of the types of fabric that should be used, recommending Peter Pan™ gingham, colorfast calico, and scraps from summer dresses. She even suggested colors for each flower. At one point, there was much discussion as to whether the flowers in the first and third vines should be the same but worked in different colors. Half of the members disagreed, arguing that "in the quilts which our grandmothers made much of the beauty lay in the repetition. If we make the flowers different colors in all four vines, aren't we going to lose some of the beauty and simplicity which would come from repetition?"[12] The group finally agreed to let each person work out her own ideas. But in all cases the patterns for the flowers on the first and third lengthwise vine were identical. The second and fourth vines grew identical flowers which were different from those on the first and third vines. When the time came to begin work on

Block 14, the Poppy, Nancy explained a new technique: "For here we are doing something we have not done before – turning the material over for a part of a petal so that we get both wrong and right side showing in the same flower."[13] When the blocks were completed, Nancy explained her method for assembling and finishing. LaGanke reported that some members were sure that they wanted a straight edge because the scallops seemed to be too much work. But Nancy told them that "with a quilt as beautiful as the

---

PLATE 136. MAGIC VINE, c.1930, appliqué, 84" x 102". Made by Mildred Hornby Moryl (1899-1980), Culver City, California. This charming quilt was made from a Nancy Page pattern, which also suggested the vine border and the scalloped edge. The flowers in the first and third vines are the same and include evening primrose, arrowhead, phlox, and blue eyed grass, among others. The second and fourth vines display different flowers, several of which are shooting star, poppy, and tulip. Mildred, who was born in New Jersey, made this quilt as a wedding gift for her sister, Evelyn Hornby Looker, and sent it to her in New Jersey in 1932. Owned by Gail Looker McKenna, niece of the maker.

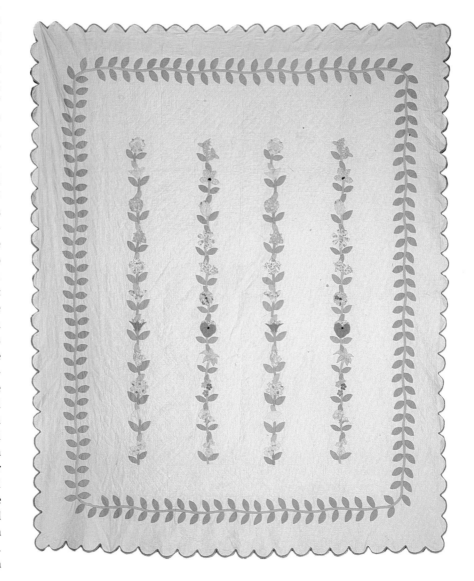

Magic Vine, it was best to put the last bit of work in as good form as the appliquéing."[14]

Following the Magic Vine series, *The Sunday Call* immediately published the pattern for Nancy's Leaf quilt. The series ran from March 22, 1931, through April 12, 1931, and featured four leaf blocks: Oak, Maple, Thorn, and Sumach. Because the members felt the need for some kind of book or file to store the many quilt patterns they had accumulated, Nancy gave instructions for the Nancy Page Scrap Book on April 19 and 26, 1931.

Later quilt patterns which ran in LaGanke's column were for the Western Star (May 5, 1931), Double Trouble and Others (May 10, 1931), Double Nine Patch (May 17, 1931), and the Wreath (May 24, 1931). After a summer of smaller needlework projects, the Garden Bouquet quilt series began on October 4, 1931.

While it is sometimes difficult to identify with certainty quilts that were made from newspaper patterns, the Project documented Nancy Page's Garden Bouquet, also known as the Bird and Urn,[15] and two Wreath quilts, in addition to the Magic Vine quilt shown in Plate 136. While the Magic Vine and Garden Bouquet quilts were made outside of New Jersey, both variations of the Wreath quilts were made in Essex County. The Wreath quilt in Plate 137 was made from the actual patterns that appeared in *The Sunday Call* from May 24, 1931 through June 14, 1931, which featured four different floral wreaths: Crocus, Yellow Rose, Lily, and Tulip. Another quilt featuring a similar Tulip Wreath can be seen in Plate 133.

During its publication, LaGanke's Nancy Page and Nancy Page Club provided many new ideas and presented a host of original designs to quiltmakers all across the country. It helped develop a national style which can now be recognized, and provided both the lone quiltmaker and the quilt group with a feeling of belonging to a vital and modern organization. ∎

PLATE 137. WREATH QUILT, c.1940, appliqué, 70" x 87". Made by May Gerweck Prochaska (1888-1985), Irvington, Essex County, New Jersey. This Nancy Page design displays a variety of pastel flowers forming appliquéd wreaths. It was made as a gift for the maker's daughter. Outline quilting was done around the wreaths, and stencil quilting done in the alternate blocks. Owned by Norma L. Prochaska, daughter of the maker.

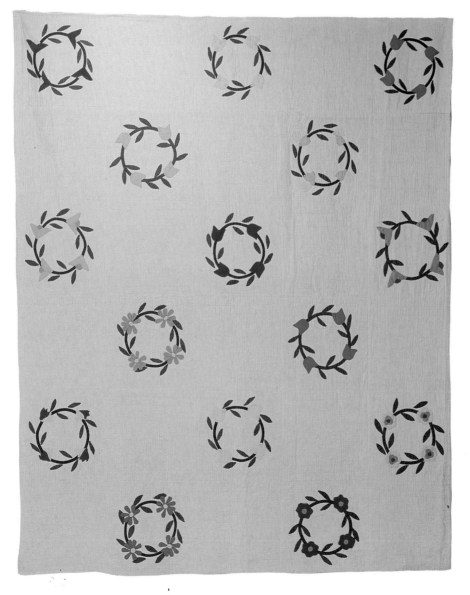

FIG. 36B. May Gerweck Prochaska

Quilt Patterns from Batting Manufacturers

The patterns printed on batting wrappers became an important source of designs for quilters.

To quilters, both past and present, perhaps one of the best known manufacturers of quilt batting and printed patterns has been The Stearns & Foster Company of Cincinnati, Ohio. The company became incorporated in 1882 and continues to this day to produce batting, stuffing, and wadding products in their mill in Lockland, Ohio. They became known for creating a new concept in marketing by giving their bales of batting trade names such as Boone, Homestead, Governor, Star, Cardinal, Crozier, and Miter, which were later printed on the products' wrappers.[16]

By the 1940's, the Lockport Cotton Batting Company in Lockport, New York, was producing three types of batting – Colonial Maid, Chinook, and Martha Washington.[17] At about the same time, the Taylor Bedding Mfg. Co. in Taylor, Texas, offered Hong Kong, Sanidown, White Chief, Blue Ribbon, Peerless, Leader, Ideal, Low Grade Cotton, and the still popular Morning Glory batts. Wool batts such as Purwool, Wooltan[18] and Wooltex were also available.

These batting companies also provided quilt patterns. Stearns & Foster began printing their patterns on the inside of the wrappers of Mountain Mist, a name they adopted in the early 1930's to identify their product. The wrappers have not changed much since then, featuring quilt designs in full color that, at one time, could be had for the regular price of 35¢, or 20¢ with a specially provided coupon on the inside.[19] The Lockport Batting Company advertised their patterns as "replicas of famous quilts and modern quilting designs" and at one time offered eleven for 25¢ but later sold them in groups of four at the same price. One side of their pattern sheet gave complete directions for making a quilt, including a fabric yardage chart, and the other listed a selection of grouped patterns that could be ordered. One particular sheet featured the appliqué pattern called Springtime on one side with the following pattern groups on the other: Group 1 – Wreath of Roses, Mrs. Cleveland's Choice, Springtime, and The Chief; Group 2 – Dutchman's Puzzle, Flower Garden,

Slumberland, and White Lily; Group 3 – Wild Rose, Pine Tree, Holland Tulip, and Star and Crescent.[20] During the 1930's and the 1940's different groups of patterns continued to be added to their collection of designs.

Later, Taylor-Made offered a catalog for 10¢ which advertised on its cover, "31 Quilt Designs with Complete Cutting Charts and Easy to Follow Directions for Making Luxurious, Long-wearing Quilts and Comforts." Inside, their patterns were categorized as "Quaint Colonial Patchwork Patterns," "Perennial Favorites," "Dainty Desirable Designs for Miss Teen-Age," "Picturesque Patterns for the Ranch Style Room," "Seven Modern Variations of Heirloom Designs," and "Four Outstanding Prize Winning Designs." In addition to providing printed patterns for making quilts featured in these categories, instructions were given for making tufted comforters.

Of the printed patterns available to New Jersey quiltmakers, those provided by batting companies seem to be the most popular. While some quilts were made following the original instructions, others were changed to meet the creativity of the individual maker. Quilt patterns such as Painted Poppies (Plate 140), Hollyhocks (Plate 138), Mexican Feather (Plate 134), and Pomegranate (Plate 139) can all be attributed to Stearns & Foster. A variation of the Lockport pattern known as White Lily can be seen in Plate 127 (bottom center) where it is called Peony, and another Lockport design, Star and Crescent, can be seen in the top quilt in Plate 146.

Because identical or similar designs appeared under various names in different batting company catalogs, it is sometimes difficult to define the origin of individual patterns. However, we do know that batting manufacturers played an important role in the development and distribution of patterns and various grades of batts to quiltmakers across the country. ∎

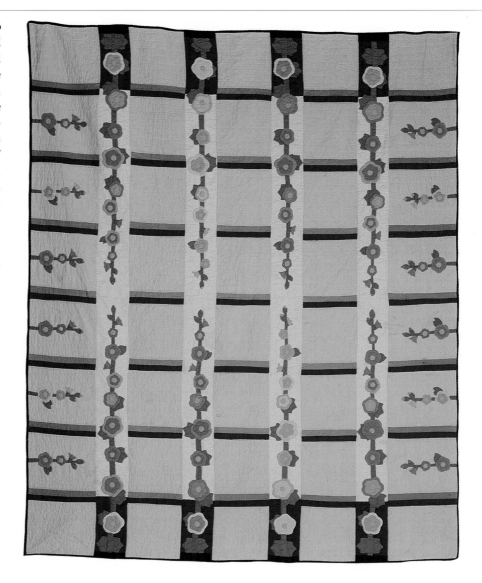

PLATE 138. HOLLYHOCKS, c.1935, appliqué, 71½" x 84". Made by Ann G. Bering (1914-), Somerset, Somerset County, New Jersey. This Mountain Mist pattern combines a bold and graphic background with quaint and colorful stalks of appliquéd hollyhocks that grow toward the center from opposite ends of the quilt. The pattern for this charming quilt is still available through Stearns & Foster. Another quilt by the same maker is Painted Poppies (Plate 140). Owned by the maker.

PLATE 139 (Detail). POMEGRANATE, c.1935, appliqué, unquilted, 76"x 79". Made by Jennie Smith Garretson (1879-1941), Middlebush, Somerset County, New Jersey. This striking quilt top was made from Mountain Mist pattern #31, although the maker added her own border. Its bright red, white, and green color scheme is typical of mid-nineteenth century quilts that found renewed popularity during the quilting revival in the 1930's. The quilt was made for the current owner, Ann G. Bering, daughter of the maker, who also made the same quilt at the same time.

PLATE 140 (Shown Sideways). PAINTED POPPIES, c.1935, appliqué, 72" x 84". Made by Ann G. Bering (1914-), Somerset, Somerset County, New Jersey. The graceful curved lines in this quilt are nicely complemented by the pleasing symmetrical arrangement of the bright yellow and orange poppies. Ann made this quilt during her first marriage when she was "setting up house." The Hollyhock quilt, shown in Plate 138, is another example of her fine work. Owned by the maker.

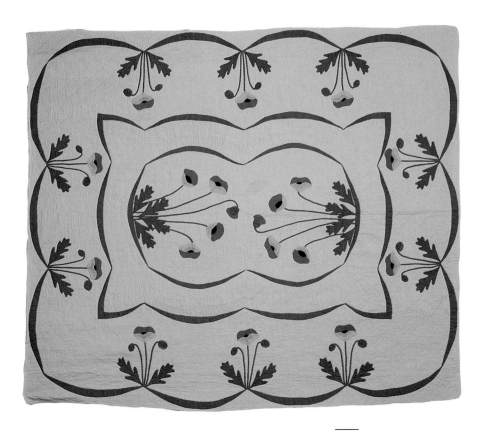

Mail-Order Quilts & Supplies

More and more patterns and kits for making quilts became available through newspapers and mail-order catalogs.

Aunt Martha, Alice Brooks, Grandma Dexter, and Hope Winslow were fictional names for some of the many women across the country whose quilt patterns appeared in newspapers or were sold through mail order catalogs. In 1933, *Hope Winslow's Quilt Book* was published by the Needleart Company of Chicago, which was known for its central medallion star quilts designed by the owner of the company, H. Ver Mehren.[21] Through this catalog, readers could purchase not only quilt patterns, but also ready-stamped appliqué patches and quilt tops, quilting designs, stamping supplies, ready-cut quilts, and bedroom sets which included embroidered pillowcases and dresser scarves.

The catalog also offered fabrics such as, "old-fashioned calico in plain colors and red, yellow, blue, or green backgrounds with gay prints." French sateen, Peter Pan™ gingham, and bleached sheeting were also available. All fabric was 25¢ per yard and came in a 25" width except for the sheeting which was 81" wide and 50¢ per yard. Stamping powder in yellow or blue was offered at 25¢ per package, as was stamping wax for use on perforated patterns.

Quilt patterns were offered at 10¢ each or 3 for 25¢. If readers were interested in reproducing a worn or tattered family heirloom, they could write to "Hope Winslow" directly, giving full particulars about the quilt and its history, to see if the pattern was in her library of designs. If it wasn't, she could advise as to the cost of making one.

The pattern for the Lone Star quilt was advertised in *Hope Winslow's Quilt*

PLATE 141. A variety of 1930's patterns, catalogs, needlecases, and stencils.

FIG. 37. Mary Plum Cornish Taylor

PLATE 142. LONE STAR, c.1930, 76½"x 82". Made by Mary Plum Cornish Taylor (b.1869), Newark, Essex County, New Jersey. This familiar star pattern is worked in four shades of sateen that range from yellow-gold to cream. The four borders were increased to seven at the upper and lower edges, giving added length. The quilt is aglow as it is enhanced by the density of quilting which includes straight line, outline, and stencil designs. The pattern is similar to one that was available through the mail order catalog, Hope Winslow's Quilt Book, which also offered pre-cut pieces for making quilts such as this. Owned by Phyllis R. Pearson, granddaughter of the maker.

Book as "an exact reproduction of one of the loveliest quilts I have ever seen." In addition, readers were told it "comes stamped ready to cut and match up lines. You will like this simple new way of making quilts."[22] The quilt could be worked up in four shades of pink, blue, orchid, or yellow and was available in three qualities of materials – sateen, fine gingham, and vat-dyed Cleona cloth. Everything needed for the top and border, ready-stamped on four shades of sateen, cost $5.95; on gingham, $4.50; and on Cleona cloth, $3.50.

While it is not certain that the Lone Star quilt in Plate 142 was made from the pattern in *Hope Winslow's Quilt Book*, it does provide a lovely example of a quilt made from a kit. The shaded sateen emphasizes the stencil-type quilting in the white space around the star as well as in the border's hanging diamond design. One other quilt, identical to this but made in shades of pink, was documented by the Project. ■

The Quilts of Clarence B. Lashley

Made from clothing and mill scraps, his spirited works have been treasured by five generations of his family.

Clarence B. Lashley, the tenth of Henry and Mary Jane Lashley's twelve children, was born in Scullville, Atlantic County, New Jersey, on May 18, 1884. Clarence's health was poor as a child, so while the other children helped on the farm, he was kept home. His mother, who dyed sugar and feed bags to make quilts, taught Clarence the art of needlework. He enjoyed all types – crocheting, embroidery, sewing – but his true love was quiltmaking. He had a keen eye for using colors and fabrics in striking combinations, which gave a one-of-a-kind quality to the wide variety of traditional patterns he used in his quilts. Clarence's quilts and love of quiltmaking have lived through five New Jersey generations.

As Clarence grew older, he was able to work on the family farm in Scullville. In 1912, he married Anna Mary English Lashley, the widow of his first cousin, Mark Lashley. Clarence raised Anna Mary's two small children, Beatrice and Myron, and became the only father they truly knew. In 1913 Clarence and Anna Mary's daughter, Emma, was born.

In 1920, the Lashley family moved to Mays Landing, Atlantic County, New Jersey, where Clarence worked for the Mays Landing Water Power Company, a manufacturer of sheeting and toweling from raw cotton, which operated from 1865-1949. Anna Mary helped out with expenses by taking in boarders, mostly school teachers.

Advancing from the shipping department to supervisor of the cloth room, Clarence continued his love of quiltmaking, shared by Anna Mary. The Basket quilt (Plate 96) is one they made together: he pieced the blocks, she put them together, and the top was quilted by a church group. Clarence would rise early in the morning to cut out quilt pieces before he had to go to work at 7 a.m. After dinner, he would be back at the cutting board working with muslin scraps from the mill and scraps from clothing made by Anna Mary for the family. For the most part, he pieced tops which other hands backed and quilted, some perhaps at the Methodist church in Scullville. He pieced by hand or machine, depending on the intricacy of the pattern.

Daughters Beatrice and Emma and granddaughter Miriam can recognize scraps from their clothes in some of the many quilts Clarence made. He also purchased fabrics specifically for his quilts. Miriam can remember driving him to the M. E. Blatt Company in Atlantic City where they spent hours looking through the fabric department. Clarence preferred riding with his granddaughter; he had a driver's license but was a terrible driver.

An avid gardener, Clarence's love of color showed in the prize-winning garden he cultivated. He regularly attended the Sunday evening service at the Scullville Methodist Church and had a great knack for storytelling.

Clarence Lashley died in 1945, but his quilt legacy continues. Some of his quilts have been handed down to his great-grandchildren, Constance and Patricia, and their children. The family still has a number of boxes filled with pieces, blocks, and quilt tops. As his granddaughter Miriam continues to complete those tops as treasures for his great-great-grandchildren, another generation will come to know and appreciate Clarence Lashley's love of quilts. ■

From family history provided by Patricia P. Mayhew, great-granddaughter of Clarence B. Lashley.

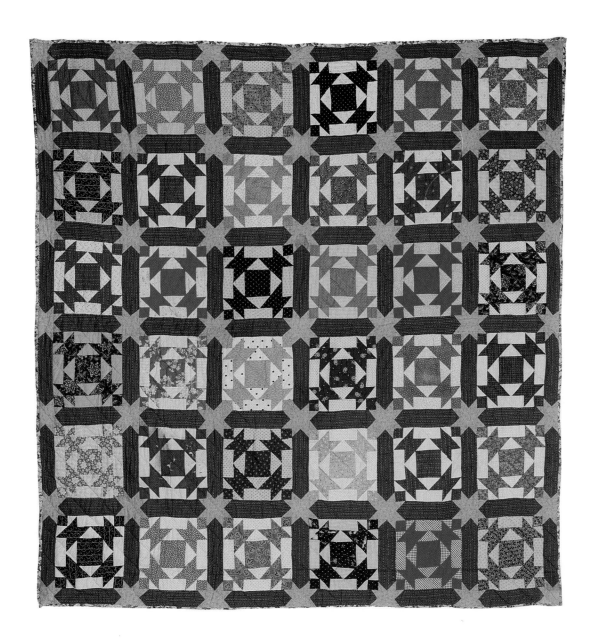

PLATE 143. DOUBLE X VARIATION, c.1895, 77¾"x 79¼", made by Clarence Lashley (1884-1945), Scullville, Atlantic County, New Jersey. A profusion of well-known fabrics from the 1870's to the 1890's are included in this quilt, probably one of the first made by Clarence. His sense of color and design is already apparent in the way he has placed the double-pink stars so they shine within the dark-green-and-blue striped lattice to give this quilt a slight three dimensional quality. The effect of the combination must have been satisfying to the maker, because he used it in another quilt. In the 1930's the top was quilted by hand in simple diagonal lines and bound by bringing the back to the front with machine top stitching. Owned by Emma L. Cline, daughter of the maker.

FIG. 38. Clarence B. Lashley

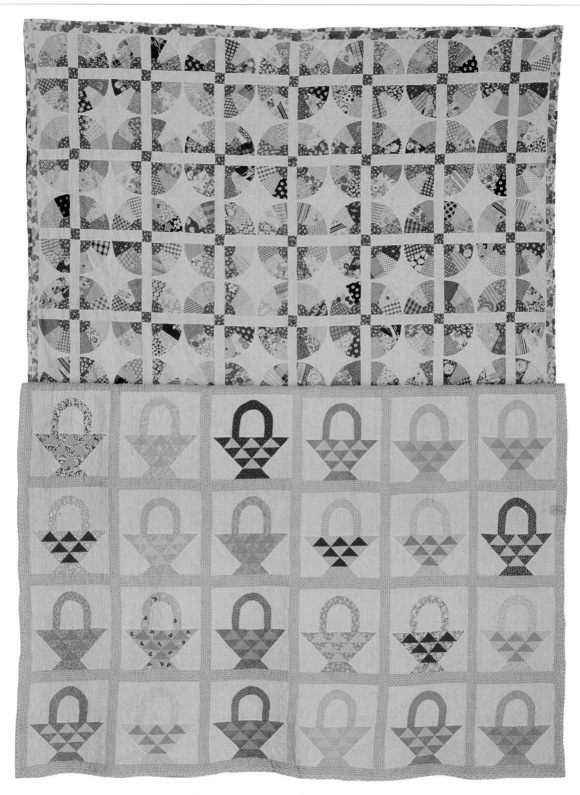

PLATE 144 (Top, Folded). FAN VARIATION, c.1930, 77" x 96". Made by Clarence Lashley (1884-1945), Mays Landing, Atlantic County, New Jersey. Mill and dress scraps have been used to great advantage in this spirited interpretation of a traditional block. While an individual block has a fan in each corner, the lively red used for the bottom of each fan and for the intersections of the lattice draws the fan together to form circles. In this way, the maker has pulled a multitude of scraps typical of the 1930's into a dashing quilt. The top was later backed with a large floral fabric brought to the front by machine top stitching and quilted in simple, diagonal lines in the 1940's. Owned by Patricia P. Mayhew, great-granddaughter of the maker.

(Bottom, Folded). BASKET, c.1930, 77"x79". Made by Clarence Lashley (1884-1945), Mays Landing, Atlantic County, New Jersey. Even though typical 1930's prints and a traditional pattern have been used, this quilt has a vivacity and sparkle because of the colorful interplay between solids and prints. In the late 1970's, the top was backed and bound with machine zigzag stitch back-to-front binding. At that time it was also machine quilted in an elaborate curlicue pattern. Owned by Constance M. Reynolds, great-granddaughter of the maker.

Mill Scraps & Salesmen's Samples

New Jersey quiltmakers used to great advantage the fabric scraps they were able to obtain from regional industries.

By the start of this century, new fabrics could be purchased by the yard from local dry goods stores or by mail from such catalogs as those of Montgomery Ward, Sears, and smaller companies like the Needleart Company of Chicago, which specialized in needlework and quilting supplies. New Jersey quilters also continued to make use of scraps from their own scrapbags and a variety of other sources available to them.

In 1925 the Report of the Census of Manufacturers shows that New Jersey made 36.7% of the nation's linen goods, 21.4% of its dyed and finished textiles, 13.2% of its worsted goods, 12% of its corsets, 11.8% of its fur felt hats, and 7.4% of its millinery and lace goods.[23] In 1954 each New Jersey county had important apparel plants, including 91 hosiery factories, 300 dress factories, 225 makers of ladies' suits and coats, 19 makers of men's suits, 40 button makers, 15 corset manufacturers, and 60 underwear plants.[24] The state's strong manufacturing tradition filled the quiltmaker's scrapbag with textile remnants, apparel scraps, salesmen's samples, and homesewing leftovers that provided an endless source of materials and inspiration.

The New Jersey textile mills that manufactured cotton, silk, and wool often sold remnants by the pound. Scraps of towelling and sheeting manufactured by the Mays Landing Water Power Company in Mays Landing were used in the Fan Variation quilt in Plate 144. Silk scraps from a Paterson silk mill were used in the Rainbow quilt in Plate 98. Wool scraps from a mill in Burlington County were used in the pastel crazy quilt in Plate 92. A quilt from curtain fabric manufactured in Keyport, Monmouth County, was also documented.

As the twentieth century approached, important apparel factories migrated to the Paterson area because of its textile mills. One factory, the Manhattan Mills, started putting its labels on Paterson shirts in 1879. Shirting fabrics featuring small-scale florals, geometrics, baseball bats, and sometimes horses on a white or off-white ground are found in quilts dating from 1870 to 1925, most often in small quantities in scrap quilts such as the Bowtie in Plate 97. Menswear manufacturers also contributed to the variety of fabrics found in New Jersey quilts, as can be seen in the suit linings that were used for the crazy quilt in Plate 89. New Jersey hat-making, which began in 1790 in Orange, Essex County, became a booming business by the Civil War, at which point it produced almost one-fourth of all the nation's hats.[25] The crazy quilt in Plate 99 contains several pieces cut from the linings of men's hats, including some from Thornton's and Lurch's, two Newark companies.

Many clothing manufacturers provided free scraps. Known as one of the largest manufacturers of pajamas, the Steiner Pajama Manufacturing Company in Manasquan, Monmouth County, boasted on its building, "We Put the World to Sleep." At its peak in the 1920's, the company employed 300 people and even built homes for some of its employees. At the end of the work day scraps were available for the taking. When the evening clean-up crew came in, they took the leftover cutaways and brought them home to their wives or neighbors who used them in quilts such as the Dresden Plate in 146. Plate 146 also shows a Sixteen Patch made with scraps from a local apron factory in Bergen County and a Star and Crescent made with scraps from a girdle manufacturer in Plainfield, Union County. A quilt using lingerie fabric from a Hackettstown, Warren County, manufacturer was also documented by the Project.

For many quilters, a common source of fabric was salesmen's samples. Many times these samples could be had for the asking or were sometimes acquired through a family acquaintance. One quiltmaker remembers how she got the fabric to make the Grandmother's Flower Garden shown in Plate 147:

I worked at the time [1936] for W. T. Grant on Washington Street in Hoboken, N.J. in the drapery and materials department. I noticed when the manager made up an order he looked through the sample books, I asked what happened to the books when he was finished. He said they threw them out, I asked if I could have them and so I began cutting 6-pointed cardboard patterns and decided one day I will try and make a quilt. The books laid around for a while until one day my mother said she was going to throw them out. Well, needless to say I tried making a quilt, the cardboard that I used as a pattern would fall apart. I asked a carpenter if he could cut me a pattern out of steel, which he did, and so I made my quilt. I was about 20 or 21 years. I said one day I will marry and have it for my trousseau. I made quite a bit and it did not look finished, when I decided I need[ed] a solid color for the border.

My grandparents had a chicken market and the feed that was fed to the chickens came in feed bags. My Mom used to make aprons and pillow cases out of them. I asked my Mom for some of the materials and so I made the border out of the feed bags.[26]

Several other quilts made from samples were documented by the Project. The Bricks quilt in Plate 148 uses baseball uniform fabric samples cut into brick shapes and assembled in a random zigzag design. Easily recognizable are the gray flannels of the uni-

form and the bright colors of the jerseys. The Nine Patch quilt in Plate 145 is made from sample pieces of dress-weight cotton using prints with the same design but in different color combinations. Usually the samples were cut into smaller pieces, but sometimes the brick-shaped samples were used unaltered, still displaying the hole in the corner of each piece where the ring had been attached.

When the Singer Company presented its innovative $3-a-month hire-purchase plan in 1873, more New Jersey women were encouraged to sew

commercially in their homes. The homesewing industry created leftover scraps not only from the construction of new garments, but also from the reshaping or restyling of outdated clothing. Fashion dictated what fabrics were "in" each year or season, and the quilts of the time tended to reflect the apparel industry's choices.

Because of the state's strong manufacturing tradition, New Jersey quiltmakers had a wealth of sources for fabric scraps. With great ingenuity, they used these scraps to their best advantage. ■

PLATE 145 (Detail). NINE PATCH, c.1940, 60"x 70½". Made by Mary Allerton, originally from Syracuse, New York. This quilt, along with several others, came down through the family of Dorothy Allerton Eden, a long time resident of Montclair, Essex County, New Jersey, and great-niece of the maker. Fabric samples that display the same print but in different colors are creatively put to use. Owned by Robert Reynolds, a friend of the Eden family.

PLATE 146 (Top, Folded). STAR AND CRESCENT, c.1930, appliqué, 79"x 91". Made by Mary Fortuna (e.b.1883-1967), Marquette, Michigan. This is a delightful piece which was made from girdle fabric. The peach brocade, a fabric once used for women's undergarments, is again brought to life in this machine appliquéd quilt. The fabric is thought to have come from a local New Jersey manufacturer in the Plainfield area of Union County. Mary Chabock, daughter of the maker, sent the fabric to her mother in Michigan. In 1950, Mary Fortuna returned the finished quilt to her daughter in New Jersey. Owned by Mary Della Sala, granddaughter of the maker.

(Bottom, Left, Folded). SIXTEEN PATCH, c.1930, 55½"x 85½". Made by Frances Elizabeth Taylor (1855-1940), Park Ridge, Bergen County, New Jersey. Hundreds of scraps from a local apron factory are pieced together in this tidy looking quilt. The individual squares were cut out by Frances' son when he came to visit. Owned by Frances Manning, granddaughter of the maker.

(Bottom, Right, Folded). DRESDEN PLATE, c.1930, appliqué, 57"x 82½". Made by Caroline L. Goddard (1885-1963), Manasquan, Monmouth County, New Jersey. The soft appearance of this Depression era quilt has been achieved through the use of cotton fabric that was used for making pajamas. The Steiner Pajama Manufacturing Company in Manasquan, New Jersey, was the last to produce pajamas with their label: "We put the world to sleep." New Jersey clothing manufacturers afforded quiltmakers the opportunity to obtain quantities of small pieces which were then sewed into quilts such as this. Owned by Helen Danskin.

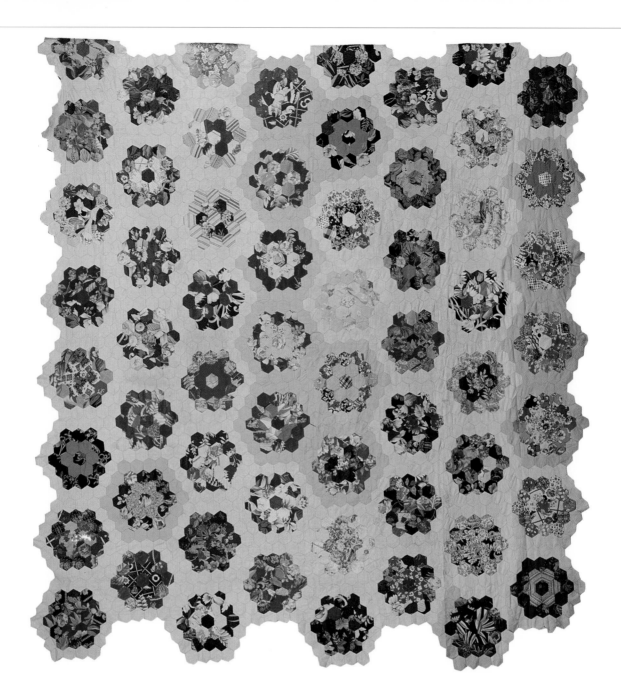

PLATE 147. GRANDMOTHER'S FLOWER GARDEN, c.1940, unquilted, 96" x 107." *Made by Bea Fleischman (1916-), Hoboken, Hudson County, New Jersey. A position working in the drapery and material department for W. T. Grant on Washington Street in Hoboken led Bea to ask for the sample books which eventually provided the fabrics for the flowers in her quilt. The solid color used in the "paths" between the flowers came from chicken-feed bags from her grandparents' chicken market. Bea was 20 years old when she made this quilt and remembers going out on dates and bringing her bag of materials with her to work on. Four years in the making, the quilt was constructed using the English paper piecing technique. Owned by the maker.*

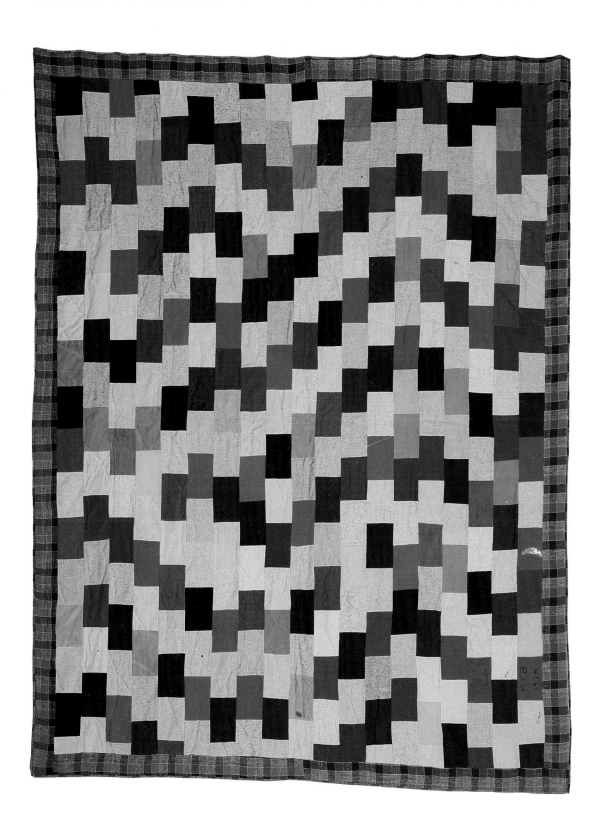

PLATE 148. BRICKS, 1939, 64" x 83". Made by Martha Emily Buckson Dawson (1915-), Newport, Cumberland County, New Jersey. Brightly colored bricks interspersed with gray are actually salesman's samples of baseball uniform fabric. Use of this unusual fabric adds to the variety of fabric samples found in New Jersey quilts. The bricks are pieced in vertical rows which form a random zigzag pattern when set together. The original swatches were twice the size used in the quilt and were obtained from a friend of Martha's employer. The plaid border adds a feeling of warmth as it carries out the geometric theme. The quilt is signed and dated by the maker, "M.E.B. 1939" and was made before her marriage in 1940. Owned by the maker.

FIG. 39. Martha Emily Buckson Dawson

Quilted by the Ladies of the Church

In New Jersey as elsewhere church groups have made quilts to raise funds or to honor ministers.

Two types of quilts – presentation and fund-raising – are traditionally associated with church groups. During the mid-nineteenth century, church groups made album and friendship quilts that were then formally presented to the minister either upon his leaving the congregation or as tokens of friendship. One example is the appliqué sampler made by ladies of the Old First Church in Monmouth County, New Jersey (Plate 45).

Quilts made for missionaries seem to have been popular in northern New Jersey in the early 1850's and may have had a fund-raising function. One such quilt made in Newark, Essex County, is shown in Plate 55. Next door to Newark, in Elizabeth, Union County, alone, three quilts were made for missionaries in 1852 and 1853 by Methodist and Presbyterian church groups. These three Elizabeth quilts share several of the same makers' names and also include several of the same patterns, fabrics, geometric and floral motifs, and religious and patriotic themes. These three quilts are now

in the collections of the Museum of American Folk Art in New York City; the Newark Museum in Newark; and the American Museum in Britain in Bath, England.[27] The idea of a quilt made for a minister was continued in 1896 in the southern part of New Jersey with the wool quilt shown in Plate 87.

The tradition of fund-raising quilts was often used by churches in order to support some specific need such as repairs or rebuilding. Churchwomen worked on quilts as a group, most often under the auspices of the Ladies Aid Society, the Sewing Society, or the Mission Society. "These women had the needle skills, they had the organization, they loved their churches, and they could produce fund-raising quilts so quickly that their husbands had no time to protest until it was too late."[28] The largest number of fund-raising quilts made by churches were made by Methodist women.[29] The Ohio Star quilt in Plate 149 and the Double Irish Chain Medallion quilt in Plate 150 are examples of fund-raising quilts.

For many church groups in New Jersey, the quilting of tops for other

people provided another means of raising money. The Sew and Sews quilting group of Tabernacle Methodist Church, Tabernacle, Burlington County, New Jersey, has been in existence for over 50 years. They meet at the home of Rachel Gerber, whose grandmother's and great aunt's quilts are the Rambler Variation and Oak Leaf and Reel in Plates 38 and 4. This group has often completed as many as 25 quilts a year. Because they live in the farmlands in southern New Jersey, their quilting season may come to a halt in the spring when it is time to pull the first crop of asparagus.[30]

Today, many churches in New Jersey still have quilt groups associated with them. These groups not only provide important funds for their churches but also educate people in the history of quiltmaking. ▫

PLATE 149 (Top). SNOW BALL, c.1940, 74½" x 94". Made in the Manasquan United Methodist Episcopal Church, Manasquan, Monmouth County, New Jersey. The pattern of this appealing two-color quilt requires exact piecing. Careful placement of the colors shows they are reversed in each of the two blocks that make up this design. Each unit is made up of four blocks. The present owner's grandmother, Grandmother Norris, helped make the quilt. Owned by Debbie Robinson.

(Bottom). OHIO STAR, c.1920, 60½" x 82½". Made by Frances Van Schoick (1880-1960), Manasquan, Monmouth County, New Jersey. This time-honored pattern is presented in a crisp blue and white color combination. Made for a fund-raiser, it was quilted at a quilting bee held at the Presbyterian Church in Manasquan. Straight line quilting is typical of the style found in many New Jersey quilts. Owned by Alice Jean Newman, daughter of the maker.

It is interesting to note that in Manasquan both the Methodist and Presbyterian churches were quilting to raise funds.

The First Congregational Church of Chester

One of the oldest New Jersey church groups in continuous service, the quilters of the First Congregational Church of Chester, Morris County, New Jersey, were first documented in the late 1800's by the minutes of the Ladies Aid Society. Beginning with "a quilting" to earn funds for missionaries, later notations recorded that earnings of the early twentieth century were primarily for local church support, salaries, and general finances. By 1956 the structure of the post-Victorian women's church activities had changed from three separate groups – Missionary Society, Ladies Aid Society, and general women members – into a merged Women's Fellowship with many smaller circle groups holding day and evening meetings and a larger monthly meeting for all. The smaller interest groups varied and included one where quilting was the major focus. Between 1963 and 1977 over 22 active quilters were making or finishing quilts

for clients. Frequently they met for two- to three-day sessions in various homes or in the Chapel if a quilt exceeded the size of available living rooms. Today, under the guidance and support of honorary chairpersons Mrs. Mabel Rockefeller Hoffman and Mrs. Mae Rockefeller Conklin (98-year-old twin sisters), the quilters of the First Congregational Church continue to meet and encourage others to join them.

While information on the early work of this group can be found in Ladies Aid Society minutes or personal journals, it wasn't until 1972 that Dorothy C. Morton began to keep formal records on the quilts themselves for the group and its clients. A permanent listing of participants, piecers, quilters, family history, and owners plus pattern history and the date of completion was prepared for each work, written on cloth with permanent ink, and sewn to the back of the quilt.

Many quilts quilted by this group

prior to 1972 can be identified by a stitch configuration called a "sparkle" (Fig. 41), which was developed by Mrs. Mabel Hoffman in the 1930's. The "sparkle" is a linear progression of 3 to 6 lines which radiate from a central point on another stitch line. Each individual line is 7 to 12 stitches long. The "sparkle" was most often used with parallel straight outlines or geometric patterns to hold the layers in place or increase the interaction of light on the surface of the fabric.

For over one hundred years, the quilters of the First Congregational Church in Chester have fostered personal growth through their endeavors of cooperation and service. As the skills and love of quiltmaking are nurtured and handed down, ecumenical fellowship grows, too. ▫

From information provided by Merry Morton, Historian, First Congregational Church of Chester.

FIG. 40 (Left to right). Mae Rockefeller Conklin and Mabel Rockefeller Hoffman, 98-year old twins

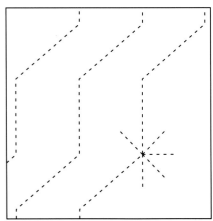

FIG. 41. Sparkle Stitch diagram

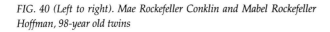

The First Presbyterian Church of Hanover

When the centennial celebration of the Hanover Presbyterian Church in Hanover, Morris County, New Jersey, began on October 11, 1935, the Ladies Aid Society, in collaboration with the Pastor, Rev. Robert Lawson, sponsored exhibitions of local historical records, a reception, and a pageant. One of the exhibits, "Agriculture and Handwork," was divided into two parts: modern and antique.

According to an article written by one of the participants in the celebration, this exhibit was "a revival of one of the Church activities which had been discontinued for a number of years. Much interest was shown in this modern exhibit where there were about 150 entries, including quilts (patchwork and appliqué), knitting and crochet work, embroidery, weaving, hooked, braided, and crochetted [sic] rugs, coverlets, canned goods, baking, jellies, jams, fruits and vegetables. The quilts were hung around the sides of the room making a colorful and attractive background for the other entries which were displayed on tables."[31]

The antique, or second part of the exhibit was held on December 6, 1935. It consisted of articles of interest to the Church and community covering the period of the history of the Church. Quilts and coverlets were hung around the walls. Mrs. Thomas Cook, church member, loaned a historical quilt for the exhibit. The flax was grown, spun, and dyed and the quilt made on the farm of Job Burnet, in what is now Whippany, New Jersey.

One year later, in the fall of 1936, the Ways and Means Committee of the Ladies Aid Society met to discuss fund-raising plans and the following account has become part of the church's history. The chairman suggested making a quilt in the Garden Path design, using alternating plain blocks for 10¢-a-name signatures. When the Society voted to accept the recommendation of the committee, two subcommittees were formed: one to make the quilt, the other to solicit names.

In January 1937, scaled drawings and patches were distributed. But when completed blocks were returned, there were problems: many did not carry out the Garden Path design, the seams on some were too wide, and others had to be made over. As the quilt did not progress with speed or enthusiasm, the chairman became discouraged and resigned.

Then Mrs. Thomas Cook, President of the Society, found herself as Chairman of the Ways and Means Committee and decided to change ideas altogether. Her plan was to make a historical quilt with the names of ministers, officers, and members of the congregation as far back as present church families were willing to go. She also decided to use only old-fashioned prints, most of them browns, for the patchwork.

When the Society changed officers, Mrs. Wallace Griffith was elected President. She also became a member of the quilt committee. She felt that in order to have colors blend and to keep pat-

FIG. 42. First Presbyterian Church of Hanover

tern and blocks correct, it was best for one person to be responsible for making blocks and putting them together. Mrs. Cook volunteered and became infatuated with her task, even though it was a case of change after change and doing over to make it right. Several members donated some very lovely old prints and Mrs. Robert Lawson, the minister's wife, donated new muslin. At the committee meetings it was a toss-up between Mrs. Herbert Smith and Mrs. Winans as to which one could tell the best stories about the renowned characters of the church and community.

Mrs. Sidney Winans volunteered to write to the Ely, Kitchell, and Green families telling them of the quilt and asking for names and donations for family blocks. The Elys, an old Livingston, New Jersey, family, contributed $10.00 for their block. The Kitchell block brought in $15.00 and the Green block $5.00. With names of her own family and others, Mrs. Winans had raised $40.00, the most raised by any individual, for which she was highly commended.

Mrs. J. Hopping volunteered to write all the family names on the blocks but the most difficult part of all was to get the names embroidered because so many of the ladies had some sort of eye trouble. The working of the names fell mostly to Mrs. Hopping, Mrs. Burleigh,

Mrs. Griffith, and Mrs. Cook.

While the quilt was being assembled, it received publicity not only from the pulpit, but also from solicitations for it and from its exhibition at all the church functions and in the vestibule of the Church. The quilt that was started in January 1937 was finished in November 1941 "thus making almost five years of tedious work."

There are about 800 names embroidered on this quilt, all of whom were people interested in the church at some time. The quilt's central medallion contains an embroidered picture of the church which was drawn by Miss Sidney Winans Tompkins, considered by ladies of the society to be one of the "young" members of the church. She signed her name, "S. Tompkins," in ink beneath the lower right corner of the building. Names of all the pastors along with their dates of service are embroidered underneath the church. The names of the pastors who served the church the longest are placed in blocks on either side of the central medallion. Names of church members, both past and present, were embroidered on many of the blocks, while names of the members of the various departments within the church were stitched on others. These included the Ladies Aid Society and the Parish Sewing Society, the Missionary Society,

the Sabbath School, 40-year members, the Young People's Fellowship, Music, and the Gospel Teams. One of the Ely family blocks lists "Smith Ely, ex-mayor New York City" and when Mrs. Kitchell embroidered the name "William D. Kitchell" on her family block, she made sure everyone knew who he was, by adding "my son" after his name.

The Quilt Fund of the Society raised $89.50 and Mrs. Winans suggested that the money be used for some permanent improvement in the Church interior. Ten of the original Communion Chairs, which were deteriorating in the basement, were repaired and refinished by two of the church members at a cost of $29.20, and were then used on Communion Sundays. Three original pulpit chairs were repaired at a cost of $37.00 and were placed in the Church Auditorium.

At the June 1943 meeting of the Ladies Aid Society, the quilt was formally placed in Mrs. Lawson's hands for safekeeping. It was to remain in the Manse and be brought out for exhibition as occasions arose.

As Mrs. LeMoyne Burleigh wrote, "Much thought, interest, time and research has been put into this work, and we are leaving it to our descendants with the hope that it will be of interest and historic value."[32] ∎

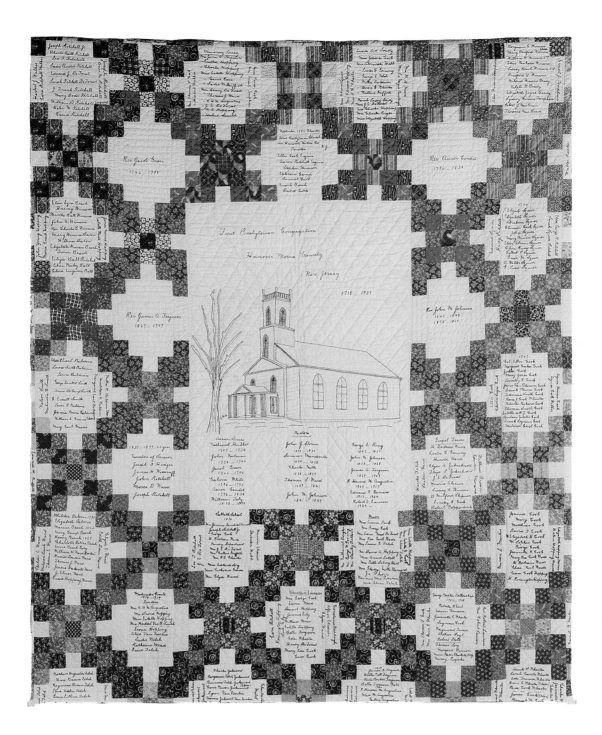

PLATE 150 (Detail). DOUBLE IRISH CHAIN WITH MEDALLION, 1936-1941, 83" x 115". Made by the Ladies Aid Society of the First Presbyterian Church of Hanover, East Hanover, Morris County, New Jersey. This popular pattern was personalized with the addition of a central medallion which features an embroidered picture of the church and the names and dates of all the ministers who served over the years. Embroidered within the plain blocks are names of the ministers who served the church the longest, officers and members of the church's organizations, and members of the congregation. Made as a fund-raiser, money was collected for each block, not per name as was so often the case in quilts of this type. Owned by the First Presbyterian Church of Hanover, Morris County.

Chapter Six

Little Treasures

Grandma said I've some
Patches you know
a needle thread
And a thimble so
Go take your naps
Now children do
and I'll make you
A Patchy Zoo

–Carrie Odgers Rinehart, quiltmaker, 1942

PLATE 151. *PATCHY ZOO, 1942, appliqué, 54" x 65". Made by Carrie Odgers Rinehart (b.1872), Newport News, Virginia. This quilt of animals is an enchanting original design. Each animal is accompanied by an original poem of information and description. The quilt shows a creative and fanciful use of the fabrics of the time, such as green plaid for the walrus and yellow and blue stripes for the zebra. Embroidered details decorate the blanket-stitched animals. The quilt is embroidered with the following inscription: "Original design for James De Groodt from his great Aunt Carrie Rinehart, Seventy years old, February 14, 1942." The quilt was mailed to James, who was living in Mendham, Morris County. Owned by Lynn Richter, great-niece of the maker.*

& Small Delights

Children's Quilts & Other Small Pieces

Quilts for children featured traditional patterns until the 1920's, when specific juvenile themes began to appear.

The existence of a small quilt made for a child implies that at least part of the time the child slept alone rather than with parents, siblings, or a nurse. Cradles and associated bedding appear in American inventories of furnishings before 1700. For example, in 1732 a Massachusetts "children's chamber" inventory included "2 quilts, 4 blankets, a small Rugg and 2 feather beds." Despite records of early cradle bedding, some children apparently continued to sleep with their parents until well into the 1800's; in 1841, Catharine Beecher wrote advice to the housewife: "It is better for both mother and child that it not sleep on the mother's arm at night, unless the weather be extremely cold....A crib beside the mother is best for the child...."[1]

Until the early 1900's, quilts intended for children can usually be identified only by their size. They normally incorporate the designs of full-scale quilts with little modification of block size. A few small quilts of a size suitable for cribs were recorded by the New Jersey Project from the period before the Civil War. The Chips and Whetstones quilt (Plate 152) and the

Diamond in a Square strip quilt (Plate 154) both use blocks that are full size or even slightly larger than full size. The crib size quilts recorded from this period are rectangular with average dimensions of about 40" x 48". A particularly interesting small quilt is the little appliquéd sampler (Plate 153) which includes two laurel leaf wreaths, one apparently with the parents' names, Julia H. and Joseph Ashbrook, and a smaller one with the child's name, Samuel C. Ashbrook. The simplicity of some of the other appliqués suggests that children may have participated in making this backed but unquilted spread.

The casually executed Star Appliqué top (Plate 156) and the precisely pieced Tumbling Blocks (Plate 155) were both made around the time of the Civil War, and both use such small pieces that they could be considered miniatures. The exquisite silk Tumbling Blocks piece is only 18" x 20". The handwritten note attached to the back bears the date July, 1860, and indicates that it was made by E. Warner, then 81 years old, for her daughter, B. Woolston. Its small size suggests that it may be a forerunner of

the purely decorative silk pieces made in abundance later in the 1800's. At the other end of the spectrum technically, is the crib size cotton Star Appliqué top made of three-inch blocks with somewhat erratically shaped appliquéd stars set with alternate blocks. Although the quilt is still in its family of origin, its history is no longer remembered, but it has a charming casualness of construction.

From the period of about 1870 to about 1925, the Project recorded a few quilts with embroidered inscriptions such as "Grandpa" or "1893 Charlie 6 years" (Plate 90). But these were full size quilts, indicating that, although some quilts were being made specifically for children, they would be indistinguishable from quilts made for adults if their inscriptions did not indicate that a child was to be the recipient.

Although children, particularly Kate Greenaway figures, were often embroidered on crazy quilts of the 1890's and farm animals or birds may be seen on the embroidered quilts made from the 1890's through the 1920's or 1930's, children's motifs are not generally the main focus of quilts until the mid-1920's when figures for children appear, first as stamped embroidery designs and then as appliqué. Stamped designs for the blue or Turkey red embroidered picture quilts and stamped or pieced alphabet block designs could be ordered from the catalogs of such companies as Ladies Art Company or Valley Supply Company, both located in St. Louis, Missouri.[2] From these quilts children could become familiar with the alphabet and exotic animals.

Commercial kits of the 1920's, 1930's, and 1940's offered a wide range of familiar designs made to appeal to children because of their familiarity: Raggedy Ann and Andy, the Three Bears, toy soldiers, dolls and marionettes. The Carousel and Cowboy quilts (Plate 158 and 160) recorded by the Project are, by their maker's information, from kits available at a local department store and by mail, respectively. On the other hand, the Patchy Zoo (Plate 151) quilt bears an embroidered inscription to tell the world that the maker designed the quilt herself. One look at any of these quilts is enough to confirm that by the 1930's children were no longer thought of as little adults. ■

PLATE 152. CHIPS AND WHETSTONES/STARBURST, c.1840, 40" x 49". Made by a relative of Paul Apgar, New Jersey. This unusually lovely small quilt has many well preserved examples of early chintz. Indeed a treasure, it has been in the Apgar family for many years. Cherished by Mabel Apgar, mother of the late Paul Apgar, the quilt is now owned by Ann Apgar.

PLATE 153. APPLIQUÉ SAMPLER, c.1850, unquilted coverlet, 38" x 50½". Made in New Jersey. A miniature labor of love, this crib-size coverlet has a primitive charm with its many original designs. One can surmise that the two names "Joseph and Julia H. Ashbrook" in the large laurel leaf wreath in the center were those of the parents, while the name "Samuel C. Ashbrook" in the matching smaller leaf wreath was their son for whom the quilt was made. Natural as well as whimsical flowers, leaves, and birds decorate the blocks. The handwork includes broderie perse, cross-stitch, and petit point. This quilt is housed in Fleming Castle, which was built in 1756 and is the oldest house in Flemington, Hunterdon County. The house and quilt are owned by the Colonel Lowery Chapter, D.A.R.

PLATE 154. DIAMOND IN A SQUARE, c.1840, 41" x 45". Made by Mary Tabor. The maker of this early small quilt used average-size blocks, but fewer of them to create this child's quilt. A simple block was given added interest with the use of Sawtooth sashing and borders. It is bound with white twill tape. Owned by the Hopewell Museum, Mercer County.

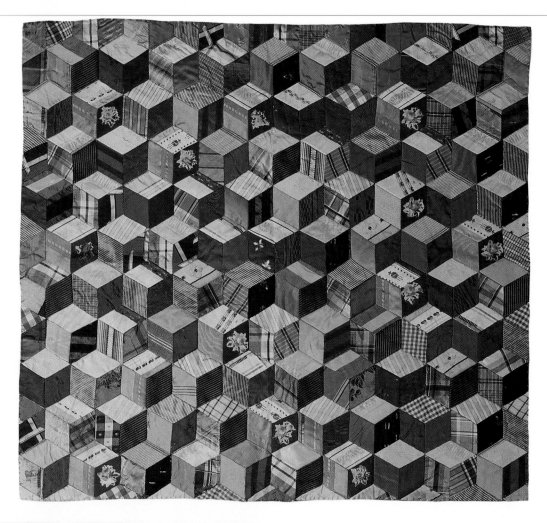

PLATE 155 (Above). TUMBLING BLOCKS, c.1860, silk, 17¾" x 19½". Made by E. Warner (b.1779). This exquisite small quilt was probably made as a decorative piece. A hand-written note attached to the back of the quilt says, "This piece of work done by E. Warner in the eighty-first year of her age and presented to her daughter, B. Woolston, July 1860." The back of the quilt is glazed blue cotton. Owned by Oscar Appel.

PLATE 156 (Left). STAR APPLIQUÉ, c.1870, unquilted, 34¼" x 41¾". Made in Ringoes or Reaville, Hunterdon County, New Jersey. Miniature free-form appliqué stars alternate with 2¾" blocks of a fine red and white stripe. The primitive shapes of the stars cause one to wonder if this was a child's learning piece. However, the stitching is better than one might expect if that were the case. The quilt came from the home of Cornie Browne, the owner's grandmother. Owned by Susanne Browne.

PLATE 157 (Left). WHOLE CLOTH, 1930, satin, 33¾" x 57½", Ramsey, Bergen County, New Jersey. Quilted satin quilts in all sizes enjoyed a popularity in the 1930's and were made commercially as well as at home. A friend or relative of the owner's mother made this quilt for the owner's birth on March 19, 1930. Decorative quilting designs include a flower and leaves in the center and bows at the top and bottom. Owned by Mary Ann Corring.

PLATE 158 (Right). CAROUSEL, 1941, appliqué, 33½" x 47". Made by Elsie Hatfield (1916-), Newark, Essex County, New Jersey. This is an example of a juvenile quilt made from a commercial kit. The kit was purchased from Bamberger's Department Store in Newark and made by the owner's mother for her daughter's birth in 1941. It was backed and quilted in the 1980's. Owned by Judith Wentworth, daughter of the maker.

PLATE 159. EMBROIDERED QUILT, 1925, 50½" x 61½". Made by Evelina Sickles Stratton (1863-1934), Elberon, Monmouth County, New Jersey. The blocks of this quilt are made from transfer designs that have been embroidered in chain stitch. These designs were popular at the time and readily available for purchase. Chosen to appeal to a child, they include a variety of scenes of children at play, animals, and several depicting Dutch children in costume. Each block is quilted in circles around the figures. One of the delights of quilts made for children is that they seem to be more frequently signed and dated, as this one is with the penned inscription on the back, "Grandmother Stratton to Margaret Truax 1925." Made for the owner's mother, Margaret Truax Clayton, the quilt is now owned by Nancy Clayton Burroughs, great-granddaughter of the maker.

FIG. 43. Evelina Sickles Stratton

PLATE 160. COWBOY, 1948, appliqué, 69½" x 86¾". Made by Elizabeth N. Hunt (1926-), Swedesboro, Gloucester County, New Jersey. This quilt was made from a mail-order kit for the maker's son, John. Its western theme was a popular one at the time for children's clothing and bedding. The Project documented several prints with a western theme in other quilts. Owned by Elizabeth N. Hunt, the maker.

FIG. 44. Elizabeth Hunt, her husband Donald, and son John

Chapter Seven

Politics, Patriotism

"O Lady Martha Washington
   Has come to Morristown,
And we must go and quickly so,
   Each in her finest gown,
And call at Colonel Ford's to see
   That dame of great renown."

So spake the dames of Hanover
   And put on their array
Of silks to wit, and all that's fit
   To grace a gala day,
And called on Lady Washington
   In raiment bright and gay.

Those were the days of scarcity
   In all our stricken land,
When hardships tried the country-side;
   Want was on every hand,
When they called on Lady Washington
   In fine attire so grand.

"And don't you think! we found her with
   A speckled homespun apron on;
With knitting in hand – that lady so grand –
   That stately Lady Washington!
When we came to Morristown that day
   With all our finest fixin's on!

She welcomed us right graciously
   And then, quite at her ease,
She makes the glancing needles fly
   As nimbly as you please;
And so we found that courtly dame
   As busy as two bees."

"For while our gallant soldiers bear
   the brunt of war," quoth she,
"It is not right that we delight
   In costly finery."
So spake good Martha Washington,
   Still smiling graciously.

"But let us do our part," quoth she,
   "And speedily begin
To clothe our armies on the field
   And independence win" –
"Good-bye! Good-bye!" we all did cry –
   "We're going home to spin!"

Charles D. Platt
Ballads of New Jersey in the Revolution
Morristown, New Jersey, 1896

PLATE 161. Detail of PRESIDENTS MEDALLION, c.1830 (Plate 163).

& Patchwork

Flags, Banners, & Commemorative Fabrics

Quilters working with patriotic and political themes often incorporated commemorative fabrics that preserve a part of history.

Many early American quilts featured commemorative textiles or were created to honor important events. When a quilt contains fabric specifically made to celebrate an historic occasion, not only is the quilt easier to date but it also gives a clearer sense of the times in which it was created. Early commemorative fabrics depicted the battles and leaders of the American Revolution. In the early nineteenth century, fabrics and ribbons were made as souvenirs to be given away at political campaigns. The Centennial Exposition of 1876 was a great incentive to produce fabric commemorating a century of American independence. The 1939 World's Fair continued the commemorative tradition into the twentieth century. No matter when the textiles were made, they offered a variety of printed subjects in cloth that were meant to serve as "reminders and keepsakes" of both national and individual events that have affected our lives.[1]

According to Herbert Ridgeway Collins, author of *Threads of History*, event handkerchiefs and banners were being made in America, France, and England beginning in the final quarter of the eighteenth century.[2] The earliest recorded reference was found in an estate inventory in Spotsylvania County, Virginia, in 1770, where "three printed handkerchiefs" were among the items listed in the estate of Charles Colson.[3] A favorite subject to appear in cloth was George Washington, who has been honored in handkerchiefs, bandannas, and yard goods from the time of his inauguration in 1789 and continuing long after his death in 1799.

Some of the first objects to present partisan politics to the electorate appeared during the heated 1828 presidential campaign between Andrew Jackson and John Quincy Adams. In addition to cloth ribbons and bandannas, there were snuff and thread boxes, metal tokens, and garment buttons. Jackson himself inspired a variety of memorabilia including silk bandannas, yard goods or chintzes, and silk ribbons. Indeed, the earliest piece of a commemorative textile found by the Project appears in the Presidents Medallion quilt (Plate 163). The original roller printed fabric from which the portraits were cut features the first six U.S. presidents – Washington, John Adams, Jefferson, Madison, Monroe, and John Q. Adams. Two versions are known to have been produced in 1829 – one without the portrait of Andrew Jackson and the other with. The earlier version, a French toile, was inscribed "Les Presidents des Etats-Unis" and does not show the portrait of Jackson.[4] The other is from yard goods manufactured in England for Jackson's 1829 inauguration and features a military bust with the words "Andrew Jackson, President of the United States from 1829 to [left blank], Supreme Commander of the Army and Navy." Beneath the portrait it reads, "Magnanimous in Peace, Victorious in War." It also features the American eagle and the frigate U.S.S. Constitution.

During the 1840 presidential contest of William H. Harrison and Martin Van Buren, textiles and other souvenirs were issued in such great quantity that it set the style for campaigns to come. Added to the numerous items sold and given away by Harrison supporters were "walking sticks, beanies, skimmers, neckties, ribbon badges, banners, kerchiefs, posters, and many others."[5] Printed banners featured Harrison's well-known campaign symbols – a log

PLATE 162 (Detail). CRAZY QUILT, 1887, unquilted, 80" x 87". Made by Emma Cordilla McIntire (1856-1937), Camden, Camden County, New Jersey. This lovely crazy quilt is placed in an historical context by the maker, who notes the Constitutional Centennial. Proudly she records the number of pieces (1,000) as well. Months of the year are featured, as well as fans and Oriental figures. Owned by the Camden County Historical Society, Camden County.

cabin and hard cider – as well as portraits of the candidate himself. In fact, the Variable Star pattern gained new popularity when it was given the political slogan "Tippecanoe and Tyler, Too."[6] Shown in the Log Cabin Courthouse Steps quilt (Plate 165) are fragments of an early political banner which originally featured a portrait of Henry Clay in the center of a blue field of 26 stars. The legend between the stripes reads "Clay and Frelinghuysen."[7] Women couldn't vote, but they formed strong opinions which could be expressed in their quilts.

Such quilt patterns as Whig's Defeat, Clay's Choice, Lincoln's Platform, Log Cabin, Whig Rose, and Democrat Rose are all names that bear political reference. The President's Wreath pattern is said to have originated in New Jersey in the mid-nineteenth century and was probably inspired by an 1845 Currier and Ives lithograph that commemorated George Washington's inaugural parade in April 1789. The print, entitled "Washington's Reception by the Ladies...on passing the bridges at Trenton, New Jersey..." depicts women with rose wreaths in their hair strewing blossoms in front of Washington's procession along streets that were decorated with rose garlands.[8]

PLATE 163. PRESIDENTS MEDALLION, c.1830, 85" x 88½". Made in New Jersey. This exquisite quilt of glazed cotton chintz features prominent appliqué cut-outs of the first six presidents of the United States. Fabric printed with these portraits was produced in both France and England for sale in America. The portraits are framed with diagonal borders of clamshell and geometric patchwork made of flowered chintz. Squares in the center medallion are half-inch. Owned by Eva Ryder.

The bandannas, handkerchiefs, and kerchiefs that were popular from 1840 to 1848 enjoyed renewed appeal in the late nineteenth century. Rallies and parades produced posters, silk ribbon badges, floats, and a variety of cloth banners. The banners and bunting used to decorate streets and platforms were later fashioned by home sewers into aprons, uniforms,

and clothing: single banners were sewn together or uncut bolts of bandanna cloth were used to create this commemorative clothing.[9]

New Jersey's advantageous location between New York City and Philadelphia made it easy to travel a reasonable distance to attend major exhibitions in either city. By the late nineteenth century, the state's railway

system was "one of the densest in the country,"[10] thereby making it easy for travelers to attend the 1876 Centennial Exposition in Philadelphia which commemorated a century of American independence. To set the mood for the festivities, the city of Philadelphia was decorated with flags from all nations and enveloped in banners and bunting. The Stars and Stripes hung every-

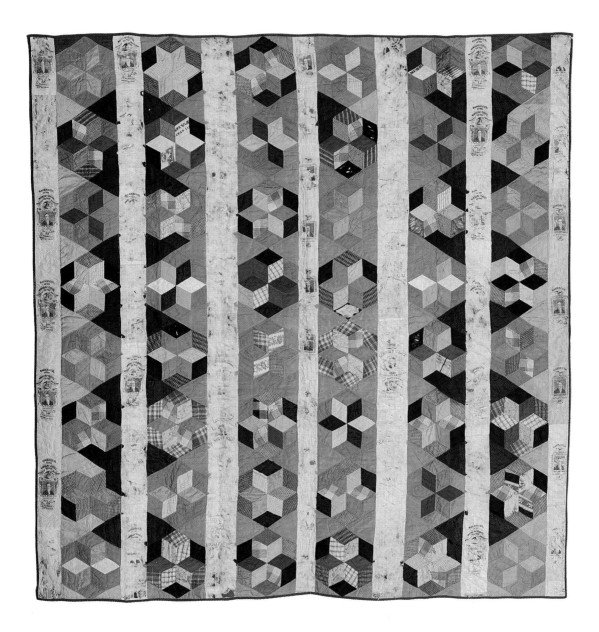

PLATE 164. SIX POINTED STAR IN STRIP SET, 1845, silk, 49½" x 49½". Made in Belvidere, Warren County, New Jersey. This fascinating, even though somewhat deteriorated, early silk quilt has strips made of several different campaign ribbons, all featuring Henry Clay and Theodore Frelinghuysen (a New Jersey native son), the Whig party's unsuccessful candidates for President and Vice President in 1844. One ribbon reads, "Barbeque by the Whigs of Ohio to the Whigs of Kentucky at Dayton. Sept. 29th 1842." Clay's name is printed above his picture with the date 1844 below. A farmer and a team of horses is shown, promoting Clay's image as a farmer. Remnants of other ribbons mention "Clay now, Polk never" and "Henry Clay, Nation's Choice." Owned by Veronica Mitchell.

---

where. Men and women wore red, white, and blue neckties and scarves; little girls tied tri-colored ribbons in their hair; even dogs and horses wore flags in their collars.[11] A great amount of fabric printed with Liberty bells, shields, flags, eagles and George Washington was manufactured for the Cen-

tennial. Bandannas and pennants were produced that pictured the fairground buildings, the Declaration of Independence, flags of all participating nations, and, of course, George Washington. While many were printed as souvenirs, some were actually printed on the grounds before the Exhibition closed

on November 9, 1876. One example of a quilt made from Centennial cloth and documented by the Project is the Centennial Quilt in Plate 167. It features banners of George Washington with his horse and the flags of the nations participating in the Centennial celebration. In addition, two other quilts documented by the Project were made by Rebecca Coles Glover who was born in 1843 in Medford, Burlington County, New Jersey. She stitched two Centennial fabric quilts by stitching three panels of uncut banner cloth together to form the tops of her quilts. One featured the same George Washington banners mentioned before and the other featured the Stars and Stripes. Both quilts had other printed flag designs used for the backing.

The Centennial fairgrounds had more than 150 buildings representing nations and activities from all over the world. The Women's Pavilion exhibited products created by or for women. Here, female artists and artisans exhibited their talents in floral decoration, painting, embroidery, and tapestry. French textiles, English furniture and household decorations, German porcelains, Japanese bronzes and lacquerware, and Indian shawls and jewelry contributed to the arts and crafts of the world that were on display. The great

interest in the Japanese pavilion in general and in the British needlework display in particular influenced American quiltmakers in developing the crazy quilt fad.[12]

Ribbons have been popular campaign items since the early part of the nineteenth century. The Project's earliest documented ribbon dates to the Whig Party of 1844 and is shown in the Six Pointed Star quilt (Plate 164). Very popular from 1876 to 1892, campaign ribbons contributed greatly to the variety of textiles appearing in quilts, especially the crazy quilts that were so fashionable. Early ribbons were simple with background colors ranging from white or light pastels (see crazy quilt, Plate 171) to vivid reds and blues. Later ribbons reflected the heavy velvet draperies and upholstery favored in Victorian homes. A military ribbon appearing in a fragment of a crazy quilt bears the printed inscription, "23rd N. J. Regiment Yahoos, May 3, 1905." The owner of this piece recalls

that the quiltmaker's father was in Col. E. Burd Grubb's 23rd New Jersey Regiment during the Civil War and each year thereafter a regimental reunion was held on a river bank (probably the Delaware River) in Edgewater Park, Burlington County, New Jersey.[13]

In preparation for the 1939 New York World's Fair, two time capsules were buried on the fairgrounds on September 23, 1938, with instructions for raising them on September 23, 6938. With the cooperation of over 2,000 libraries worldwide, the capsules contained artifacts of importance to civilizations five thousand years in the future and included needles and thread.[14] The focal points of the fair, the Trylon and the Perisphere, were reproduced on many souvenir items including clothing, scarves, handkerchiefs, and yard goods. The Project documented a quilt that was backed in the multi-colored version of yard goods produced for the fair. The front of the quilt was a Spider Web variation c.1930 that contained many examples of dress fabrics of the time, including rayon, voile, and seersucker as well as the more common printed cottons.[15]

New Jersey manufacturers were important contributors to the production of commemoratives. The Passaic Print Works which was established in 1877 in Passaic, Passaic County, New Jersey, claims to have set a world record in cotton printing when in 1927 it produced in 17 hours 5000 yards of fabric commemorating Charles Lindbergh.[16] Another manufacturer, B. B. Tilt & Son, from Paterson, Passaic County, New Jersey, had been one of the few American textile concerns to exhibit at L'Exposition Universelle in Paris in 1878. The silk ribbon it produced featured the Statue of Liberty, signifying the friendship between the United States and France, and was probably made at the fair and sold as a souvenir.[17] In addition, the Taylor Silk Manufacturing Company, also from Paterson, produced a silk handkerchief which commemorated the Electric Tower, the centerpiece of the fairgrounds of the Pan American Exposition which was held in Buffalo, New York, in 1901.[18]

PLATE 165 (Reverse side, folded and with bottom right corner turned up). LOG CABIN COURTHOUSE STEPS, c.1885, unquilted, 44" x 56". Some of the foundation squares of this quilt have been cut from an 1844 Whig presidential campaign flag showing a portrait of Henry Clay and the names of both Clay and New Jersey native son Theodore Frelinghuysen. The excitement of having a local son on the national ticket stirred the pride of New Jerseyans, and Clay was popular as well. In the voting, the Whigs won a majority in New Jersey, although losing at the national level by a slim margin. A quilt made of identical complete banners is in the collection of the Old Barracks Association, Trenton, Mercer County. Owned by Lorraine Apel.

In addition to using such commemorative textiles as banners, handkerchiefs or ribbons, a surge of patriotism or a strong political movement was all the inspiration a quilter needed to make her own personal statement. One-of-a-kind patriotic quilts or quilts made through group efforts in support of various causes continue to be made to this day.

The tradition of making quilts in support of war efforts spans the decades from the Civil War to World War II. The United States Sanitary Commission was established in the North during the Civil War to improve the conditions of the Union soldiers, and in the fall of 1863 began a series of Sanitary Fairs (see Plate 171) intended to provide funds to sustain its efforts.[19] The story of a Civil War quilt documented by the Project, as told by the owner, is of her Turkey Tracks quilt and how it was made by a girl who said years later that she would "never forget walking through a near-by Civil War battlefield when she was twelve and getting blood stains on her shoes."[20] Red Cross quilts were a specific type of fund-raising quilt that was made after the start of World War I in 1914 (Plate 110, Right). Relief committees actively sought the inclusion of patchwork quilts in packages sent to war-torn Europe.[21] Ladies Aid Societies and other church sewing circles made quilts for their missionaries or for victims of disaster. Today's quilters appear to have continued this tradition by making quilts in support of Desert Storm.

Patriotic symbols, particularly flags and eagles, have appeared in quilts throughout the nineteenth and twentieth centuries. As Barbara Brackman states in *Clues in the Calico*, "The flag as a quilt motif does not seem to date as early as the eagle (possibly because the eagle is supposed to symbolize the country in commercial and decorative arts while the flag is reserved for official purposes)."[22] Other symbols used as quilt motifs include the Liberty Bell, the rooster (a symbol used by the Democratic Party in 1880), and the chick and egg (symbols of the new nation). Quilts that featured

PLATE 166 (Detail). CENTENNIAL QUILT, c.1876, unquilted, 79½" x 79½". Made by Mary M. McDermitt (b.1845), Newark, Essex County, New Jersey. A Nine Patch block is set with lattice strips of material made in celebration of the U.S. Centennial. The alternate strips show repeats of two designs. One is a shield with the word "PEACE" and the date "1876" with an eagle below the shield and a dove flying overhead. Behind the shield is a cap on a pole, a symbol of liberty. The second design shows a cannon, a flag and a drum, and a Liberty Bell inscribed "1776." Both motifs are surrounded with leafy scrolls. The quilt is signed and dated by the maker. Owned by Gail Looker McKenna, great-great-niece of the maker.

important events or patriotic symbols that were documented by the Project were varied. The patriotic flag quilt in Plate 169 is a fine example of the use of Civil War banners and the flag quilt in Plate 168 might well be an original interpretation of a design attributed to *Peterson's Magazine* in 1861.[23] The crazy quilt (Plate 162) commemorates the Constitutional Centennial, and the Centennial quilt top in Plate 166 makes use of 1876 fabric that features the Liberty Bell and shield. A small amount of Centennial fabric also appears in the

Log Cabin quilt in Plate 170.

Looking to events of the past such as George Washington's inauguration or the 1876 Centennial and comparing them to the 1986 centennial celebration of the Statue of Liberty or the impact of Desert Storm, it is evident that quilters have continued the tradition of using patriotic and political themes as avenues of expression. The presence of commemorative textiles in a quilt enables us not only to date a quilt but also to preserve a part of history. ■

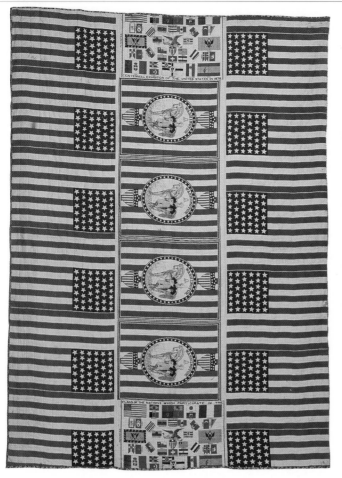

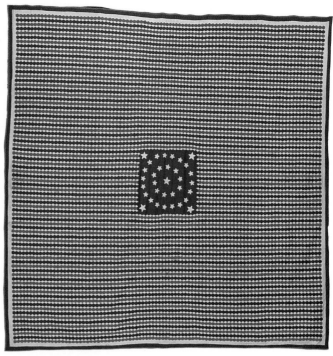

PLATE 167 (Top, Left). CENTENNIAL QUILT, 1876, 72" x 95". Made in New Jersey. This patriotic quilt is sewn from 18 printed Centennial banners. Each of the twelve banners on the outside edge has thirteen red and white stripes and thirty-nine white stars on a blue field. The four center banners show the same stylized portrait of George Washington as a young man in military uniform: he is posed in a jaunty stance, leaning against his horse with his right leg crossed in front. He points to a message reading "Washington/victory is ours/Paul Jones." Above his head is the Liberty Bell with the crack showing. An oval is set upon a flag with thirteen red and white stripes with two shields on top and bottom, inscribed "Shield of U.S. America." The remaining two banners are identical, showing a variety of flags and containing the inscription, "Flags of the Nations which participate in the Centennial Exhibition of the United States in 1876." Owned by Mr. and Mrs. W.J. Benjamin, it was passed down from Mr. Benjamin's grandmother, Carrie Angleman Bodine, who was a young girl at the time the quilt was made.

PLATE 168 (Top, Right). FLAG QUILT, 1861, unquilted, 90" x 92". Made by Ivy Purcell, Atlantic City, Atlantic County, New Jersey. This striking flag is painstakingly hand stitched of approximately 7,000 tiny hexagons and diamonds. The center medallion containing 34 stars indicates a probable date of 1861 to 1863. The center is similar to the center of a quilt in the collection of The Smithsonian's National Museum of American History that also has a center design of 34 stars and was made in 1861 by a woman whose son was a soldier in the Civil War. The maker, Ivy Purcell, was the wife of a doctor. Owned by Margaret E. Risley, whose grandmother, Margaret Leeds Risley, acquired the quilt from the maker.

PLATE 169 (Left). PATRIOTIC FLAG QUILT, c.1865, 78" x 84". Made in New York. This graphic quilt is said to have been made of material from flags originally decorating New York City buildings at the end of the Civil War. Saved when fire threatened, the flags were later used to create this bold and patriotic piece. Owned by Diane Clark, great-great-great-granddaughter of the maker.

PLATE 170 (Top, Detail). LOG CABIN, BARN RAISING VARIA-TION, c.1876, unquilted, 82½" x 83". Made by Mary Lewis Tracy Jennings (1845-1889) and friends, New London, Connecticut. A close-up of this quilt reveals Centennial print fabric. Individual letters of the word "Centennial" are printed in white on blue and red stars. The background is made up of similar blue and red shooting stars. The oriental look of the crane fabric begins to show the influence of Japanese design following the exhibitions of Japanese culture in London in 1862 and at the Philadelphia Centennial in 1876. Family history recalls that Mary Lewis Tracy was fond of a man named Crane; hence the four cranes in the center of the quilt. However, she later married Charles Jennings. Owned by B. J. Stephen, granddaughter of the maker.

PLATE 171 (Left, Detail, Folded). CRAZY QUILT, c.1890, 72" x 79". Made by Mary Carroll, Brooklyn, New York. The subtle inclusion of political ribbons, flags, and fair ribbons adds to the overall collection of fabrics in this well cared for quilt. Quiltmakers often sewed personal mementos such as these into their quilts as keepsakes or remembrances of national events. Here, portraits of Democrats Grover Cleveland (a New Jersey native son) and Allan G. Thurman are shown on a white ribbon which bears a red, white, and blue shield flanked on either side by the American flag and topped by the American eagle. It announces their candidacy for President and Vice President in the campaign of 1888. Also shown are opposing candidates, the Republican team of Benjamin Harrison and Levi P. Morton, who won the election. A less noticeable ribbon commemorates the New Jersey Sanitary Commission's Metropolitan Fair of 1864. Established during the Civil War, these fairs were intended to provide funds to help improve the conditions of the Union soliders. Owned by Dorothy M. Holmes whose husband's aunt was the maker.

Chapter Eight

Documenting the

"I was using this quilt for years, as a throw, tossed over the back of my sofa!" said Jane Lutz of Stockton, as three quilt appraisers from the Heritage Quilt Project of New Jersey fingered the fabric, and declared her quilt to be the oldest seen that day. [See Plate 26]

"Between 1830 and 1840" was the final pronouncement on the quilt's date of origin, and Mrs. Lutz was shocked. "I had no idea!" she said.

– Fran Miller, "Project Pinpoints Antique Quilt Origins,"
Hunterdon County Observer, April 22, 1989

FIG. 45 (Left). THE HERITAGE QUILT PROJECT OF NEW JERSEY.
Front row (left to right): Marti Porreca, Barbara Schaffer, Rita Erickson, Barbara Finch.
Back row (left to right): Winifred Friese, Veronica Mitchell, Rachel Cochran, Natalie Hart.
Other active members not pictured: Helen Burkhart, Aleta Johnson, Janet Krache, Olive Loper,
Mariann Loughlin, Kay Lukasko, Leona Pancoast, and Peggy Sloan.

PLATE 172 (Below). Some of the many printed materials The Heritage Quilt Project of New
Jersey's activities involved.

Disappearing Heritage

The Quilt Documentation Effort

The Heritage Quilt Project of New Jersey contributed to a growing nationwide volunteer effort.

The idea of recording quilts as an aspect of a state's history originated in Kentucky in the late 1970's when Louisville quilt dealer Bruce Mann realized that part of his state's heritage was being lost as quilts were sold to out-of-state buyers. The Kentucky Quilt Project was designed by four Kentucky women to implement Mr. Mann's idea. The Kentucky Project's founders devised a plan to record family quilts at several locations throughout the state, organize a museum exhibit, and publish a book to present some of the most interesting quilts they had recorded.[1]

When the Kentucky Project presented its book in 1982, groups throughout the country began to organize similar quilt documentation projects for their states. Although the Kentucky Project served as a model, the documentation effort has been a true grassroots movement with no nationwide planning committee to standardize projects from state to state. Therefore, each state has been free to set its own goals, design its own questionnaires, establish its own parameters for the quilts to be recorded, and face its own funding and organiza-

tional problems. For example, Kentucky did not record quilts made after 1900 but New Jersey chose 1950 as its cut-off date in order to determine whether or not its quilters participated in the quilt revival of the 1930's. Some states designed 10-page questionnaires while others limited their surveys to one tightly spaced page of basic information with narrative information being given on additional sheets as needed. Some state projects operated under the auspices of a major university or museum while others were conducted by local quilters or local businesswomen without institutional support. In some states one group made a concerted effort to cover the entire state while in other areas the task was handled by several groups acting independently.

The New Jersey Effort – Getting Organized

The New Jersey Project began in late 1986 when Barbara Schaffer sent letters of inquiry to Katy Christopherson, a member of the original Kentucky Project, as well as to the presidents of the California, Ohio, and Kansas Projects. Helen Gould, the

president of the California Project, arranged to have several members of her board meet with Barbara in April 1987, at the American Quilters' Society show in Paducah, Kentucky. In May of the same year Helen came to New Jersey for a family visit and met with a small group of interested New Jersey quilters to explain the California Project's organization and Quilt Day procedures. With the information that Helen provided, members of the initial New Jersey group determined that, in order to begin the project, they would need to:

- Write a charter and by-laws, become incorporated, acquire non-profit status, and select officers.
- Identify additional quiltmakers and other interested people throughout the state who could help to make the Project a statewide effort.
- Determine the guidelines and procedures by which the quilts would be recorded.
- Develop an explanatory brochure, design a documentation questionnaire, and prepare other written materials.
- Locate local co-sponsors for an initial series of Quilt Days.

• Seek sources of funding.

These start-up tasks were accomplished in Fall 1987 and Spring 1988. Legal matters, such as incorporation and non-profit status, were resolved with the valuable assistance of a Trenton-based organization, The Center for Non-Profit Organizations. The New Jersey Project heard about its services through the newsletter of the New Jersey Designer Craftsmen, a statewide organization for contemporary craft artists. Contacts with quiltmakers in other parts of the state were established through two organizations for quilting teachers, The New Jersey Quilting Teachers in the northern part of the state and The Tri-State Quiltmaking Teachers in the west central area of the state. The Mid-Atlantic Quilt Guild Network, an organization for quilt guild presidents and program chairs, also provided several contacts and hosted some of the Project's annual meetings.

As quiltmakers from additional locations joined the Project, meetings were held to select officers and to decide which quilts were eligible to be recorded. The cut-off year of 1950 was chosen because it appeared to present a logical break in quilt styles and because it might allow the Project to contact some quilters of the 1930's. The Project members also decided to record unquilted tops and to document quilts made outside of the state if they were brought into the state by 1950. At the first Board of Directors meeting in October 1987, the Project established its goals and purposes, which were to:

• Conduct Quilt Discovery Days in all 21 counties to which New Jerseyans would be invited to bring their quilts and share the stories that went with them.

• Encourage documentation and preservation of quilts in New Jersey.

• Work toward exhibits and a publication on quilts and quiltmakers in New Jersey.

• Establish archives on New Jersey quilts and quiltmakers.

In Spring 1988 the Project received a seed money grant from the Montclair Craft Guild, a statewide organization for contemporary craftspeople. This

FIG. 45. Nancy Castner

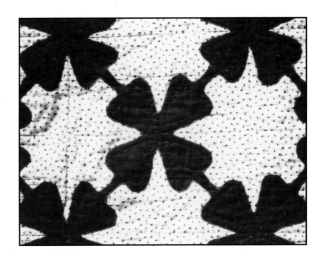

PLATE 173. DOUBLE HEARTS, Detail, c.1880, 72½" x 73½". Made by Nancy Castner (Mrs. Andrew) (b.1833), Spruce Run, Hunterdon County, New Jersey. One of the discoveries of state documentation projects has been the prevalence of visible machine stitching in 1870-1900 quilts, such as the machine stitched binding and appliqué in this quilt owned by Betty Cawley Connlain, great-great-granddaughter of the maker.

money allowed the project to print explanatory brochures and other materials, and to send these brochures to every quilt guild and county Heritage and Cultural Commission in the state.

Quilt Discovery Days –
The Documentation Begins

In June 1988 the Rebecca's Reel Quilters of Monmouth County hosted a Quilt Discovery Day which allowed the Project to test and refine its procedures. In Fall 1988 the same quilt group plus two other quilt guilds in the northern part of the state hosted the Project's first series of actual Quilt Discovery Days.

One of the goals of the Project was to conduct at least one Quilt Discovery Day for each of the 21 counties of the state. Following the model of many other states, a local co-sponsor was sought in each location. The local co-sponsor was needed to find a suitable space for the Quilt Discovery Day, to conduct local publicity, to provide additional volunteers, and to invite local quilt owners, including historic houses and museums, to bring their quilts in for documentation. Initially, most co-sponsors were local quilting groups. In counties where no local quilting groups were available, historical societies, museums, and restorations were often able to fill this role. The Project's original intent was to

record quilts owned by private individuals. But as the Project became more familiar with the patterns of quilt ownership in the state, it also documented the quilt collections of small museums and historic societies, especially when those local organizations were the co-sponsors of public Quilt Discovery Days. In deference to weather conditions and vacation schedules, Quilt Discovery Days were normally held during the spring and the fall. The required space was found in such locations as church halls, auditoriums, historic houses, meeting halls, libraries, museums, and school gymnasiums.

Expenses and Funding

The primary expenses of the New Jersey Project during the start-up and documentation phases were for printing, film, and photographic developing. The Project did not pay outside consultants, reimburse workers for their transportation expenses, or award monetary prizes to quilt owners as some other states did. The Project's major sources of income were donations from quilt guilds, historic societies, and private individuals and grant awards from the Montclair Craft Guild, the National Quilting Association, the East Coast Quilters' Alliance and Johnson & Johnson. Members of the Project gave lectures to quilt groups and historical societies, which not only served the Project's mission of increasing public knowledge of antique quilts, but also contributed to the Project's fund-raising efforts. A donation jar was placed near the exit at each Quilt Day to encourage quilt owner donations. During the early part of the Project's existence, it offered enameled Oak Leaf logo pins to donors who gave over $25. During the later Quilt Discovery Days, the Project allowed quilt owners to purchase photographs of their quilts at $3.50 for a 4" x 6" color print. These small-scale fund-raising efforts permitted the Project to emerge from the documentation phase in the black, though with little surplus.

In Spring 1991, after three years of Quilt Discovery Days, the Project met its goal of holding Quilt Discovery Days that covered every county of the state. When the documentation phase ended, the Project had recorded over 2,100 quilts at 32 locations. Although Project members recognized that many New Jersey quilts were yet to be recorded, it was time to turn attention to the preparation of a book and the organization of a museum exhibit.

Preparing the Book and
Planning the Museum Exhibit

The Morris Museum in Morris County, which had hosted a Quilt Discovery Day and had previous experience in presenting successful quilt exhibits, agreed to be the originating museum for the Project's exhibit, which was to travel to several museums within the state. After also having hosted successful Quilt Discovery Days, the Noyes Museum in Atlantic County and the Jersey City Museum in Hudson County expressed interest in having the exhibit travel to their facilities. The Monmouth Museum in Monmouth County also asked to be included in the traveling exhibit.

An exhibit opening date of December 19, 1992, required that the book, serving as the exhibit catalog, be in the hands of the publisher by November 1991. At the beginning of 1991, even before the schedule of Quilt Discovery Days had been completed, a committee of Project members began the demanding task of reviewing each

of the 2,100 quilts recorded by the Project for possible inclusion in the book. A tentative book outline was drafted to aid in the selection process. The committee's goal was to select about 175 quilts that were either typical of New Jersey quilts recorded or were in some way unusual among the quilts documented. The quilts chosen were to represent every area of the state, and the entire time period documented: 1777 to 1950. Some quilts were chosen because they illustrated an aspect of New Jersey life, such as the Grange fund-raising quilt from Sussex County or the quilt made of silk mill scraps from Paterson. Although many of the quilts selected were made by or for New Jerseyans, quilts made outside the state, such as the dated pre-Civil War silk quilt from nearby Philadelphia, were included if they contained some feature of unusual interest. The condition of the quilts was frequently a factor in the selection process. Many New Jersey families seem to have used and washed their quilts often rather than keeping them "for show." Thus, many interesting quilts could not be included in the book because of their fragile or faded condition. In planning the focus of this book, the New Jersey Project chose not to present an extensive biography of every quiltmaker, but rather to provide readers with the social and historical context in which the quilts were made. Detailed biographies are featured for a few quiltmakers who produced an outstanding collection of works.

During the first review of the quilt slides the book committee reduced the number under consideration from 2,100 to 700, about one third of the quilts documented. After hours of comparison, the committee eventually reduced the number of slides to 350, then 225, and then to the required 175. A further reduction in the total number of photographs was achieved by combining some quilts into a single photograph. Throughout the quilt selection process, as the theme of the book developed, Project members and invited authors began to write text for the book. The end result is a true collaborative effort.

In order to help finance the book's photography costs, the Project established contact with Pro Bono: Volunteers in Public Relations, a Morris County organization that assists nonprofit groups in writing publicity, preparing annual reports, and so forth. Through the efforts of this organization, the Project obtained the services of professional photographer Chip Greenberg, whose enthusiasm and involvement made the book possible.

With the book photographs and text in the hands of the publisher, the Project members returned to the difficult job of selecting 35 of the book's 175 quilts for the museum exhibit. This time the task was to identify quilts in good condition that had a particular story to tell and could be made available for an extended period of time.

The Final Phase – The Archives

An article about the New Jersey Project in the New Jersey Historical Commission's Spring 1990 newsletter, brought the Project an invitation to donate its material to the Special Collections and Archives of the Rutgers University Libraries in New Brunswick, New Jersey. In September 1991, an interview with the Library's Director of Special Collections, Ronald Becker, and New Jersey bibliographer Bonita Craft Grant, assured Project members that the archives would be arranged and described according to standard archival practice, catalogued into a national database, housed in acid-free containers in a climate controlled facility, and made available to the public for research. Individual names and addresses of quilt owners would not be divulged without the Project's permission. Photographic duplicating services would be made available through the Library. As the Project materials are turned over to the Library, the Project will continue to accept quilt registrations by mail to be included in the Library's files. These mail registrations will be accepted by the New Jersey Project until December 31, 1995, and can be mailed to the following address: The Heritage Quilt Project of New Jersey, Inc., P. O. Box 341, Livingston, NJ 07039. ■

Quilt Discovery Days

**The New Jersey Project used
a six-step process to document quilts.**

At each Quilt Discovery Day, the New Jersey Project provided a photographer and several trained consultants who would acquaint local volunteers with Quilt Day jobs and procedures. The six-step documentation process adopted by the Project included: registration, labeling, consultation, interview, photography, and check-out. As quilt owners proceeded through the steps of quilt documentation, they were able to hear consultant's comments about the age and condition of their quilts and ask any questions they might have about care or restoration.

A numbering system was devised that would help the Project easily identify the quilt day location, quilt owner, and quilt. For example, the first two digits of the number 52-001-01 represent the location, the next three digits identify the quilt owner, and the last two digits identify the quilt. If more than one quilt was brought in by the same person only the last two digits changed. For example, three quilts brought in by one person might be numbered 52-001-01, 52-001-02, and 52-001-03.

At the **registration** table, the quilt owners were asked to sign the registration log after the volunteer verified that their quilts were made in New Jersey or brought to New Jersey prior to 1951. Each quilt was then given a permanent registration number which was recorded on the Project's Documentation Form and fabric label.

While the quilt owner filled out the top portion of the documentation form, a volunteer sewed the **label** to the back left corner of the quilt.

A Project textile consultant, assisted by a volunteer recorder, examined each quilt at the **consultation** station. Size, name of pattern (if known), condition, technique used, construction style, types of fabrics used and overall quality were recorded on the documentation form. Based on the information gathered, an estimated date range was recorded, unless a family event or marriage suggested a more specific one. As an example, a quilt that was given a date c.1870 could have been made somewhere within the period 1860-1880. Later, pattern names and quilt dates were researched and verified by Project members.

Volunteer **interviewers** prompted the quilt owners to talk about their quilts by asking such questions as:

- Was this quilt made in New Jersey? If not, when and how did it come to New Jersey?
- Does this quilt have any special historic or family significance?
- Was the quilt made for a particular event or person?
- Were the fabrics or design chosen for a particular reason?
- Does the quilt have any dates or lettering?
- Does the family have any documentation about the quilt or quiltmaker such as pictures, letters, diaries?

This information was also recorded on the documentation form.

Each quilt was then **photographed** with its identification number at the photography station. Both black-and-white photographs and color slides were taken.

At the **check-out** station, a volunteer checked the identification number on the quilt label against the documentation form. The quilt owner received a copy of the completed form and was also given the Project's prepared information on recommended quilt care procedures.

After each Quilt Discovery Day,

slides and photographs were developed, identified, and filed. The black and white photographs were assembled and sent to the co-sponsoring group for their records, along with copies of the documentation form. The Project retained its own copy of the form and the slides which were to become part of a permanent archive. In addition, a summary sheet of each day was made which included the following information for each quilt documented: the identification number; date made; state or country of origin; the maker, if known; whether the quilt had remained in the family; the pattern name; the condition of the quilt (excellent, good, fair, poor, deteriorating); the overall quality rating (1 to 5, 1 being lowest and 5 the highest); and the textile consultant's brief description of an overall impression of the quilt including such points as the variety of fabrics used, workmanship, unusual design. ∎

Quilt Discovery Days

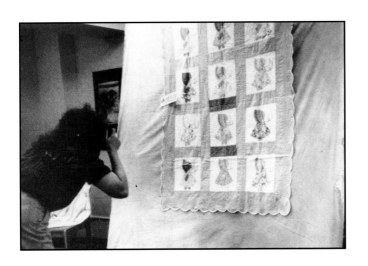

Six Steps to Documentation

Six steps led to the documenting of quilts at the Project's Quilt Discovery Days. At the registration table, quilt owners registered and each of their quilts was assigned a permanent three-part number (Far Left). As the owner completed the form, a volunteer sewed a label on the quilt (Left, Top). The owner was then interviewed, with a volunteer recording notes on the documentation form (Left, Bottom). At the consultation station, a consultant examined the quilt and discussed it with the owner, and this information was also recorded (Right, Top). The quilt was photographed with its identification number (Above), and the owner then proceeded to the check-out station to receive a copy of the documentation, along with information on caring for the work (Right, Bottom).

Quilt Day Locations

MAP LOCATIONS

County	Quilt Discovery Day Locations
Sussex	Sparta
Passaic	West Milford
Bergen	(I) Rutherford
	(II) Haworth
	(III) Upper Saddle River
Warren	Washington
Morris	(I) Morristown
	(II) Chester
Essex	Bloomfield
Hudson	Jersey City
Somerset/Union	Plainfield
Union II	Plainfield
Somerset/Middlesex	Bound Brook
Hunterdon	(I) Flemington
	(II) Clinton
Mercer	(I) Pennington
	(II) Hopewell
Monmouth	(I) Middletown
	(II) Middletown
	(III) Lincroft
Ocean/Monmouth	Manasquan
Cape May	Cape May
Burlington	(I) Cinnaminson
	(II) Medford
Salem	Pennsville
Cumberland	Millville
Atlantic	Oceanville
Gloucester	Mullica Hill
Camden	Camden

This form may be duplicated

DATE: _____

COUNTY: _____

MAIL REGISTRATION FORM – The Heritage Quilt Project of New Jersey

(PLEASE INCLUDE PHOTO)

To be Completed by Quilt Owner or Representative (Please Print)

1. Present Owner _____

   Address _____ City _____ State _____ Zip Code _____

2. Your name, if not owner _____ Relationship _____

   Address _____ City _____ State _____ Zip Code _____

3. Name of Quilt _____

   Approximate Date Made _____ Where ? _____

4. Name of Quiltmaker _____ Relationship to owner _____

   Date of Birth _____ Marriage _____ Death _____

To the best of my knowledge this quilt was made in or brought to New Jersey before 1951. Permission is given for The Heritage Quilt Project of New Jersey to use the photograph of the quilt and the information given on this form for purposes of research and education.

Signature _____ Date_____

Please answer the following questions: (You may attach a sheet if you need more space.)

1. Was this quilt made in New Jersey?   Yes ___   No ___
   If yes, where? _____

2. If not made in New Jersey, where was it made? _____

   When did it come to New Jersey? _____
   How did it come to New Jersey? _____
   _____

3. Does the quilt have any special historic or family significance? _____
   _____

4. Was the quilt made for a particular event or person?
   _____

5. Was the design or fabric chosen for a particular reason?
   _____

6. Does the quilt have any dates or lettering?   Yes ___   No ___
   What does it say? _____

7. Does the family have any documentation about the quilt or the quiltmaker such as pictures, letters, diaries, genealogical records, etc.?   Yes ___   No ___
   If yes, describe. _____

8. Does the family have any old quilting materials (quilt blocks, quilting stencils, newspaper clippings, etc.)?
   If yes, describe. _____

Please describe your quilt

1. Size: _____ (width) x _____ (length)

2. Overall condition: _____ (good, fair, poor, etc.)

   Noticeable stains _____ Deterioration _____

   Rips or holes _____ Repairs _____

3. Dominant colors:_____

   Fabrics: cotton _____ wool _____ silk _____

   Any unusual fabrics: _____

4. Construction: block style _____ one fabric _____

   strips _____ medallion (central block) _____

5. Do you know if it was pieced by hand? _____ machine? _____

6. If embellished: stuffed or corded _____ painted/stenciled _____ beaded or sequined _____
   chenille _____ cross-stitch _____ signed in ink _____ signed in embroidery _____

7. Number of borders: pieced (triangles, squares, etc.) _____ appliquéd _____ plain strips _____

8. Edge of Quilt: straight _____ scalloped _____ follows design _____

9. Corners: square _____ curved _____ cut out _____

10. Binding: applied _____ back brought to front _____
    front brought to back _____ edges turned in _____

11. Is this a quilt top only? yes _____ no _____
    Is this quilt quilted? yes _____ no _____
    Are three layers present? yes _____ no _____
    Is it thick _____ medium _____ thin _____

12. Quilting designs: straight lines _____ outline (follows piecing or appliqué) _____
    stencil (leaves, flowers, other designs) _____ What color is the quilting thread? _____

13. Back of quilt: one fabric _____ more than one fabric _____ printed design _____

    solid color _____ What color? _____

    Any special features? _____

    Signature? _____

14. Comments_____

    _____

    _____

    _____

    _____

    _____

    _____

    _____

    _____

    _____

Thank you for taking the time to fill out this questionnaire. Please mail it along with a snapshot to:
The Heritage Quilt Project of New Jersey, Inc., P. O. Box 341, Livingston, New Jersey 07039.
The deadline for accepting mail registrations is December 31, 1995.

Benefactors & Sponsors

Support from benefactors & sponsors – and many volunteers – made it possible for the Project to document quilts from all 21 New Jersey counties.

Benefactors/Patrons
Johnson & Johnson
Eastcoast Quilters Alliance
Fred R. Alleman
The Heritage Quilt Project Lecture Series
Molly Pitcher Stitchers Guild
Montclair Craft Guild

Donors/Sponsors
Brownstone Quilters
Martha Calderwood
Rachel Cochran
Carol Esch/true colors
Barbara Finch
Winnie Friese
Garden State Quilters
The Hopewell Museum
Kay Lukasko
National Quilting Association (NQA)
New Jersey Quilting Teachers
Pieced Together Quilters Guild

Friends/Contributors
Evelyn F. Balusins
Elizabeth K. Basile
Berry Basket Quilters
Jacqueline Biegel
Hilda E. Bluhm
In Memory of Louise Briggs
Helen Burkhart
Annette Burns
Frances E. Camoosa
Chester Historical Society, Inc.
Vikki Chenette
Elizabeth Cochran
Contented Heart
The Coterie Club
Nance Cruikshank
Judy Dales
Sally B. Davis
S. L. Dorrbecker
Donna Edwards
Gertrude G. Frey
Aleta Johnson
Marian B. Koob
Mary E. Koob
Janet C. Krache
Russ and Carol McConnell
Jane D. MacFarland
Ronnie Mitchell
Frieda M. Murch
Annette Murricane

Betty B. Nelson
Mary Lou Nichols
Old First Church of Middletown
Alison M. Petersen
Piecers of Warren
Mary Jane Pozarycki
Mary Ann Reynolds
Mildred Sanford
Barbara Schaffer
Kathryn W. Schmidt
Gay Wise Scott
Alice J. Senger
Beryl S. Sortino
Janet Spencer
Doris L. K. Stein
Jean C. Steinberg
Eileen Stokes
Doris C. Sutterley
Mary W. Taylor
Helen Tiger
Elizabeth D. Turner
Turtle Creek Quilters
Mr. and Mrs. Charles B. Wallace
Lynn Warner
Warren County Needlearts Guild
Betty L. Wells
Marge Wetmore
Jean Wickstead
M. Carolyn Wyckoff

Appendix A

New Jersey Quilt Day Locations

I.D. #: 11 DATE: June 4, 1988 TYPE: PUBLIC DAY
COUNTY(IES): MONMOUTH (I)
LOCATION: PORICY PARK NATURE CENTER, OAK HILL ROAD,
MIDDLETOWN, NJ
SPONSOR: REBECCA'S REEL QUILTERS OF PORICY PARK
COORDINATORS: LYNN KOUGH, JOY BOHANAN, MARTI PORRECA

I.D. #: 12 DATE: OCTOBER 22, 1988 TYPE: PUBLIC DAY
COUNTY(IES): WARREN
LOCATION: WARREN COUNTY VOCATIONAL & TECHNICAL SCHOOL,
ROUTE 57 WEST, WASHINGTON, NJ
SPONSOR: WARREN COUNTY NEEDLEARTS WITH HELP FROM PIECERS OF
WARREN AND EVENING STAR QUILTERS
COORDINATOR: WINNIE FRIESE

I.D. #: 13 DATE: NOVEMBER 5, 1988 TYPE: PUBLIC DAY
COUNTY(IES): MONMOUTH (II)
LOCATION: PORICY PARK NATURE CENTER, OAK HILL ROAD,
MIDDLETOWN, NJ
SPONSOR: REBECCA'S REEL QUILTERS OF PORICY PARK
COORDINATORS: MARTI PORRECA, JOY BOHANAN

I.D. #: 14 DATE: NOVEMBER 19, 1988 TYPE: PUBLIC DAY
COUNTY(IES): SUSSEX
LOCATION: SPARTA LIBRARY, 22 WOODPORT ROAD, SPARTA, NJ
SPONSOR: HANDS OF FRIENDSHIP QUILT CLUB
COORDINATORS: HELEN BURKHART, MARY LOU NICHOLS

I.D. #: 21 DATE: APRIL 1, 1989 TYPE: PUBLIC DAY
COUNTY(IES): BERGEN (I)
LOCATION: RUTHERFORD LIBRARY, PARK AVE., RUTHERFORD, NJ
SPONSOR: MEADOWLANDS MUSEUM
COORDINATOR: HELEN TIGER

I.D. #: 22 DATE: APRIL 8, 1989 TYPE: PUBLIC DAY
COUNTY(IES): UNION AND SOMERSET
LOCATION: YWCA OF PLAINFIELD/NORTH PLAINFIELD, 232 E. FRONT ST.,
PLAINFIELD, NJ
SPONSOR: YWCA QUILT GROUP
COORDINATOR: ANN EELMAN

I.D. #: 23 DATE: APRIL 15, 1989 TYPE: PUBLIC DAY, PRIVATE DAY
COUNTY(IES): HUNTERDON(I)
LOCATION: RARITAN TOWNSHIP FIREHOUSE (STATION 21),
SOUTH MAIN STREET, FLEMINGTON, NJ
PUBLIC DAY SPONSOR: HUNTERDON COUNTY QUILTING GUILD
PRIVATE DAY DOCUMENTATION: QUILT COLLECTION OF THE HUNTERDON
COUNTY HISTORICAL SOCIETY
COORDINATOR: RONNIE MITCHELL

ID. #: 24 DATE: APRIL 22, 1989 TYPE: PUBLIC DAY
COUNTY(IES): CAPE MAY
LOCATION: CAPE MAY COUNTY MARINE MUSEUM,
HISTORIC COLD SPRING VILLAGE, 735 SEASHORE ROAD, CAPE MAY, NJ
SPONSOR: HISTORIC COLD SPRING VILLAGE
COORDINATOR: JOHN D. ALLEN, PAST CURATOR

I.D. #: 25 DATE: MAY 13, 1989 TYPE: PUBLIC DAY, PRIVATE DAY
COUNTY(IES): MORRIS (I)
LOCATION: THE MORRIS MUSEUM, 6 NORMANDY HEIGHTS ROAD,
MORRISTOWN, NJ
PUBLIC DAY SPONSOR: THE MORRIS MUSEUM
PRIVATE DAY DOCUMENTATION: QUILT COLLECTION OF THE
MORRIS MUSEUM
COORDINATOR: SHEILA MARINES, CURATOR OF HISTORY

I.D. #: 26 DATE: JULY 19, 1989 TYPE: PRIVATE DAY
COUNTY(IES): HUNTERDON (II)
LOCATION: CLINTON HISTORICAL MUSEUM, 56 MAIN ST., CLINTON, NJ
DOCUMENTATION: QUILT COLLECTION OF THE CLINTON
HISTORICAL MUSEUM
COORDINATOR: KATHY JORDAN, CURATOR

I.D. #: 31 DATE: AUGUST 19, 1989 TYPE: PUBLIC DAY
COUNTY(IES): MONMOUTH AND OCEAN
LOCATION: UNITED METHODIST CHURCH, CHURCH & SOUTH STREETS,
MANASQUAN, NJ
SPONSOR: THE HERITAGE QUILT PROJECT OF NJ, INC.
COORDINATOR: MARTI PORRECA WITH HELP FROM THE MANASQUAN
UNITED METHODIST CHURCH QUILTING BEES

I.D. #: 32 DATE: OCTOBER 7, 1989 TYPE: PUBLIC DAY
COUNTY(IES): MORRIS (II)
LOCATION: CONGREGATIONAL CHURCH, HILLSIDE ROAD, CHESTER, NJ
SPONSOR: CHESTER HISTORICAL SOCIETY, INC.
COORDINATOR: ANITA RHODES

I.D. #: 33 DATE: OCTOBER 21, 1989 TYPE: PUBLIC DAY
COUNTY(IES): SOMERSET AND MIDDLESEX
LOCATION: BOUND BROOK HIGH SCHOOL, WEST UNION AVE.,
BOUND BROOK, NJ
SPONSOR: PIECED TOGETHER QUILTERS, SOMERSET COUNTY
HISTORICAL SOCIETY
COORDINATORS: JANET KRACHE, DOROTHY STRATFORD

I.D. #: 34 DATE: NOVEMBER 4, 1989 TYPE: PUBLIC DAY
COUNTY(IES): ESSEX
LOCATION: OAKESIDE BLOOMFIELD CULTURAL CENTER,
240 BELLEVILLE AVENUE, BLOOMFIELD, NJ
SPONSOR: OAKESIDE BLOOMFIELD CULTURAL CENTER
COORDINATOR: LISA MOLLE, EXECUTIVE DIRECTOR

I.D. #: 41 DATE: MARCH 31, 1990 TYPE: PUBLIC DAY
COUNTY(IES): BURLINGTON (I)
LOCATION: CINNAMINSON COMMUNITY CENTER, MANOR ROAD &
RIVERTON MOORESTOWN ROAD, CINNAMINSON, NJ
SPONSOR: CINNAMINSON QUILTERS
COORDINATOR: MAE PRAY

I.D. #: 42 DATE: APRIL 21, 1990 TYPE: PUBLIC DAY
COUNTY(IES): SALEM
LOCATION: TRINITY UNITED METHODIST CHURCH, SOUTH BROADWAY,
PENNSVILLE, NJ
SPONSOR: PENNSVILLE TOWNSHIP HISTORICAL SOCIETY
COORDINATORS: LEONA PANCOAST, OLIVE LOPER, ELISABETH GALLAGHER

I.D. #: 43   DATE: APRIL 28, 1990   TYPE: PUBLIC DAY
COUNTY(IES): PASSAIC
LOCATION: CHURCH OF THE INCARNATION, 253 MARSHALL HILL RD.,
WEST MILFORD, NJ
SPONSOR: WEST MILFORD HERITAGE QUILTERS, INC.
COORDINATOR: LESLIE TALLAKSEN

I.D. #: 44   DATE: MAY 20, 1990   TYPE: PUBLIC DAY
COUNTY(IES): BERGEN (II)
LOCATION: HAWORTH MUNICIPAL LIBRARY, 300 HAWORTH AVE.,
HAWORTH, NJ
SPONSOR: HAWORTH MUNICIPAL LIBRARY
COORDINATOR: JUNE LEWIN

I.D. #: 51   DATE: JULY 16, 1990   TYPE: PRIVATE DAY
COUNTY(IES): BERGEN (III)
LOCATION: HOPPER-GOETSCHIUS HOUSE, 363 E. SADDLE RIVER RD.,
UPPER SADDLE RIVER, NJ
DOCUMENTATION: QUILT COLLECTION OF THE UPPER SADDLE RIVER
HISTORICAL SOCIETY
COORDINATOR: KAY YEOMANS

I.D. #: 52   DATE: OCTOBER 13, 1990   TYPE: PUBLIC DAY
COUNTY(IES): BURLINGTON (II)
LOCATION: FRIENDS MEETING HOUSE, UNION ST., MEDFORD, NJ
SPONSOR: BERRY BASKET QUILTERS
COORDINATORS: ALETA JOHNSON, PEGGY SLOAN

I.D. #: 53   DATE: OCTOBER 20, 1990   TYPE: PUBLIC DAY
COUNTY(IES): ATLANTIC
LOCATION: THE NOYES MUSEUM, LILY LAKE ROAD, OCEANVILLE, NJ
SPONSOR: THE NOYES MUSEUM
COORDINATOR: ANNE FABBRI, PAST DIRECTOR,
ROBERT J. KOENIG, PRESENT DIRECTOR

I.D. #: 54   DATE: OCTOBER 27, 1990   TYPE: PRIVATE DAY, PUBLIC DAY
COUNTY(IES): CAMDEN
LOCATION: CAMDEN COUNTY HISTORICAL SOCIETY, PARK BOULEVARD &
EUCLID AVE., CAMDEN, NJ
PRIVATE DAY: QUILT COLLECTION OF THE CAMDEN COUNTY
HISTORICAL SOCIETY
PUBLIC DAY SPONSOR: CAMDEN COUNTY HISTORICAL SOCIETY
COORDINATOR: COURTNEY GANZ, PAST CURATOR,
MARY DABNY, PRESENT CURATOR

I.D. #: 55   DATE: NOVEMBER 3, 1990   TYPE: PUBLIC DAY
COUNTY(IES): GLOUCESTER
LOCATION: FRIENDS SCHOOL GYM, HIGH STREET, MULLICA HILL, NJ
SPONSORS: GLOUCESTER COUNTY ARTS COUNCIL, GLOUCESTER COUNTY
CULTURAL AND HERITAGE COMMISSION, THE HARRISON TOWNSHIP
HISTORICAL SOCIETY
COORDINATORS: DORIS RINK AND DR. JAMES TURK

I.D. #: 56   DATE: NOVEMBER 17, 1990   TYPE: PUBLIC DAY
COUNTY(IES): CUMBERLAND
LOCATION: WHEATON VILLAGE ARTS & CRAFTS BUILDING, OFF RT. 55 ON
WHEATON AVE., MILLVILLE, NJ
SPONSOR: CHARLOTTE MACKIE
COORDINATOR: CHARLOTTE MACKIE

I.D. #: 61   DATE: MARCH 2, 1991   TYPE: PUBLIC DAY, PRIVATE DAY
COUNTY(IES): MERCER
LOCATION FOR PUBLIC DAY: PENNINGTON SCHOOL, DELAWARE AVE.,
PENNINGTON, NJ
SPONSOR: THE HERITAGE QUILT PROJECT OF NJ, INC.
LOCATION OF PRIVATE DAY: THE HOPEWELL MUSEUM, BROAD STREET,
HOPEWELL, NJ
DOCUMENTATION: QUILT COLLECTION OF THE HOPEWELL MUSEUM
COORDINATOR: RONNIE MITCHELL WITH HELP FROM
COURTHOUSE QUILTERS

I.D. #: 62   DATE: JUNE 8, 1991   TYPE: PUBLIC DAY
COUNTY(IES): HUDSON
LOCATION: THE JERSEY CITY MUSEUM, 472 JERSEY AVE., JERSEY CITY, NJ
SPONSOR: THE JERSEY CITY MUSEUM
COORDINATORS: SUSAN MILES, GWEN STOKES

I.D. #: 63   DATE: SEPTEMBER 3, 1991   TYPE: PRIVATE DAY
COUNTY(IES): MONMOUTH (III)
LOCATION: MONMOUTH COUNTY PARK SYSTEM
DOCUMENTATION: QUILT COLLECTION OF THE MONMOUTH COUNTY
PARK SYSTEM
COORDINATOR: PHYLLIS MOUNT

I.D. #: 64   DATE: SEPTEMBER 27, 1991   TYPE: PRIVATE DAY
COUNTY(IES): UNION (II)
LOCATION: THE DRAKE HOUSE, 602 W. FRONT ST., PLAINFIELD, NJ
DOCUMENTATION: QUILT COLLECTION OF THE HISTORICAL SOCIETY OF
PLAINFIELD
COORDINATOR: JEANNE TURNER

IN SOME INSTANCES, SEVERAL OF THE MUSEUMS AND/OR HISTORICAL
SOCIETIES THAT SPONSORED A QUILT DISCOVERY DAY ALSO REGISTERED
QUILTS FROM THEIR COLLECTION WITH THE PROJECT. IF THIS WAS THE CASE,
THEY ARE LISTED ABOVE AS THE SPONSOR AND BELOW AS A PARTICIPANT.
VARIOUS OTHER HISTORICAL GROUPS ALSO BROUGHT QUILTS TO QUILT
DISCOVERY DAYS FOR DOCUMENTATION. LISTED BELOW ARE ALL THE OR-
GANIZATIONS WHO SHARED THEIR QUILTS WITH US:
CAMDEN COUNTY HISTORICAL SOCIETY
CLINTON MUSEUM VILLAGE
COLONEL LOWERY CHAPTER NSDAR
HADDONFIELD HISTORICAL SOCIETY
HARRISON TOWNSHIP HISTORICAL SOCIETY
HISTORIC ALLAIRE VILLAGE
HISTORICAL SOCIETY OF MOORESTOWN
HISTORICAL SOCIETY OF PLAINFIELD
HOPEWELL MUSEUM
HUNTERDON COUNTY HISTORICAL SOCIETY
JERSEY CITY MUSEUM
MEADOWLANDS MUSEUM
MONMOUTH COUNTY PARK SYSTEM
THE MORRIS MUSEUM
OAKESIDE BLOOMFIELD CULTURAL SOCIETY
ROXBURY TOWNSHIP HISTORICAL SOCIETY
UPPER SADDLE RIVER HISTORICAL SOCIETY
VINELAND HISTORICAL SOCIETY
WARREN COUNTY HISTORICAL SOCIETY

Appendix B

Additional New Jersey Quilts in Print

QUILTS FROM 1777 - 1840
Linsey-Woolsey Quilt. c. 1770. Houck, *American Quilts*, p. 8.
Tree of Life Quilt. c. 1777. *New Jersey Quilters*, p. 18.
Simple Star. c. 1800. Houck, *American Quilts*, p. 77.
Star of Bethlehem. c. 1815. Curtis, *American Quilts Newark*, p. 42.
All White Quilt. c. 1820. *New Jersey Quilters*, p. 7.
Tree of Life. 1825-1830. *Nineteenth Century Quilts*, p. 13.
Candlewick Spread. 1822. Bishop, *New Discoveries*, p. 94-95.
Trade and Commerce Bedcover. c. 1830. Fox, *Antiques*, p. 582-583.
Chintz Applique. c. 1830-1840. Curtis, *American Quilts Newark*,
    p. 44.
The Eagles Quilt. c. 1830-1840. Orlofsky, *Quilts*, p. 277.
Sixteen and Four Patch. 1830-1870. Herr, *Quilt Digest*, p. 32.
Embroidered Coverlet. 1835. *Quilt Calendar* 1988, June 5.
Stenciled Quilt. c. 1835. Bishop, *Quilts, Coverlets, Rugs*, plate 248.
Lend and Borrow. 1839-1843. Swanson, *Silber Collection*, p. 19.
Star of Bethlehem. 1839. *Quilt Calendar* 1979, Nov. 19.

QUILTS FROM 1840 - 1870
Delectable Mountains. 1840-1860. *New Jersey Quilters*, p. 20.
Basket Quilt. 1840-1850. *New Jersey Quilters*, p. 13.
Album Patch. 1841-1852. Nicoll, *Quilted*, fig. 3.
The Randolph Quilt. 1842 - 1848. Laury, *California*, p. 28.
Hancock Album Quilt. 1842 - 1843. Nicoll, *Quilted*, plate IV.
Sampler Presentation. 1842-1844. Orlofsky, *Quilts*, p. 173.
Appliqué Friendship Quilt. 1843, Kolter, *Gallery*, p. 22.
Campaign Flag Quilt. c. 1844. *New Jersey Quilters*, p. 30.
Oak Leaf and Reel. 1844. Brackman, *Quilter's Newsletter* 206, p. 37.
Friendship Album Quilt. 1844-1852, Kolter, *Forget Me Not*, p. 43.
Album Quilt. c. 1845. *New Jersey Quilters*, p. 14.
Star of Bethlehem. c. 1845-1848. Peck, *American Quilts Metropolitan*,
    p. 188.
Eastwood Quilt. c. 1848. *New Jersey Quilters*, p. 10.
Cherry Wreaths. 1850. Orlofsky, *Quilts*, p. 88.
Irish Chain. c. 1850. Curtis, *American Quilts Newark*, p. 46.
Friendship Quilt. c. 1850. *New Jersey Quilters*, p. 21.
Bay Leaf Applique Quilt. 1850-1860. Bishop, *New Discoveries*, p. 78.
Friendship Album. 1852. Bishop, *New Discoveries*, p. 70.
Kiggins Pieced Quilt. 1852. Duke, *Glorious Quilts*, p. 275.
Tumbling Blocks. 1852. Betterton, *Quilts American Museum*, p. 50.

Mrs. Waterbury Album Quilt. 1853. Betterton, *Quilts American
    Museum*, p. 85.
Black Family Album Quilt. 1854. Duke, *Glorious Quilts*, p. 26.
Appliqué Quilt. c. 1855. *New Jersey Quilters*, p. 4.
Flower Basket Quilt. c. 1855. *New Jersey Quilters*, p. 36.
The Ackerman Quilt. 1859. Fox, *Wrapped in Glory*, p. 82.
Flower Basket. c. 1860-1862. Curtis, *American Quilts Newark*, p. 48.
Emeline Dean Quilt. c. 1860. Curtis, *American Quilts Newark*, p. 35;
    Kolter, *Forget Me Not*, p. 52; and Orlofsky, *Quilts*, p. 89.
Star Quilt. c. 1860. *Lady's Circle* Summer 1983, p. 9.
Presentation Quilt. c. 1860-1862. Kolter, *Forget Me Not*, p. 68.
Red Baskets. c. 1860-1870. Betterton, *Quilts American Museum*, p. 18.
Album Quilt Top. 1862. Betterton, *Quilts American Museum*, p. 79.
Tumbling Blocks. 1870. *Lady's Circle* Summer 1983, p. 8.
Variable Star. c. 1870. *Quilt Calendar* 1979, April 9.
Log Cabin Variation. c. 1870. *Quilt Calendar* 1979, October 1.
Broken Dishes. c. 1870. *Quilt Calendar* 1990, December 9.

QUILTS FROM 1870 - 1925
Double T. 1870-1880. Laury, *California*, p. 72.
Garden of Eden. 1874. Bishop, *New Discoveries*, p. 86.
Victorian Album Quilt. 1875-1900. Orlofsky, *Quilts*, p. 280.
Civil War Quilt. 1875-1900. Bishop, *All Flags*, p. 28 and Carlisle,
    Quilts Shelburne Museum, p. 42.
Friendship Medley. c. 1876. Curtis, *American Quilts Newark*, p. 50.
Embroidered Floral Album Crazy Quilt. c. 1880. Duke,
    Glorious Quilts, p. 161.
Lilies. c. 1880. *Lady's Circle* Summer 1983, p. 13.
Victorian Silk. c. 1880. *Lady's Circle* Summer 1983, p. 21.
Appliqué Album Quilt. c. 1880. Kolter, *Forget Me Not*, p. 53.
Memory Quilt. 1884. *Quilts Nebraska*, plate 21.
Delectable Mountains. c. 1885. Woodard, *Crib Quilts*, p. 38.
Railroad Quilt. 1885. *Lady's Circle* Summer 1983, p. 23.
Four Patch Variation. c. 1890. Bishop, *Quilts, Coverlets, Rugs*,
    plate 32.
Double Irish Chain. 1890-1910. Laury, *California*, p. 93.
Burgoyne Surrounded. 1891-1928. Bishop, *New Discoveries*, p. 33.
Central Medallion with Birds in Air. c. 1895. *Quilt Calendar* 1980,
    October 5.
Oak Leaf and Currants. c. 1910. Bishop, *New Discoveries*, p. 81.

Endnotes

Two Centuries of Quilts in New Jersey
1. Richard P. McCormick, *New Jersey from Colony to State 1609-1789* (Newark: New Jersey Historical Society, 1981), p. 89.

The New Jersey Quilt Style
1. Karoline P. Bresenhan and Nancy O. Puentes, *Lone Stars, A Legacy of Texas Quilts, 1836-1936* (Austin: University of Texas Press, 1986).
2. Jonathan Holstein, "The American Block Quilt," in *In the Heart of Pennsylvania Symposium Papers,* edited by Jeannette Lasansky (Lewisburg, PA: The Oral Traditions Project of the Union County Historical Society, 1986), p. 22.
3. Bets Ramsey, lecture presented at the Great American Quilt Festival III., New York, 1991.
4. Richard P. McCormick, *New Jersey from Colony to State 1609-1789* (Newark: New Jersey Historical Society, 1981), p. 81, and Patricia Herr, "In All Modesty and Plainness," in *Quilt Digest 3,* edited by Michael M. Kile (San Francisco: The Quilt Digest Press, 1985), p. 33.
5. Jonathan Holstein, *The Pieced Quilt, An American Design Tradition* (Boston: Little Brown and Co., 1973), p. 53.

CHAPTER ONE: CONTRIBUTIONS TO AN AMERICAN TRADITION
1. Florence M. Montgomery, *Printed Textiles: English and American Cottons and Linens 1700-1850* (New York: The Viking Press, 1970), p. 36.
2. Florence H. Pettit, *America's Indigo Blues: Resist-printed and Dyed Textiles of the Eighteenth Century* (New York: Hastings House Publishers, 1974), p. 146.
3. Florence H. Pettit, *America's Printed and Painted Fabrics 1600-1900* (New York: Hastings House Publishers, 1970), p. 158.
4. Pettit, *Indigo,* p. 150.
5. Pettit, *Indigo,* p. 152.
6. Pettit, *Indigo,* p. 148.
7. Montgomery, p. 85.
8. Pettit, *Printed,* p. 241.
9. Pettit, *Indigo,* p. 150.
10. Pettit, *Printed,* p. 203.
11. *Trenton Federalist* (17 April 1815), p. 1: an advertisement for carpenters, masons, and other mechanics to improve Bloomsbury Village, Trenton, noting "where extensive Cotton Factories are now established, made by Daniel W. Coxe."
12. Letters by Robert Waln to Gideon Wells between 5 March 1814, and 16 December 1814.
13. Louise Hewitt, *Historic Trenton* (Trenton: The Smith Press, 1916), p. 15.
14. *Trenton Federalist* (17 April 1815), p. 1.
15. Letters of Robert Waln.
16. 1820 U. S. Census of Manufactories, AM/Film m23-136/135.
17. "Trenton in Bygone Days," *Sunday Times Advertiser* (30 Jan. 1944), vol. 5, p. 57.
18. Thomas F. Meehan, Stephan Farrelly, and Joseph F. Delany, *Historical Records and Studies* (NY: U.S. Catholic Historical Society, 1919), vol. 13, p. 83.
19. Montgomery, p. 96.
20. "J. L. Shreve et al., vs. The Trenton Calico Manufacturing Co.," *Judicial Records, Supreme Court Judgement Book,* No. 38691 (BAH, NJSL), pp. w-38.
21. *State Gazette,* Trenton, New Jersey (16 October 1854), p. 2.
22. *The True American* (11 March 1826), p. 4.
23. Lloyd E. Griscom, "Shreves in Black Horse, Shreveville, and Shreveport," *Burlington County Herald* (Mount Holly, New Jersey, no date), photocopy by Burlington County Historical Society.
24. Zilpah Burtis, *Ledger,* begun April 1, 1825, collection of Phyllis Mount.
25. *Lady's Circle Patchwork Quilts* (Summer 1983), p. 10.
26. Jessica F. Nicoll, *Quilted For Friends: Delaware Valley Signature Quilts 1840-1855* (Winterthur: The Henry Francis DuPont Winterthur Museum, 1986), p. 12.
27. William C. Bolger, *Smithville: the Results of Enterprise* (Mount Holly, NJ: Burlington County Cultural and Heritage Commission, 1980), p. 53.
28. Bolger, p. 53.
29. Griscom, p. 20.
30. *Book W of Mortages,* 3738 (BCCO, April 19, 1954), pp. 217-268.
31. Bolger, p. 30.
32. Caroline Sloat, "The Dover Manufacturing Company and the Integration of English and American Printing Techniques 1825-29," in *Winterthur Portfolio 10,* edited by Ian M. G. Quimby (Charlottesville: University Press of Virginia, 1975), p. 52.
33. George R. Prowell, *History of Camden County* (Philadelphia: L.J. Richards & Co., 1886), p. 591.
34. An 1854 dated signature quilt from Gloucester County (HQPNJ 55-025-01) includes a square signed by Samuel Chew as well as by former State Governor Charles Stratton. It is speculated that this quilt may have been done in memory of those lost in a mass tragedy, possibly a shipwreck.
35. "The Ancona Printing Company," *The Daily Graphic Illustrated Evening Newspaper* (New York: 4 January 1875), clipping included in Harry F. Green Collection, vol. 2, Gloucester County Historical Society.

36. Prowell, p. 591.

37. *Design for Women, A History of the Moore College of Art* (Wynnewood, PA: Livingston Publishing Company, 1968).

38. John T. Cunningham, *Made in New Jersey: The Industrial Story of a State* (New Brunswick: Rutgers University Press, 1954), pp. 37-38.

39. Montgomery, p. 9.

40. Dena S. Katzenberg, *Baltimore Album Quilts* (Baltimore: The Baltimore Museum of Art, 1982), p. 17.

41. Pettit, *Printed*, pp. 237-238.

42. G. R. Merrill, A. R. Macormac, and H. R. Mauersberger, *American Cotton Handbook* (New York: American Cotton Handbook Company, 1941), pp. 8-9.

43. Grace Rogers Cooper, *The Invention of the Sewing Machine* (Washington, DC: The Smithsonian Institution, 1968), pp. 8-9.

44. Cunningham, p. 37.

45. Cooper, p. 216.

46. Charles Cummings, *Newark, An American City* (Newark: Newark Bicentennial Commission, 1979), p. 21.

47. J. Palmer Murphy and Margaret Murphy, *Paterson & Passaic County* (Northridge, CA: Windsor Publications, Inc., 1987), p. 64.

48. Cunningham, p. 37.

49. Cunningham, p. 38.

50. Wright's Brochure.

51. Cooper, p. vii.

52. Cooper, p. 11 and 217.

53. Cooper, p. 220.

54. Suellen Meyer, "Early Influences of the Sewing Machine," in *Uncoverings 1989*, edited by Laurel Horton (San Francisco: American Quilt Study Group, 1990), p. 39.

55. Cooper, p. 34.

56. Cooper, p. 41.

57. Cooper, p. 221.

58. Christine Blazina, "The Social Effects of the Sewing Machine," Master's paper, George Washington University, 1990, p. 4.

59. Meyer, p. 40.

60. Blazina, p. 4.

61. Cunningham, p. 131.

62. Virginia Avery, "Florence Peto, Pathfinder," *Lady's Circle Patchwork Quilts* (Summer 1983), p. 14ff.

63. Joyce Gross, "Four Twentieth Century Quiltmakers" in *Uncoverings 1980*, edited by Sally Garoutte (Mill Valley, CA: American Quilt Study Group, 1981), pp. 36-40.

64. Gross, pp. 36-40.

65. Newark Museum Association, *A Survey: 50 Years of the Newark Museum* (Newark: The Newark Museum Association, 1959), p. 54.

66. Gordon B. Bishop, *Greater Newark: A Microcosm of America* (Northridge, CA: Windsor Publications, Inc., 1989), p. 146.

67. Phillip H. Curtis, *American Quilts in the Newark Museum Collection* (Newark: The Newark Museum Association, 1973), p. 2.

68. Margaret DiSalvi, telephone conversation with Barbara Schaffer, 27 August 1991.

69. Curtis, p. 16.

70. Curtis, p. 9.

71. DiSalvi.

72. Curtis, p. 31.

73. "American Patchwork Quilts," *The Museum* (January 1930), pp. 89-92.

74. "Review of Exhibits," *The Museum* (February 1930), p. 107.

75. DiSalvi.

76. Margaret E. White, *Quilts and Counterpanes in the Newark Museum* (Newark: Newark Museum Association, 1948), p. 70.

77. "Early American Quilts and Coverlets," *Antiques* (May 1947).

78. DiSalvi.

79. Curtis, p. 61.

CHAPTER TWO: NEW JERSEY BEGINNINGS – 1777 to 1840

1. Gloria Seamen Allen, *First Flowerings: Early Virginia Quilts* (Washington, DC: D.A.R. Museum, 1987) and Ellen Fickling Eanes et al., *North Carolina Quilts* (Chapel Hill and London: The University of North Carolina Press, 1988).

2. Allen, pp. 16-37.

3. Carter Houck and Myron Miller, *American Quilts and How To Make Them* (New York: Charles Scribner's Sons, 1975), p. 77.

4. Phillip Curtis, *American Quilts in the Newark Museum Collection* (Newark: The Newark Museum Association, 1973), pp. 62-63.

5. Janet Rae, *The Quilts of the British Isles* (New York: E. P. Dutton, 1987), p. 13.

6. Rae, p. 13.

7. Dorothy Osler, *Traditional British Quilts* (London: B. T. Batsford Ltd., 1987), p. 83.

8. Osler, p. 84.

9. Josette Bredif, *Printed French Fabrics, Toiles de Jouy* (New York: Rizzoli, 1989), pp. 18-20.

10. Patsy Orlofsky and Myron Orlofsky, *Quilts in America* (New York: McGraw Hill Book Co., 1974), p. 6.

11. Osler, p. 93.

12. Osler, p. 106.

13. Sally Garoutte, "Early Colonial Quilts in a Bedding Context," in *Uncoverings 1980*, edited by Sally Garoutte (Mill Valley, CA: American Quilt Study Group, 1981), pp. 18-25.

14. Allen, p. 6.

27. Barbara Cunningham, ed., *The New Jersey Ethnic Experience* (Union City, NJ: Wm. H. Wise and Co., 1977), pp. 4-7.

28. John T. Cunningham, *Made in New Jersey: The Industrial Story of a State* (New Brunswick: Rutgers University Press, 1954), pp. 34-35.

29. Delight W. Dodyk, "Women's Work in the Paterson Silk Mills: A Study in Women's Industrial Experience in the Early Twentieth Century," in *Women in New Jersey History*, edited by Mary R. Murrin (Trenton: New Jersey Historical Commission, 1985), p. 12.

CHAPTER FOUR: EXPANDING HORIZONS – 1870 to 1925

1. Patricia Herr, "In All Modesty and Plainness," in *Quilt Digest 3*, edited by Michael M. Kile (San Francisco: The Quilt Digest Press, 1985), p. 33.

2. *New Jersey Quilters: A Timeless Tradition* (Convent, NJ: The Morris Museum of Arts and Sciences, 1983), cover.

3. John T. Cunningham, *Made in New Jersey: The Industrial Story of a State* (New Brunswick: Rutgers University Press, 1954), p. 93.

4. J. Palmer Murphy and Margaret Murphy, *Paterson & Passaic County: An Illustrated History* (Northridge, CA: Windsor Publications, Inc., 1987), p. 13.

5. Kevin Dann, *25 Walks in New Jersey* (New Brunswick: Rutgers University Press, 1982), p. 70.

6. Murphy, p. 61.

7. Florence H. Pettit, *America's Printed and Painted Fabrics 1600-1900* (New York: Hastings House Publishers, 1970), p. 240.

8. Murphy, p. 62.

9. Cunningham, p. 89.

10. Murphy, p. 63.

11. Cunningham, p. 90.

12. Murphy, p. 64.

13. Murphy, p. 64.

14. Murphy, p. 124.

15. Murphy, p. 136.

16. Murphy, p. 140.

17. Murphy, p. 140.

18. Cunningham, p. 94.

19. Cunningham, p. 95.

20. Bets Ramsey, lecture presented at the Great American Quilt Festival III, New York, 1991.

21. Jeannette Lasansky, lecture presented at the Great American Quilt Festival III, New York, 1991.

22. Museum of American Folk Art, *The Clarion* (Summer 1991), p. 2.

23. Nancy Roan, "Quilting in Goschenhoppen," in *In The Heart of Pennsylvania Symposium Papers*, edited by Jeannette Lasansky (Lewisburg, PA: The Oral Traditions Project of the Union County Historical Society, 1986), pp. 51-52.

24. Jonathan Holstein, *The Pieced Quilt: An American Design Tradition* (Boston: Little Brown and Co., 1973), p. 53.

25. Glenn Cunningham, "Curiosity Leads to Discoveries in Black History," *New York Times* (2 February 1992).

26. Unless otherwise noted, material in this section refers to Clement Alexander Price, *Freedom Not Far Distant* (Newark: The New Jersey Historical Society, 1980).

27. Murphy, p. 44.

28. G. Cunningham, "Discoveries."

29. G. Cunningham, "Discoveries."

30. Cunningham, p. 34.

31. Susanna Pfeffer, *Quilt Masterpieces* (New York: Hugh Lauter Levin Associates, Inc., 1988), dust jacket.

32. Mavis Fitzrandolph as quoted in Dorothy Osler, *Traditional British Quilts* (London: B. T. Batsford Ltd., 1987), p. 121.

33. Osler, pp. 110-121 and Janet Rae, *The Quilts of the British Isles* (New York: E. P. Dutton, 1987), p. 22.

34. Laurel Horton, "South Carolina Quilts and the Civil War," in *Uncoverings 1985*, edited by Sally Garoutte (Mill Valley, CA: American Quilt Study Group, 1986), pp. 53-67 and Virginia Gunn, "Quilts for Union Soldiers in the Civil War," in *Uncoverings 1985*, edited by Sally Garoutte (Mill Valley, CA: American Quilt Study Group, 1986), pp. 95-117.

35. Dorothy Cozart, "The Role and Look of Fundraising Quilts, 1850-1930," in *Pieced by Mother: Symposium Papers*, edited by Jeannette Lasansky (Lewisburg, PA: The Oral Traditions Project of the Union County Historical Society, 1988), p. 87.

36. Cozart, p. 93.

CHAPTER FIVE: THE GREAT REVIVAL – 1925 to 1950

1. Virginia Gunn, "Quilts for Milady's Boudoir, " in *Uncoverings 1989*, edited by Laurel Horton (San Francisco: American Quilt Study Group, 1990), p. 81.

2. Marcia Loeb, *Art Deco Designs and Motifs* (New York: Dover Publications, 1972), p. iii.

3. Harold W. Grieve, "A Budget House for a Box Office Beauty, " *American Home* (May 1942), pp. 14-15.

4. David Bond, *The Guinness Guide to 20th Century Homes* (Enfield, England: Guinness Superlatives Ltd., 1984), p. 131.

5. Mary Cross, "Reflections on an Oregon Quilt Contest," in *Bits and Pieces: Textile Traditions*, edited by Jeannette Lasansky (Lewisburg, PA: The Oral Traditions Project of the Union County Historical Society, 1991), p. 101.

6. *The Philadelphia Record*, 14 May 1932.

7. Zelma Bendure and Gladys Pfeiffer, *America's Fabrics: Origin and History, Manufacture, Characteristics and Uses* (New York: The MacMillan Company, 1946), pp. 617, 631, 641.

8. *The Sunday Call*, 28 September 1930.

9. *The Sunday Call*, 23 November 1930.

10. *The Sunday Call*, 7 December 1930.

11. *The Sunday Call*, 16 November 1930.

12. *The Sunday Call*, 9 November 1930.

13. *The Sunday Call*, 4 January 1931.

14. *The Sunday Call*, 15 March 1931.

15. Barbara Brackman, "Who Was Nancy Page?" *Quilter's Newsletter* (September 1991), p. 24.

16. "The Stearns and Foster Company," *American Quilter* (Winter 1985), pp. 15-17.

17. File of Lockport Cotton Batting Company patterns. Collections of Winnie Friese and Barbara Schaffer.

18. Taylor Bedding Mfg. Co., *31 Quilt Designs by Taylor-Made* (Taylor, TX: Taylor Bedding Mfg. Co., undated), p. 15.

19. File of Mountain Mist wrappers, 1933-1974. Collection of Winnie Friese.

20. Lockport patterns. Collections of Friese and Schaffer.

21. Merikay Waldvogel, *Soft Covers for Hard Times: Quiltmaking and the Great Depression* (Nashville: Rutledge Hill Press, 1991), p. 20.

22. H. Ver Mehren, *Hope Winslow's Quilt Book* (Des Moines: Needleart Company, 1933).

23. Floyd W. Parsons, editor, *New Jersey: Life, Industry and Resources of a Great State* (Newark: New Jersey State Chamber of Commerce, 1928), p. 284.

24. John T. Cunningham, *Made in New Jersey: The Industrial Story of a State* (New Brunswick: Rutgers University Press, 1954), p. 39.

25. Cunningham, p. 33.

26. Letter from Bea Fleischman to HQPNJ, 25 June 1991.

27. Lee Kogan, "The Quilt Legacy of Elizabeth, New Jersey," *The Clarion* (Winter 1990), pp. 58 - 64.

28. Dorothy Cozart, "The Role and Look of Fundraising Quilts, 1850-1930, " in *Pieced by Mother: Symposium Papers*, edited by Jeannette Lasansky (Lewisburg, PA: The Oral Traditions Project of the Union County Historical Society, 1988), p. 93.

29. Cozart, p. 87.

30. Rita Zorn Moonsammy, David S. Cohen, and Lorraine E. Williams, *Pinelands Folklife*, (New Brunswick: Rutgers University Press, 1987), p. 221.

31. Oliver W. Chapin, "A History of the First Presbyterian Church of Hanover, 1718-1968: 250 Years of Christian Service," East Hanover: Hanover Church Library, pp. 54-55.

32. Mrs. LeMoyne Burleigh and Mrs. Wallace Griffith, Hanover Church Quilt documentation, Hanover, NJ, August 13, 1944.

CHAPTER SIX: LITTLE TREASURES & SMALL DELIGHTS

1. Thos. K. Woodard and Blanche Greenstein, *Crib Quilts and Other Small Wonders* (New York: E. P. Dutton, 1981), p. 8.

2. Nancy J. Martin, *Threads of Time* (Bothell, WA: That Patchwork Place, 1990), p. 97.

CHAPTER SEVEN: POLITICS, PATRIOTISM & PATCHWORK

1. Diane L. Fagan Affleck and Paul Hudon, *Celebration and Remembrance: Commemorative Textiles in America, 1790-1990* (Washington, DC: Museum of American Textile History, 1990), p. 23.

2. Herbert Ridgeway Collins, *Threads of History: Americana Recorded on Cloth, 1775 to the Present* (Washington, DC: Smithsonian Institution Press, 1979), p. 2.

3. Charles Colson, estate inventory, October 18, 1770, Spotsylvania County, Virginia, Book D, 1760-1772, p. 446.

4. Collins, p. 78.

5. Robert Fratkin, "Political Souvenirs: Reminders of Old Campaigns," in *The Encyclopedia of Collectibles*, edited by Andrea Dinoto (Alexandria, VA: Time-Life Books, Inc., 1979), p. 64.

6. Florence H. Peto, "Age of Heirloom Quilts," *Antiques* (July 1942), pp. 32-35.

7. Collins, p. 117.

8. Diane Hill, "The Story Behind the Stitches: An Historic Look at America's Patriotic and Political Quilts," lecture presented at Brownstone Quilt Festival, Montvale, NJ, July 20, 1991.

9. Roger A. Fischer, *Tippecanoe and Trinkets Too: The Material Culture of American Presidential Campaigns, 1828-1984* (Urbana and Chicago: University of Illinois Press, 1988), pp. 115-116.

10. The Women's Project of New Jersey, Inc., *Past and Promise: Lives of New Jersey Women* (Metuchen and London: The Scarecrow Press, Inc., 1990), p. 96.

11. Dee Brown, *The Year of the Century: 1876* (New York: Charles Scribner's Sons, 1966), p. 114.

12. *America's Quilts*, (Lincolnwood, IL: Publications International, Ltd., 1990), p. 11.

13. HQPNJ Archives.

14. Jeffrey Hart, "Yesterday's America of Tomorrow," *Commentary* 80:1 (July 1985), pp. 62-66.

15. HQPNJ Archives.

16. Fagan Affleck, p. 41.

17. Fagan Affleck, p. 47.

18. Fagan Affleck, p. 49.

19. Sandi Fox, "Comments from the Quilt," *Modern Maturity* (August-September 1990), p. 62.

20. HQPNJ Archives.

21. Nancy J. Martin, *Threads of Time* (Bothell, WA: That Patchwork Place, 1990), p. 84.

22. Barbara Brackman, *Clues in the Calico: A Guide to Identifying and Dating Antique Quilts* (McLean, VA: EPM Publications, 1989), p. 152.

23. Barbara Brackman, *An Encyclopedia of Pieced Quilt Patterns* (Lawrence, KS: Prairie Flower Publishing, 1984), p. 551.

CHAPTER 8: DOCUMENTING THE DISAPPEARING HERITAGE

1. Jonathan Holstein and John Finley, *Kentucky Quilts 1800-1900, The Kentucky Quilt Project* (New York: Pantheon Books, 1982).

Bibliography

Allen, Gloria Seamen. *First Flowerings: Early Virginia Quilts*. Washington, DC : DAR Museum, 1987.

Allen, Gloria Seamen. *Old Line Traditions: Maryland Women and Their Quilts*. Washington, DC : DAR Museum, 1985.

America's Quilts. Lincolnwood, Il: Publications International, Ltd., 1990.

"American Patchwork Quilts." *The Museum* (January 1930): 89-92.

The Art Institute of Chicago. Quilts 1990. New York: Universe, 1989.

Avery, Virginia. "Florence Peto, Path Finder" *Lady's Circle Patchwork Quilts* (Summer 1983): 14-16.

Bendure, Zelma, and Gladys Pfeiffer. *America's Fabrics: Origin and History, Manufacture, Characteristics and Uses*. New York: The MacMillan Company, 1946.

Betterton, Sheila. *Quilts and Coverlets from the American Museum in Britain*. Great Britain: The American Museum in Britain, 1978.

Bishop, Gordon B. *Greater Newark: A Microcosm of America*. Northridge, CA: Windsor Publications, Inc., 1989.

Bishop, Robert, and Patricia Coblentz. *New Discoveries in American Quilts*. New York: E. P. Dutton, 1975.

Bishop, Robert, and Carter Houck. *All Flags Flying*. New York: E. P. Dutton, 1986.

Bishop, Robert, William Secord, and Judith Reiter Weissman. *Quilts, Coverlets, Rugs, and Samplers*. New York: Alfred A. Knopf, 1982.

Blazina, Christine. "The Social Effects of the Sewing Machine." Master's paper, George Washington University, 1990.

Bolger, William C. *Smithville: The Results of Enterprise*. Mount Holly, NJ: Burlington County Cultural and Heritage Commission, 1980.

Bond, David. *The Guinness Guide to 20th Century Homes*. Enfield, England: Guinness Superlatives Limited, 1984.

Brackman, Barbara. *An Encyclopedia of Pieced Quilt Patterns*. Vol. 8. Lawrence, KS: Prairie Flower Publishing, 1984.

Brackman, Barbara. *Clues in the Calico: A Guide to Identifying and Dating Antique Quilts*. McLean, VA: EPM Publications, 1989.

Brackman, Barbara. "Distinctive Signatures." *Quilter's Newsletter Magazine* 206 (October 1988): 37.

Brackman, Barbara. "Signature Quilts: Nineteenth Century Trends." In *Uncoverings* 1989, edited by Laurel Horton. San Francisco: American Quilt Study Group, 1990.

Brackman, Barbara. "Who Was Nancy Page?" *Quilter's Newsletter Magazine* 235 (September 1991): 22.

Bredif, Josette. *Printed French Fabrics, Toiles de Jouy*. New York: Rizzoli, 1989.

Bresenhan, Karoline P., and Nancy O. Puentes. *Lone Stars, A Legacy of Texas Quilts*, 1836-1936. Austin: University of Texas Press, 1986.

Brown, Dee. *The Year of the Century: 1876*. New York: Charles Scribner's Sons, 1966.

Bullard, Lacy Folmar, and Betty Jo Shiell. *Chintz Quilts: Unfading Glory*. Tallahassee, FL: Serendipity Publishers, 1983.

Burleigh, Mrs. LeMoyne, and Mrs. Wallace Griffith. "Hanover Church Quilt Documentation." Photocopy. Hanover, NJ, August 13, 1944.

Burtis, Zilpah. Ledger. Collection of Phyllis Mount.

Carlisle, Lilian Baker. *Pieced Work and Appliqué Quilts at the Shelburne Museum*. Museum Pamphlet Series, no. 2. Shelburne, VT: The Shelburne Museum, 1957.

Chapin, Oliver W. "A History of the First Presbyterian Church of Hanover, 1718-1968: 250 Years of Christian Service." Hanover Church Library, East Hanover, NJ, 1968.

Cohen, David Steven. *The Folklore and Folklife of New Jersey*. New Brunswick: Rutgers University Press, 1983.

Colby, Averil. *Patchwork*. Newton Centre, MA: Charles T. Brandford Co., 1958.

Collins, Herbert Ridgeway. *Threads of History: Americana Recorded on Cloth, 1775 to the Present*. Washington, DC : Smithsonian Institution Press, 1979.

Colson, Charles, Estate inventory, October 18, 1770. Spotsylvania County, Virginia, Book D, 1760-1772, p. 446.

Cooper, Grace Rogers. *The Invention of the Sewing Machine*. Washington, DC: Smithsonian Institution Press, 1968.

Cozart, Dorothy. "The Role and Look of Fundraising Quilts, 1850-1930." In *Pieced by Mother, Symposium Papers*, edited by Jeannette Lasansky. Lewisburg, PA: The Oral Traditions Project of the Union County Historical Society, 1988.

Cross, Mary. "Reflections on an Oregon Quilt Contest." In *Bits and Pieces: Textile Traditions*, edited by Jeannette Lasansky. Lewisburg, PA: The Oral Traditions Project of the Union County Historical Society, 1991.

Cummings, Charles. *Newark: An American City*. Newark: Newark Bicentennial Commission, 1979.

Cunningham, Barbara, ed. *The New Jersey Ethnic Experience*. Union City, NJ: Wm. H. Wise and Co., 1977.

Cunningham, Glenn. As quoted by George M. Point in "Curosity Leads to Discoveries in Black History." *The New York Times*, February 2, 1992.

Cunningham, John T. *Made in New Jersey, The Industrial Story of a State*. New Brunswick: Rutgers University Press, 1954.

Cunningham, John T. *This is New Jersey*. New Brunswick: Rutgers University Press, 1978.

Curtis, Phillip H. *American Quilts in the Newark Museum Collection*. The Museum New Series, vol. 25, nos. 3 and 4, Summer-Fall 1973. Newark: The Newark Museum Association, 1974.

Dann, Kevin. *25 Walks in New Jersey*. New Brunswick: Rutgers University Press, 1982.

DiSalvi, Margaret. Telephone conversation with Barbara Schaffer, 27 August 1991.

Dodyk, Delight W. "Women's Work in the Paterson Silk Mills: A Study in Women's Industrial Experience in the Early Twentieth Century." In *Women in New Jersey History*, edited by Mary R. Murrin. Trenton: New Jersey Historical Commission, 1985.

Duke, Dennis, and Deborah Harding, eds. *America's Glorious Quilts*. New York: Hugh Lauter Levin Associates, Inc., 1987.

Eanes, Ellen Fickling et al. *North Carolina Quilts*. Chapel Hill and London: The University of North Carolina Press, 1988.

"Early American Quilts and Coverlets." *Antiques* (May 1947).

"Echoes of Elegant Living" *Lady's Circle Patchwork Quilts* (Summer 1983): 22 ff.

Fabend, Firth Haring. *A Dutch Family in the Middle Colonies, 1660-1800*. New Brunswick and London: Rutgers University Press, 1991.

Fagan Affleck, Diane L., and Paul Hudon. *Celebration and Remembrance: Commemorative Textiles in America, 1790-1990*. Washington, DC: Museum of American Textile History, 1990.

Fischer, Roger A. *Tippecanoe and Trinkets Too: The Material Culture of American Presidential Campaigns, 1828-1984*. Urbana and Chicago: University of Illinois Press, 1988.

Fox, Sandi. "American Figurative Quilts and Bedcovers." *The Magazine Antiques* (March 1991): 575-585.

Fox, Sandi. "Comments from the Quilt." *Modern Maturity* (August-September 1990): 62ff.

Fox, Sandi. *Wrapped in Glory. Figurative Quilts & Bedcovers 1700-1900*. Los Angeles and New York: Los Angeles County Museum of Art and Thames and Hudson, 1990.

Fratkin, Robert. "Political Souvenirs: Reminders of Old Campaigns." In *The Encyclopedia of Collectibles*, edited by Andrea DiNoto. Alexandria, VA: Time-Life Books, Inc., 1979.

Garoutte, Sally. "Early Colonial Quilts in a Bedding Context." In *Uncoverings* 1980, edited by Sally Garoutte. Mill Valley, CA: American Quilt Study Group, 1981.

Grieve, Harold W., decorator. "A Budget House for a Box Office Beauty." *The American Home* (May 1942): 14-15.

Griscom, Lloyd E. "Shreves in Black Horse, Shreveville, and Shreveport." *Burlington County Herald* (no date).

Gross, Joyce. "Four Twentieth Century Quiltmakers." In *Uncoverings* 1980, edited by Sally Garoutte. Mill Valley, CA: American Quilt Study Group, 1981.

Gunn, Virginia. "Quilts for Milady's Boudoir." In *Uncoverings* 1989, edited by Laurel Horton. San Francisco: American Quilt Study Group, 1990.

Gunn, Virginia. "Quilts for Union Soldiers in the Civil War." In *Uncoverings* 1985, edited by Sally Garoutte. Mill Valley, CA: American Quilt Study Group, 1986.

Harris, Florence LaGanke. "Nancy Page Quilt Club Magic Vine." *The Philadelphia Record*, 14 May 1932 - 29 October 1932.

Harris, Florence LaGanke. "Overheard At Our Needlework Meetings." *The Sunday Call*, June 1929 - June 1931.

Hart, Jeffrey. "Yesterday's America of Tomorrow." *Commentary* 80:1 (July 1985): 62-66.

The Heritage Quilt Project of New Jersey, Inc., Archives, 1988-1991.

Herr, Patricia T. "In All Modesty and Plainness." In *Quilt Digest 3*, edited by Michael M. Kile. San Francisco: The Quilt Digest Press, 1985.

Hersh, Tandy. "The Evolution of the Pennsylvania Dutch Pillowcase." In *Bits and Pieces: Textile Traditions*, edited by Jeannette Lasansky. Lewisburg, PA: The Oral Traditions Project of the Union County Historical Society, 1991.

Hewitt, Louise. *Historic Trenton*. Trenton: The Smith Press, 1916.

Hill, Diane. "The Story Behind the Stitches: An Historic Look at America's Patriotic and Political Quilts." Lecture presented at Brownstone Quilt Festival, Montvale, New Jersey, July 20, 1991.

Holstein, Jonathan. "The American Block Quilt." In *In the Heart of Pennsylvania Symposium Papers*, edited by Jeannette Lasansky. Lewisburg, PA: The Oral Traditions Project of the Union County Historical Society, 1986.

Holstein, Jonathan. *The Pieced Quilt: An American Design Tradition*. Boston: Little Brown and Co., 1973.

Holstein, Jonathan, and John Finley. *Kentucky Quilts 1800-1900, The Kentucky Quilt Project*. New York: Pantheon Books, 1982.

Horton, Laurel. "South Carolina Quilts and the Civil War." In *Uncoverings* 1985, edited by Sally Garoutte. Mill Valley, CA: American Quilt Study Group, 1986.

Houck, Carter. *The Quilt Encyclopedia*. NY: Harry N. Abrams, 1991.

Houck, Carter, and Myron Miller. *American Quilts and How to Make Them*. New York: Charles Scribners Sons, 1975.

Katzenburg, Dena S. *Baltimore Album Quilts*. Baltimore: The Baltimore Museum of Art, 1982.

Kogan, Lee. "The Quilt Legacy of Elizabeth, New Jersey." *The Clarion* (Winter 1990): 58-64.

Kolter, Jane Bentley. *Forget Me Not*. Pittstown, NJ: The Main Street Press, 1985.

Kolter, Jane Bentley. *A Gallery of Friendship and Album Quilts*. Pittstown, NJ: The Main Street Press, 1985.

Lady's Circle Patchwork Quilts (Summer 1983), New York, NY: Lopez Publications.

Lasansky, Jeannette. Lecture presented at the Great American Quilt Festival III. New York 1991.

Laury, Jean Ray, and the California Heritage Quilt Project. *Ho For California! Pioneer Women and Their Quilts*. New York: E. P. Dutton, 1990.

Lipsett, Linda Otto. *Remember Me: Women and Their Friendship Quilts*. San Francisco: The Quilt Digest Press, 1985.

Lockport Cotton Batting Company, File Patterns. Collections of Winnie Friese and Barbara Schaffer.

Loeb, Marcia. *Art Deco, Designs and Motifs*. New York: Dover Publications, 1972.

Lubell, Cecil, ed. *Textile Collections of the World. Vol. I., United States and Canada*. New York: Van Nostrand Reinhold Co., 1976.

McCormick, Richard P. *New Jersey from Colony to State 1609-1789*. Newark: New Jersey Historical Society, 1981.

McKendry, Ruth. *Quilts and Other Bed Coverings in the Canadian Tradition*. Toronto: Van Nostrand Reinhold Ltd., 1979.

Martin, Nancy J. *Threads of Time*. Bothell, WA: That Patchwork Place, 1990.

Merrill, G. R., A. R. Macormac, and H. R. Mauersberger. *American Cotton Handbook*. New York: American Cotton Handbook Company, 1941.

Meyer, Suellen. "Early Influences of the Sewing Machine." In *Uncoverings 1989*, edited by Laurel Horton. San Francisco: American Quilt Study Group, 1990.

Montgomery, Florence M. *Printed Textiles, English and American Cottons and Linens 1700-1850*. A Winterthur Book. New York: The Viking Press, 1970.

Moonsammy, Rita Zorn, David S. Cohen, and Lorraine E. Williams. *Pinelands Folklife*. New Brunswick and London: Rutgers University Press, 1987.

Mountain Mist, 1933-1974, Wrapper Collection of Winnie Friese.

Murphy, J. Palmer, and Margaret Murphy. *Paterson & Passaic County*. Northridge, CA: Windsor Publications, Inc., 1987.

Museum of American Folk Art, *Clarion* (Summer 1991): 2.

New Jersey Quilters: A Timeless Tradition. Convent, NJ: The Morris Museum of Arts and Sciences, 1983.

Newark Museum Association. *A Survey: 50 Years of the Newark Museum*. Newark: The Newark Museum Association, 1959.

Nicoll, Jessica. *Quilted for Friends: Delaware Valley Signature Quilts 1840-1855*. Winterthur: The Henry Francis DuPont Winterthur Museum, 1986.

Nineteenth-Century Appliqué Quilts. Bulletin Fall 1989. Philadelphia: Philadelphia Museum of Art, 1989.

Orlofsky, Patsy, and Myron Orlofsky. *Quilts in America*. New York: McGraw Hill Book Co., 1974.

Osler, Dorothy. *Traditional British Quilts*. London: B. T. Batsford Ltd., 1987.

Parsons, Floyd W., editor. *New Jersey: Life, Industry and Resources of a Great State*. Newark: New Jersey State Chamber of Commerce, 1928.

Peck, Amelia. *American Quilts & Coverlets in the Metropolitan Museum of Art*. New York: Metropolitan Museum of Art and Dutton Studio Books, 1990.

Pernot, Rhett. Letter to Rita Erickson, 13 September 1991.

Peto, Florence. "Age of Heirloom Quilts." *Antiques* (July 1942): 32-35.

Peto, Florence. *Historic Quilts*. New York: The American Historical Company, Inc., 1939.

Pettit, Florence H. *America's Indigo Blues: Resist-printed and Dyed Textiles of the Eighteenth Century*. New York: Hastings House Publishers, 1974.

Pettit, Florence H. *America's Printed and Painted Fabrics 1600-1900*. New York: Hastings House Publishers, 1970.

Pfeffer, Susanna. *Quilt Masterpieces*. New York: Hugh Lauter Levin Associates, Inc., 1988.

Price, Clement Alexander. *Freedom Not Far Distant*. Newark: The New Jersey Historical Society, 1980.

Prowell, George R. *History of Camden County*. Philadelphia: L. J. Richards & Co., 1886.

The Quilt Engagement Calendar. New York: E. P. Dutton, 1979.

The Quilt Engagement Calendar. New York: E. P. Dutton, 1980.

The Quilt Engagement Calendar. New York: E. P. Dutton, 1988.

The Quilt Engagement Calendar. New York: E. P. Dutton, 1990.

Quilts from Nebraska Collections. Lincoln NE: Sheldon Memorial Art Gallery, 1974.

Ramsey, Bets. Lecture presented at the Great American Quilt Festival III. New York, 1991.

Rae, Janet. *The Quilts of the British Isles*. New York: E.P. Dutton, 1987.

"Review of Exhibits." *The Museum* (February 1930): 107.

Roan, Nancy. "Quilting in Goschenhoppen." In *In The Heart of Pennsylvania Symposium Papers*, edited by Jeanette Lasansky. Lewisburg, PA: The Oral Traditions Project of the Union County Historical Society, 1986.

Safford, Carleton L., and Robert Bishop. *America's Quilts and Coverlets*. NY: E. P. Dutton, 1980.

Sloat, Caroline. "The Dover Manufacturing Company and the Integration of English and American Printing Techniques 1825-29." In *Winterthur Portfolio X*, edited by Ian M. G. Quimby, Charlottesville: University Press of Virginia, 1975.

"The Stearns and Foster Company." *American Quilter* (Winter 1985): 15-17.

Swanson, Lynne, and Marsha MacDowell, eds. *Quilts from the Albert and Merry Silber Collection*. East Lansing: Michigan State University Museum, 1988.

Taylor Bedding Mfg. Co. 31 *Quilt Designs by Taylor-Made*. Taylor, TX: undated.

Trenton Federalist, 17 April 1815.

Ver Mehren, H. *Hope Winslow's Quilt Book*. Des Moines, Iowa. 1933.

von Gwinner, Schnuppe. *The History of the Patchwork Quilt*. West Chester, PA.: Schiffler Publishing, 1988.

Waldvogel, Merikay. *Soft Covers for Hard Times: Quiltmaking and the Great Depression*. Nashville: Rutledge Hill Press, 1991.

Waln, Robert. Letters to Gideon Wells, 5 March 1814 to 16 December 1814.

Webster, Marie. *Quilts: Their Story and How to Make Them*. Garden City, NY: Doubleday Page and Co., 1915.

White, Margaret E. *Quilts and Counterpanes in the Newark Museum*. Newark: The Newark Museum Association, 1948.

The Women's Project of New Jersey, Inc. *Past and Promise: Lives of New Jersey Women*. Metuchen, NJ and London: The Scarecrow Press, Inc., 1990.

Woodard, Thomas K., and Blanche Greenstein. *Crib Quilts and Other Small Wonders*. New York: E. P. Dutton, 1981.

Woodard, Thomas K., and Blanche Greenstein. *Twentieth Century American Quilts*. New York: E. P. Dutton, 1988.

Wm. E. Wright Company, Brochure, East Warren, Massachusetts. Photocopy.

Index

Notes on the Authors

Rachel B. Cochran grew up in the Maryland suburbs of Washington, DC, and has been a second-time New Jersey resident since 1983. She began quilting in 1978. A former editorial assistant at Doubleday & Co., Inc. and assistant editor for *The Journal of the Electrochemical Society*, she is now a freelance editor. She holds a degree in English literature from Beloit College. A curator for the museum exhibition of quilts from the Project, she lives in Montclair, New Jersey, with her husband and three children.

Rita Erickson grew up in Indiana with quiltmakers on both sides of her family. She has a B.A. in history from DePauw University and an M.A. in anthropology from New York University. She has lived in Montclair, New Jersey, since 1972 and is a well-known teacher, quiltmaker, and lecturer. Vice-President of The Heritage Quilt Project of New Jersey, she is a textile consultant for the Project and for The Morris Museum, and curator for the Project's museum exhibition.

Natalie Hart was born and raised in Gorham, Maine, then moved to New Jersey in 1963. She began quiltmaking in 1974. A dealer and appraiser of antique quilts and vintage textiles, she is also a legal librarian. She is a textile consultant to The Heritage Quilt Project of New Jersey and curator for the museum exhibit. She lives in Chester, New Jersey.

Barbara Schaffer is a native New Jerseyan. She continued her mother's quiltmaking legacy when she began quilting in 1962, and has been a serious quiltmaker since 1974. Founder and President of The Heritage Quilt Project of New Jersey, she is a textile consultant for the Project's quilt discovery days, and curator for the exhibition of quilts. She resides in Livingston, New Jersey, in the historic Beach House which was built in 1730.

John T. Cunningham is a life-long New Jersey resident. What started as an assignment in 1952 to write a series of articles on New Jersey for *The Newark Sunday News* grew into the first edition of *This is New Jersey*. His twenty-four subsequent books include *Made in New Jersey, The New Jersey Sampler*, and *New Jersey: A Mirror on America*. He is a five-time winner of the Award of Merit from the American Association for State and Local History, and has served as chairman of the New Jersey Historical Commission, vice chairman of the New Jersey Bicentennial Commission, and president of the New Jersey Historical Society.

Carter Houck is a nationally known quilt expert. She began her career as a patternmaker for Butterick and was the editor of *Lady's Circle Patchwork Quilts* for fourteen years. Her eighth and latest book about quilts is *The Quilt Encyclopedia Illustrated*.

∾ American Quilter's Society ∾
dedicated to publishing books for today's quilters

These books can be found in local bookstores and quilt shops. If you are unable to locate a title in your area, you can order by mail from AQS, P.O. Box 3290, Paducah, KY 42002-3290. Please add $1 for the first book and 40¢ for each additional one to cover postage and handling. (International orders please add $1.50 for the first book and $1 for each additional one.)